. . . . THE CHANGING AMERICAN PARENT

New York · John Wiley & Sons, Inc.

London · Chapman & Hall, Ltd.

THE CHANGING AMERICAN PARENT
A Study in the Detroit Area

DANIEL R. MILLER

Department of Psychology
University of Michigan

GUY E. SWANSON

Department of Sociology
and Doctoral Program in Social Psychology
University of Michigan

Library of Congress Catalog Card Number: 58–13470

Printed in the United States of America

P<small>REFACE</small>

Of works on the rearing of children there is no end. This is yet another. How does it differ from the rest?

To begin with, this book tells something of the actual rearing of a sample of almost 600 children. It is not a book which gives advice to parents or which complains about their inadequacies. It simply reports what they do.

Even more important, this book shows that a new and evolving style of child rearing is in use in at least one American city, Detroit, and suggests why we may expect this change in methods of training children to appear more generally among families in the United States. The study described here also tries to locate some of the sources of these new developments and to forecast consequences they may have for family life and for the personalities of parents and their children.

Finally, the parents under study were chosen to represent *all* of the parents in a great *metropolitan area*. By choosing this type of sample, we have centered our attention on all the families in the community rather than on some deviant or special group of families.

In the past, the homes of delinquent children have been the subject of many important studies. The family life of the poor, the newly immigrated, the divorced, the minorities, and of many other special groups has received extensive attention. It is far more difficult to find comparably detailed pictures of life as it is lived in most American homes.

The parents in our sample live in or near a large city. We did not observe parents living in small, isolated towns or on farms.

Since the publication of *The Child in America* by William and Dorothy Thomas in 1928 (1) and the reports of the White House Conference (2) in the same period, there have been few large-scale attempts to show the effect of urban conditions on the behavior and experience of America's children. There are a number of distinguished studies of child life in small towns and in the countryside. We think of the names of Hollingshead, Warner, Sewell, and Mangus (3) as among these contributors. But the population on the farms is declining. The city increasingly determines the pace and form of the small towns. It is urban life, not the village or country neighborhood, that contains the wave of the American future. Ours is not simply a society with many city dwellers. It is an increasingly urban society in all its aspects.

We can imagine several reasons for the absence of more efforts to connect urban social conditions with the experiences of the child in and outside his family. The first of those reasons is the real difficulty of grasping a picture of events in the city. This is especially true in a great metropolis. The very size and complexity of urban settings make it hard for the scientist to trace and identify the sources of the behavior he observes. Such work is not easy in small communities. Its difficulties are multiplied many times in metropolitan areas.

Since we wanted to do precisely the kind of research that this problem of size and complexity makes forbidding, we were forced to take a preliminary step. We pieced together a picture of some important features of urban social life from such evidence as exists. Then we used this picture as a guide for making some predictions about the ways parents rear children. Feeling as we do that an urban style of living increasingly dominates the experiences of all Americans, we believe our study provides some understanding of the experiences children have, or will come to have, in all parts of the United States.

A second reason for the small number of studies of the child in *large* societies and communities is the expense of such research. We have been fortunate in having the support of an on-going research facility of the University of Michigan, the Detroit Area Study, which conducts a sample study of the Detroit metropolitan area once each year. We are indebted to the Ford Foundation, which provided the funds for the Detroit Area Study program, and to the University of Michigan's Horace H. Rackham Faculty Research Fund. The Rackham Fund gave us the money necessary to analyze the material gathered by the Detroit Area Study. Some of our own time was freed for the supervision of the work by a grant from the United States Public Health Service for studies in the ways children resolve inner conflicts (U. S. P. H. S. Project M-564). The study of the resolution of conflicts was closely geared to this one, and each has enhanced the work of the other in important ways.

We came to the present research as an outgrowth of almost five years of collaboration. In 1948 we began an extracurricular seminar aimed at translating psychoanalytic thinking into the concepts used in contemporary psychology and sociology and at discovering where such terms fail to grasp the psychoanalytic conceptions. At the same time, we tried to explore the relevance of psychoanalytic ideas for the study of social relations. In the years that followed, we worked together on an empirical investigation which wedded psychoanalytic and sociological interests.

When we were approached by the Detroit Area Study in the spring of 1952 and invited to submit a proposal for the use of their research facilities, we thought of the work reported in this monograph as an extension of our earlier joint research. In that research we studied the ways in which children resolve inner conflict. We tried to relate their resolutions of conflict to a few broad social characteristics of their families and to the specific ways in which these youngsters were reared by their parents. We hoped in the present study to discover in more detail the relation between some of the principal social positions in American society and the views and practices used by mothers in rearing their children.

The work we sketch here has implications for many topics other than the ones we specifically exploit. It suggests questions about the operation of personalities as well as societies. It provides some criteria for the student of personality, or of organizations smaller than societies, who wants to know what he must control in his studies and to what social universe he may generalize his findings. It says something about current history and tries to foresee a part of the shape of the future. We think that parents, that practitioners dealing with children and with family relations, and that a number of professional behavioral scientists will find new problems here for their consideration and some answers to old ones.

More than this, we hope the ideas in this book will be found understandable by people without long or special training in the social sciences. With this desire in mind, we have tried to tell the story of our work with more detail about each step than would normally be the case if we wrote only for other social scientists.

Our collaboration, as is common in science, extended beyond ourselves to a wide circle of friends and colleagues on whom we drew. Ronald Freedman and Morris Axelrod, as the directors of the Detroit Area Study program, gave us the well-trained interviewers and provided the carefully designed sample for our work. They also contributed much more than is required, even by the standards of duty to one's colleagues, in wise suggestions for the elaboration and implementation of our ideas, and in the essential, and patiently tactful, prodding of two men loath to begin data collection until the last interview question was honed to the edge of perfection. The Survey Research Center of the University of Michigan and William Sewell of the University of Wisconsin gave us copies of their questionnaires from previous studies. We learned much from their experiences. In developing the last revision of the interview schedule, we benefited greatly from the counsel of Morris Janowitz of the University of Michigan and Albert J. Reiss of Vanderbilt University. We received from our graduate assistant, George Witt, thorough and knowledgeable aid in tightening our thinking, in developing the schedule, and in the creation of a code for the completed interviews. Ching-Shung T. Tu and Leonard M. Lansky gave us unusually careful and imaginative assistance with machine tabulation.

We are indebted also to many readers of the early drafts of this manuscript for their perceptive comments. Those readers were: Franz Alexander, Wesley Allinsmith, John W. Atkinson, Raymond A. Bauer, Urie Bronfenbrenner, Marie R. Butler, S. N. Eisenstadt, Ronald Freedman, Alex Inkeles, Morris Janowitz, Daniel Katz, Gerhard E. Lenski, Seymour M. Lipset, Leo Lowenthal, Elton B. McNeil, Theodore M. Newcomb, Helen Peak, Albert J. Reiss, David Riesman, Harold L. Sheppard, and Harold Wilensky.

We have been especially impressed—since their commitment to the often tedious and always demanding work of research was less settled and less certain—with the graduate students who participated as trainees in the Detroit Area Study. They were involved in every step of our work. Their good judgment and faithfulness, the eagerness with which they volunteered for special pretesting of the schedule and their persistence in keeping us alert to the limitations and the areas of vagueness in our work were a help and a challenge of a high order. The members of this student group were Isaac Akita, Zoe Akselrod, Julaine Ames, William Barth, John Beresford, Jack Bloom, Katherine Butterworth, Carolyn Comings, Margaret Dennison, Henry Elsner, Jr., Albert Friedman, David Goldberg, Marjorie Guigou, Willard Hansen, Edward B. Klein, Ernest Lilienstein, Albert McQueen, John Pettibone, Sol Plafkin, Franz Samelson, James Soukup, Murray Thomson, Barbara Trask, Catherine Varchaver, Robin Weerakoon, and M. Keren Whittemore.

NOTES

1. William I. and Dorothy S. Thomas, *The Child in America* (New York: Alfred A. Knopf, 1928).

2. The summary volume from this conference is: Katherine Glover and Evelyn Dewey, *Children of the New Day* (New York: D. Appleton-Century Co., 1934). An especially important field study of American children appears in the conference publication by Ernest W. Burgess, *The Adolescent in the Family* (New York: D. Appleton-Century Co., 1934).

3. August B. Hollingshead, *Elmtown's Youth: The Impact of Social Classes on Adolescents* (New York: John Wiley and Sons, 1949); Robert J. Havighurst and Hilda Taba, *Adolescent Character and Personality* (New York: John Wiley and Sons, 1949); William H. Sewell, "Infant Training and the Personality of the Child," *The American Journal of Sociology*, 58 (September, 1952), 150–159; A. R. Mangus, "Personality Adjustment of Rural and Urban Children," *American Sociological Review*, 13 (October, 1948), 566–575.

ACKNOWLEDGMENTS

The following authors, editors, periodicals, and publishers graciously permitted quotation from their works:

Ernest Burgess, Allison Davis, Ronald Freedman, Arnold Gesell, Edgar A. Guest, Robert Havighurst, William Henry, Harvey Locke, Eleanor Maccoby, Margaret Mead, Benjamin Spock, John Watson, and Martha Wolfenstein.

The American Book Co., the *American Journal of Sociology*, *The American Mercury*, American Sociological Society, Appleton-Century-Crofts, the Detroit Area Study, Harcourt, Brace and Co., Harper and Bros., Alfred A. Knopf, the Macmillan Co., Pocket Books, the Society for the Psychological Study of Social Issues, and the University of Chicago Press.

The quotations from Edgar A. Guest's poems "Opportunity" and "A Man" are printed with the permission of the Reilly and Lee Co. They are from the *Collected Verse of Edgar A. Guest*, copyright 1934, the Reilly and Lee Co., Chicago.

CONTENTS

The Problem

The Findings

Evaluation of the Findings

. . . . *T*HE CHANGING AMERICAN PARENT

THE PROBLEM . . . .

CHAPTER ONE

. . . . *A* MERICAN CHILD TRAINING
—OLD AND NEW

Early in 1953 we had an unusual opportunity.
We were able to ask almost six hundred mothers
living in or near the city of Detroit some questions about their methods of rearing children.
Our interviewers had approximately thirty-five
minutes of conversation in each home. In that
time one can inquire about only a few things,
and we chose to ask questions especially about
those points in child rearing that are current
subjects of dispute or that have been the subjects of vigorous debate in the recent American
past. For example, we knew that many American mothers feed their new babies on a rigid

3

schedule, and allow no nursing between appointed times. We knew also that this practice has come under increasingly strong attacks. Further, there are many other aspects of child training that are widely discussed and debated in popular magazines and in newspaper columns on child care. What should the parent do if the baby or child disobeys? Is spanking wise? What about teaching the youngster to take care of his own clothes and toys? When should that begin? How does one cope with thumb-sucking? How early, if ever, should a child be forced to work out his own problems of getting along in the world? How soon is he prepared to assume such adult responsibilities as marriage and parenthood? What, if anything, should the parent do if her daughter likes to fix motors or her son enjoys cooking and sewing? Should the fathers and mothers be alarmed if a child touches his sex organs? It was principally about such matters that we inquired.

Our hope was to learn what mothers actually do as they come to each of these controversial points in their youngsters' development. We were not giving advice. We were talking with parents to learn; not to counsel. Then, having learned how mothers really behave, we wanted to try our hand at explaining why some of them care for their children in one way and why others act differently. There was no expectation that we could explain all the differences among these parents. We hoped, however, to obtain some understanding of the more important differences—differences in the broad point of view with which parents come to the task of training the young. For we felt it likely that all the debate over particular matters—matters such as age of weaning, methods of training the child to use the toilet, techniques of reward and punishment, and all the rest—were but special expressions of more fundamental disputes. The definition and explanation of some of those more fundamental controversies were our great interest.

From the beginning, we found that other writers sense the existence of a basic dispute over ways and means of rearing American children. Some of them say that it is a debate between sterner and easier ways of training youngsters. Requiring children to use the toilet before the end of the first year or spanking them reflects the sterner approach. Waiting until the child is older before teaching him to use the bathroom and trying to reason with him spring, we are told, from a preference for an easier life for the growing boy or girl. There are those who find the cause of such differences in the spreading influence of the ideas of Sigmund Freud or of modern psychologists in general. Psychoanalysis, they argue, makes a strong case for the dangers of demanding too much of a child before he is mature enough to understand the reasons for the request, or to comply. It points to some unhappy or neurotic lives as the outcome of excessive requirements imposed on the young. As these psychoanalytic ideas spread, the reasoning goes, they come in conflict with older notions that hold children to be quite capable of being trained by more stringent methods.

Despite such differences of opinion about the nature of the fundamental changes in training children, there is considerable agreement among observers that these changes are occurring and that they have a wide and spreading acceptance. Such pervasive new methods of child care are likely to spring from new social conditions that are found extensively in American life and that have an impact on parents.

What these new, widespread, underlying social conditions may be is the subject of the next chapter. But, here at the beginning, we want to make clear what seem to us the great and conflicting differences in ideas about the training of American children. Some of these ideas have their beginnings at least a century or more in the past. We will give a picture of their growth up to the 1950's. This background from earlier times helps us to understand current and conflicting approaches to rearing children. To account for those current approaches is the major problem of our study.

In Chapter Two we shall try to explain a part of what we have described, to say why some of the older methods of training American children are passing and why certain new methods are gaining currency. The principal evidence we have to offer in support of our explanations will be given in Chapters Three through Seven. Chapter Eight describes the new kind of American family that we feel is accompanying these changes in child care and the new sort of American personalities such methods of training children will produce.

. . . . . *TRAINING AMERICAN CHILDREN:*
THEN AND NOW

Just what is distinctive about the child training techniques that now seem to be emerging in the United States? We can appreciate their special characteristics only if we compare them with other methods of child care. For such a comparison we will examine the methods of rearing youngsters that seem to have been in vogue in this country for the last century and a half.

It is convenient to divide this history of American child training into four broad periods. The first extends from the middle of the

American Child Training—Old and New **5**

1700's to about the time of the Civil War. Those years saw the decline of techniques for "breaking the child's will" and the beginning of attacks on corporal punishment. In the second period, roughly from 1860 to the First World War, corporal punishment and the arbitrary use of parental authority drew less and less support. At the same time, it became increasingly permissible to nurse infants from bottles instead of at the breast. The 1920's and 1930's represent a third phase in rearing children. The great theme of those decades is the training of children who would be highly independent. The time at which Americans weaned and toilet-trained their children had always been early. Now these regimens were put on a formal schedule in the name of science, and to them was added the scheduled feeding of infants. Finally, in the fourth period, a span of years from about 1945 to the present, there occurred many drastic changes in ideas about child care. For the first time in American history, it became proper to let the child set the age at which he was ready to be disciplined, weaned, and trained to use the toilet. Thumb-sucking and genital play were tolerated. These were only symptoms of still greater changes which we shall describe and try to explain.

Before 1860

The story, as we know it, of the training of American children in the 1800's comes largely from reports in the books, magazines, and newspapers of that period. Most of it is in the form of articles that give advice to parents or that present comments on American families by foreign visitors to the United States. Rarely do the records tell us what mothers did. However, in the latter part of the nineteenth century some mothers wrote for advice to the authors of child-care pages in magazines. Sometimes their letters were printed along with the adviser's reply.

Information of this kind must be treated with some caution. The advisers of parents were usually people of some means and education, and they wrote for others like themselves. The foreign visitor who produced a memoir of his American travels was not likely to be poor, illiterate, or inarticulate. Similarly, mothers who wrote to magazines for advice were far from a representative selection of all mothers. The ideas of child care given by any one of these sources were likely to be more typical of those of middle and upper class families than those of the working classes. Such ideas more frequently represented the views of city dwellers than of farmers. The reports give the further impression, though it is hard to document, that their authors were more likely than not to be Protestants. They were almost always whites, not Negroes.

We may also wonder whether the writers practiced what they advocated. We rarely know. But the few letters and diaries of nineteenth century mothers, as well as casual references to child rearing in the novels of the period, suggest that practice, at least among the middle and upper classes, resembled the advice given in the press.

In any event, the picture that various nineteenth century writers give is fairly consistent. These writers speak with authority. They do not suggest. They offer no alternative proposals. It is as if most of them believe they have the right answers, and that parents should behave as directed.

In his study of the years from 1820 to 1860, Robert Sunley (1) finds that the training of children was then considered a rational, self-conscious process. If parents would apply the correct methods, the results they sought would inevitably appear. What are those early nineteenth century methods and results?

To begin with, writers in that period felt that the baby's life should have regularity. Feeding and sleeping and playing and all other activities should occur at routine times. While those writers did not insist on mothers adhering to a rigid schedule of nursing infants, they proposed that babies' meals should come at approximately the same times each day. They believed that overfeeding was dangerous, and discouraged parents from allowing children to eat between meals. In their opinion, the infant should be weaned at some time between eight and twelve months. However, mothers were told to make weaning a gradual process. To prevent summer illnesses, they were urged to choose the cooler months to complete the change from breast or bottle to drinking from cups and eating solid foods.

It was advocated that bodily disciplines such as toilet training begin early. For some reason, no specific age was mentioned, although one doctor was reported as praising a mother who completed her child's bowel training when he was a month old.

Babies then, as now, were likely to cry and to develop undesired habits. These early publications discuss such problems. The crying baby should be examined. If he is not in pain, he should be allowed to go on screaming until he stops of his own accord. This was commended as making the child less demanding later in life and as an aid to "breaking his will." And, of course, the child must become neat, clean, and orderly as soon as possible. He also must not be allowed to masturbate. Masturbation leads to disease, insanity, and even death. Sometimes, mothers were told, careless or vicious servants teach the

American Child Training—Old and New **7**

child to handle his genitals or do so themselves as a means of pacifying the infant.

During the 1800's many writers campaigned against the customs of dressing babies in great swaths of clothing and of binding their bodies, especially the abdomen, in heavy cloth bands. The child, they declared, should be free to move about. It was thought important that he have exercise and be allowed to learn about his world by exploring it.

The period before the Civil War also had its controversies about child care. Although most writers of that time advocated firm discipline as well as love for the child, and said that the mother indulges herself, not the child, when she does not correct his misbehavior, there was a running dispute over the desirability of using corporal punishment. Apparently, spankings were common in American homes a hundred years ago, and several studies show that they were the standard and frequent practice in the schools of that period. But the opposition was strong and growing.

Again, there was the question of whether or not babies might be fed from the bottle. The considerable majority of pre-Civil War writers decried bottle feeding. They denied that nursing at the breast spoiled a woman's figure or that it confined a mother to her home. They refuted the argument that many mothers are too nervous for breast feeding. At the same time, literature directed to "fashionable" women, while condemning the practice of bottle feeding, gave advice on formulas. It is a curious sidelight on this matter that articles appeared picturing women among the poor as able to nurse for many months with an especially plentiful supply of milk.

Finally, Sunley points to three broad and conflicting attitudes toward children that were present in the first half of the nineteenth century. The first, associated with Calvinism, saw the new infant as damned with all mankind in Adam's fall. This depraved, degenerate creature was full of rebellion against God and His laws. The child's evil, impulsive will had to be broken for his own good and for God's glory.

. . . One mother, writing in the *Mother's Magazine* (2) in 1834, described how her sixteen-month-old girl refused to say "dear mama" upon the father's order. She was led into a room alone, where she screamed wildly for ten minutes; then she was commanded again, and again refused. She was then whipped, and asked again. This was kept up for four hours until the child finally obeyed. Parents commonly reported that after one such trial the child became permanently submissive. But not all parents resorted to beatings to gain this end. One mother spoke of "constant though gentle drilling," which consisted partly of refusing to give the child an object just out of its reach, however much it cried. Another mother taught submission and self-denial at one and the same time by taking objects away from the child. Strictness in diet and daily routine was apparently frequently an accompaniment to obedience training. However, many mothers seemed to find it hard to follow out such prescriptions, and the *Mother's Magazine* carried many exhortations to mothers to do their duty toward their children (3).

Of a different spirit was a second view, coming from the teaching of John Locke and Jean Jacques Rousseau, and aimed at hardening the child for a difficult life. Included in its advice were recommendations for cold baths such as the Indians were thought to take.

The third of these conceptions of the child stood in sharp contrast to the other two in its insistence that children be led, not driven; persuaded, not commanded. Encouragement and reward were called the most important methods for guiding juvenile behavior. Corporal punishment was opposed because it was considered ineffective and because it was thought to crush the tender child. Children, this third conception held, are like flowers opening to the sunshine. Parents should water them with affection and support and protect them from damaging experiences.

Of these three, we get the impression that the first was by far the most prevalent in its time. The second seems to have had much less acceptance. The third, though not widespread, was to gain acceptance both in Europe and America.

It is striking how many of these methods of training children were described a hundred or more years *before* the period from 1820 to 1860 and how many of them persisted without serious challenge until the middle of the 1930's. In still earlier times than those we have just explored, we find Susannah Wesley (4) writing at the request of her son John, founder of Methodism, about her methods of educating children. The year of writing was 1732. The period to which she refers was about thirty years earlier.

Dear Son—According to your desire, I have collected the principal rules I observed in educating my family; which I now send you as they occurred to my mind. . . .

The children were always put into a regular method of living, in such things as they were capable of, from their birth; as in dressing, undressing, changing their linen, etc. The first quarter commonly passes in sleep. After that, they were, if possible, laid into their cradles awake, and rocked to sleep; and so they were kept rocking, till it was time for them to awake. This was done to bring them to a regular course of sleeping; which at

American Child Training—Old and New **9**

first was three hours in the morning, and then in the afternoon; afterward two hours, till they needed none at all. . . . [At six o'clock, as soon as family prayers were over, they had their supper, at seven the maid washed them.]and got them all to bed by eight; at which time she left them in their several rooms awake; for there was no such thing allowed of in our house, as sitting by a child till it fell asleep.

As soon as they were grown pretty strong, they were confined to three meals a day. At dinner their little tables and chairs were set by ours, where they could be overlooked; and they were suffered to eat and drink (small beer) as much as they would; but not to call for anything. If they wanted aught, they used to whisper to the maid which attended to them. . . .

Mornings they had always spoon-meat; sometimes at nights. But whatever they had, they were never permitted to eat, at those meals, of more than one thing, and of that sparingly enough. Drinking or eating between meals was never allowed, unless in case of sickness; which seldom happened. . . .

Susannah Wesley was also a stern disciplinarian, using the rod even for infants.

When turned a year old (and some before), they were taught to fear the rod, and to cry softly; by which means they escaped abundance of correction they might otherwise have had; and that most odious noise of the crying of children was rarely heard in the house; but the family usually lived in as much quietness as if there had not been a child among them.

All the children were taught to read at the age of five years, and were early introduced to Sabbath observance and family religious practices.

They were very early made to distinguish the Sabbath from other days, before they could well speak or go. They were as soon taught to be still at family prayers, and to ask a blessing immediately after, which they used to do by signs, before they could kneel or speak.

But, if her discipline was stern, it was even and just and leavened with kindliness. Here are some of her rules about punishment.

That whoever was charged with a fault, of which they were guilty, if they would ingenuously confess it, and promise to amend, should not be beaten. . . .

That no sinful action . . . should ever pass unpunished.

That no child should ever be chid, or beat twice for the same fault; and that if they amended, they should never be upbraided with it afterwards.

That every signal act of obedience, especially when it crossed upon their own inclinations, should be always commended, and frequently rewarded, according to the merits of the case.

That if ever any child performed an act of obedience, or did anything with intention to please, though the performance was not well, yet the obedience and intention should be kindly accepted; and the child with sweetness directed how to do better for the future.

Mrs. Wesley, herself, thought of this sternness as deeply loving.

. . . As self-will is the root of all sin and misery, so whatever cherishes this in children insures their after-wretchedness and irreligion; whatever checks and mortifies it promotes their future happiness and piety. This is still more evident, if we further consider, that religion is nothing else than doing the will of God, and not our own: that the one grand impediment to our temporal and eternal happiness being this self-will, no indulgences of it can be trivial, no denial unprofitable. Heaven or hell depends on this alone. . . .

Unlike the teaching of other skills and ideas, which had to be done gradually and adapted to the child's abilities, conquering the child's will had to begin at once and to proceed with all speed.

In order to form the minds of children, the first thing to be done is to conquer their will, and bring them to an obedient temper. To inform the understanding is a work of time, and must with children proceed by slow degrees as they are able to bear it: but the subjecting the will is a thing which must be done at once; and the sooner the better.

Thus in the 1730's as in the 1830's, we find some mothers determined to control their children's self-will for the glory of God. It seems likely, however, that there were many fewer challenges to this practice in the eighteenth century than in the nineteenth. In fact, not only efforts to crush children's self-will, but corporal punishment and, ultimately, almost any stern exercise of parental authority, came under increasing attack in the United States from 1860 to the First World War.

This challenge to adult authority caught the eye of many travelers from Europe. A review we have made of a large selection of books by these visitors in the nineteenth century shows that it is the single feature of American child care they were most likely to find of note. Frances and Anthony Trollope, mother and son, are typical and articulate. First printed in 1832, Frances Trollope's *Domestic Manners of the Americans* commented at several points on the lax discipline of American parents. She also made much of the lack of bows and courtesies, of respect and civility, on the part of their children.

. . . I have conversed with many American ladies on the total want of discipline and subjection which I observed universally among children of all ages, and I never found any who did not both acknowledge and deplore the truth of the remark. In the state of Ohio they have a law . . . that if

American Child Training—Old and New **11**

a father strike his son, he shall pay a fine of ten dollars for every such offence. . . . Such a law, they say, generates a spirit of freedom. What else may it generate (5)?

And about thirty-five years later, Anthony Trollope wrote (6):

. . . I must protest that American babies are an unhappy race. They eat and drink just as they please; they are never punished; they are never banished, snubbed, and kept in the background as children are kept with us; and yet they are wretched and uncomfortable. . . . Can it be, I wonder, that children are happier when they are made to obey orders and are sent to bed at six o'clock, than when allowed to regulate their own conduct; that bread and milk is more favourable to laughter and soft childish ways than beef-steaks and pickles three times a day; that an occasional whipping, even, will conduce to rosy cheeks: It is an idea which I should never dare to broach to an American mother. . . .

Such accounts must not be taken too literally, of course. The Trollopes were not only English, but people of considerable education and social standing. They were unhappy that America lacked the class distinctions and the respectful manners of a traditional and monarchic society. And, as one commentator points out (7), it is likely that the children of whom they spoke were those found in the streets and other public places, not necessarily the youngsters of typical American homes. Several travelers did mention that the children of upper class Americans were quite like European boys and girls in training and deportment (8).

Nevertheless, these Europeans, in stressing the "looseness" of American discipline, were underscoring an important theme. If the rule of the rod was coming under fire in the first half of the 1800's, it was more castigated than supported before that century was over. We have examined all the references listed under the headings of "Infant," "Child," "Child Study," and "Children" in the *Nineteenth Century Readers' Guide* and in Poole's *Index to Periodical Literature* (9). These articles in general periodicals, including the popular magazines for women, mark off the decline in corporal punishment. Not that corporal punishment was without support. (Well up to the present time, we can find writers who say it is good and necessary.) It must, of course, be just, be performed with calmness and restraint, but, its advocates urged, no other technique is really effective against the child's rebelliousness. However, the number of these supporters grew smaller, as the nineteenth century wore on.

The case against corporal punishment may be traced in the pages of *The Ladies' Home Journal*. In its very first year, 1884, appeared an article, titled "Hasty Mothers" (10), denying that whipping is required in order to make children careful or obedient. The theme was developed in issue after issue, by author after author. Spanking crushes the child's independence. It destroys the moral relation between parent and child by resorting to might instead of right. It awakens animal instincts in both parent and child, brutalizing both. What should take its place? Guidance, reasoning, and deprivations were recommended. It was held as even more important that the child discover, through natural consequences, the unfortunate results of his behavior. If he lies, he will find that others distrust and shun him. If he is aggressive, others will attack him in return. And, of course, the truly wise and resourceful parent will provide so rich an outlay of interesting and desirable activities for the child that he will not have the time for, or the thought of, being bad.

Our European visitors probably were right in another sense as well. The attacks on whipping and spanking probably were only part of a more general shift in attitudes toward the child. He was to be independent. Parents were not to force their ambitions and hopes on him. Once again, we can find especially telling examples in the periodicals of the time. Just at the turn of the century, a frequent contributor to *The Ladies' Home Journal* put the developing position into a series of articles (11). Children, she said, must live their own lives. They must grow. Youngsters are born good. Parents must keep them that way. The child is a plant with peculiar, individual growth tendencies of its own. It naturally reaches out and up to its maturity. If it has water, sun, and gentle pruning, it will grow to a fruitful maturity. The parent must cooperate with God, who is working in the child, and must refrain from competing with Him by oppressing the youngster.

And each child is a distinct individual, not to be put into a common mold. Parents can help by drawing the children out instead of cramming them with predigested information. They must be the friends of their children, sympathetic as well as loving.

Naturally, this position was not taken lightly at the time by supporters of older ways. In the same period an "American Mother" asked in the *Journal* (12) how mothers can advise their children when the parents no longer have authority. It was a rhetorical question. And, typical of proponents of more equalitarian relations between parents and children, a regular *Journal* columnist (13) reminded mothers that sympathy can be overdone. The child cannot become independent, she wrote, if too much pity and sympathy are displayed over its small injuries and disappointments. Mothers must teach children to bear them bravely.

As with disciplinary techniques, so the controversy over nursing children with a bottle instead of at the breast continued well through the 1800's and to our own time. Bottle feeding gained increasing acceptance. By 1900, breast feeding was still considered physically and emotionally more healthful for both mother and child, but much of the earlier polemic and vituperation were gone. The mother's milk was said to be superior in nourishment to any formula. Breast-fed babies were reported in study after study as surviving better than those nursed artificially. (It must be noted, however, that these studies never gave evidence that the babies observed were carefully matched on important characteristics other than manner of feeding.) But the mother who preferred the bottle was rarely pictured any longer as a disgrace to her sex, an unnatural degenerate who preferred books and a gay social whirl to the true and inborn responsibilities of motherhood.

1914 to 1945

While methods of discipline, independence training, and nursing had undergone some change, this is less true of other techniques of child care during the span of years from 1800 almost to the time of the Second World War. Again, we must remember that our evidence comes from books and periodicals, generally those dealing with advice rather than with observations of practice. But there is a remarkable similarity on many matters in these published sources over a long period.

Take the questions of the age of weaning and of the methods to be used. In 1928 as in 1820, the recommendation was that weaning should be gradual and the expectation was that it should be completed before the end of the baby's first year—probably around the ninth or tenth month. Or, consider toilet training. Although Sunley, who has reviewed advice from 1820 to 1860, did not find specific dates recommended for beginning bowel training, he did discover a fairly regular statement that it should begin early. In 1929, the fourteenth edition of what was then perhaps the most widely used manual of child care in the United States, that of Luther Emmett Holt and his son, had the following to say (14):

How may a child be trained to be regular in the action of the bowels?
By endeavoring to have them move at exactly the same time each day.
At what age may an infant be trained in this way?
Usually by the third or fourth month if training is begun early.
What is the best method of training?
A small chamber, about the size of a pint bowl, is placed between the nurse's knees, and upon this the infant is held, his back being against the nurse's chest and his body firmly supported. This should be done twice a day, after the morning and afternoon feedings, and always at the same hour. . . .
What advantage has such training?
The regular habit formed in infancy makes regularity in childhood much easier. It also saves the nurse much trouble and labor.

The Holts' manual said much the same thing in its first edition in 1894. And so did other books and articles from the late nineteenth century on until 1930.

The Holts, father and son, advised much else that was typical of the span of years over which they wrote. Breast feeding was greatly to be preferred to bottle feeding because it provided a superior nourishment for the infant. Weaning should begin at about nine months and generally end by the child's first birthday. Earlier weaning might occur if the child was not developing satisfactorily or if the mother became ill. However, it was assumed that children weaned at nine to ten months were trained to the bottle instead of the breast, and that nursing from either source would not end until the thirteenth or fourteenth month. The baby might have a bottle at night even after that. But, for the sake of adequate nourishment and to discourage an undesired habit, nursing should not be permitted as long as the second or third year.

If the child is two or more years old, the only effective means of weaning from the bottle is through hunger. The bottle should be taken away at once and entirely, and nothing allowed except milk from a cup until the child takes this willingly. Sometimes a child will go an entire day without food, occasionally as long as two days, but one should not be alarmed on this account and yield. This is a matter of the child's will and not of his digestion, and when once he has been conquered it is seldom that any further trouble is experienced . . . (15).

American Child Training—Old and New **15**

Although the Holts provided a schedule for feeding the typical healthy infant and warned against overfeeding, they did not go so far as to state that the child might never be fed at any other times or that only water might be given between meals. Their schedule is of some interest because it assumed that the period it takes for an infant to digest a meal should be taken into account so that the stomach has "a little time for rest just before each feeding." The Holts' regimen as reproduced below was widely advocated by other writers of pediatrics books and by the authors of child-care columns in the women's magazines (16).

Age	Hourly Interval Between Daytime Meals	Night Feedings (10 P.M. to 7 A.M.)
2nd to 7th day	2	2
2nd and 3rd weeks	2	2
4th and 5th weeks	2	1
6th to 9th week	$2\frac{1}{2}$	1
9th week to 5th month	3	1
5th to 9th month	3	0
9th to 12th month	4	0

Parents are warned by the Holts against what they called the most common bad habits of young children: sucking, nail biting, dirt eating, bed wetting, and masturbation. Sucking of fingers, thumbs, clothing, or of pacifiers and nipples must be broken early. Once the parent is certain that the child is not hungry from insufficient food, he should use such preventives as fastening the child's hands to its sides during sleep, having the infant wear mittens, or confining the elbow with splints that make it impossible for the child to get its hand to its mouth. Failure to take all necessary steps has many serious consequences. Sucking may injure the shape of the mouth or fingers. It stimulates the flow of saliva and aggravates disturbances of digestion. It may lead to mouth infections.

Nail biting and dirt eating were recognized as more frequent in nervous children or those whose general health is below average. But no cure for the nervousness was proposed. Instead, mothers were told to use "every means" to break up these habits early.

Bed wetting was thought abnormal if it occurred after three years of age. Punishments were sometimes useful when the child is three or four years old, but not afterward. Rewards were held to be more efficacious for older children. Liquids should not be given after 4 P.M., and the child should be examined to see if some local irritation might be causing the trouble.

"Masturbation is the most injurious of all the bad habits . . . (17)." Why this is so was not stated. But parents were told that punishments and mechanical restraints are of little avail except with infants. Rewards were recommended for older children: "It is of the utmost importance to watch the child closely, to keep his confidence, and by all possible means to teach self-control."

If anything, the Holt books were typical of their period in the degree of restraint with which they approach matters like the foregoing. Atypical advice was most often in the same direction as theirs, but more radical in the means to the same ends. Some classic examples of the greater extremes may be found in a book written by the prominent psychologist John B. Watson, father of behaviorism (18).

Watson saw his manual on *Psychological Care of Infant and Child* as a companion-piece to the more medically oriented works by the Holts. A baby's physical health, he suggested, may be regained in a short time by proper care, but "once a child's character has been spoiled by bad handling, which can be done in a few days, who can say that the damage is ever repaired" (19)?

Whereas the Holts opposed kissing the baby on the mouth, and kissing in general, because it transmitted disease, Watson opposed it, along with much other fondling and petting, as making the child too dependent. Mothers who "coddle" infants rob them of their opportunity for "conquering the world" (20).

There is a sensible way of treating children. Treat them as though they were young adults. Dress them, bathe them with care and circumspection. Let your behavior always be objective and kindly firm. Never hug and kiss them, never let them sit in your lap. If you must, kiss them once on the forehead when they say good night. Shake hands with them in the morning. Give them a pat on the head if they have made an extraordinarily good job of a difficult task. . . .

If you expected a dog to grow up and be useful as a watch dog, a bird dog, a fox hound, useful for anything except a lap dog, you wouldn't dare treat it the way you treat your child . . . (21).

Like the Holts, Watson urged that if the child cried, not from pain or hunger, but to be rocked, to be carried about, to have a light in its room, to suck on a bottle, or to continue any other "bad habit," it should be allowed to cry until it stops of its own accord. In dealing with other habits he was even more thorough and insistent. Take toilet training:

. . . The infant from 8 months of age onward should have a special toilet seat into which he can be safely strapped. *The child should be left alone in the bathroom without toys and with the door closed.* Under no cir-

American Child Training—Old and New **17**

cumstances should the door be left open or the mother or nurse stay with the child. This is a rule which seems to be almost universally broken. When broken it leads to dawdling, loud conversation, in general to unsocial and dependent behavior (22).

Children must be taught to play alone for considerable periods from the first. They must be exercised. They must be exposed to social contacts as soon as possible and the child and his companions should be left alone for at least an hour each day—"fights, accidents, quarrels and all" (23). To avoid habits of inferiority and shyness that may come from lack of continence, the child should be started on urinary control by the third or fifth week of life. And what will result?

. . . The end result is a happy child free as air because he has mastered the stupidly simple demands society makes upon him. An independent child because all during his training you have made him play and work alone a part of the time, and you have made him get out of difficulties by his own efforts. A child that meets and plays with other children frankly, openly, untroubled by shyness and inferiority. An original child because his perfect adjustment to his environment gives him leisure to experiment. Don't believe anyone who tells you that such insistence on routine tends to steam roller the child and to reduce the growth of his own "inward life and powers." "Spontaneity," "inward development," and the like are phrases used by those too lazy or too stupid or too prejudiced to study children in the actual making.

The only person in life who is effectively original is the person who has a routine and has mastered a technique. The person who has not these is a slave—his life is taken up in trying to keep up with the procession of those struggling to obtain just bread, meat, and a roof for shelter (24).

Martha Wolfenstein (25) has reviewed one of the most important guides to the care of babies from its first issue in 1914 to its edition for 1951. Because it bridges so much of the first half of this century and because it takes us well into current practice, this guide, *Infant Care*, published by the United States government's Children's Bureau, gives us an unusually sharp picture of the contrasts. Wolfenstein's conclusions are put like this:

. . . [In 1914] the infant appeared to be endowed with strong and dangerous impulses. These were notably autoerotic, masturbatory and thumb-sucking. This child is described as "rebelling fiercely" if these impulses are interfered with. The impulses "easily grow beyond control" and are harmful in the extreme: "children are sometimes wrecked for life." The baby may achieve the dangerous pleasures to which his nature disposes him by his own movements or may be seduced into them by being given pacifiers to suck or having his genitals stroked by the nurse. The mother must be ceaselessly vigilant; she must wage a relentless battle against the child's sinful nature. She is told that masturbation "must be eradicated . . . treatment consists of mechanical restraints." The child should have his feet tied to opposite sides of the crib so that he cannot rub his thighs together; his nightgrown sleeves should be pinned to the bed so that he cannot touch himself. Similarly for thumb-sucking, "the sleeve may be pinned or sewed down over the fingers of the offending hand for several days and nights," or a patent cuff may be used which holds the elbow stiff. The mother's zeal against thumb-sucking is assumed to be so great that she is reminded to allow the child to have his hands free some of the time so that he may develop legitimate manual skills; "but with the approach of sleeping time the hand must be covered . . ." (26).

But the bulletins issued in the period from 1942 to 1945 disagree sharply. The child no longer comes into the world with intense and preformed desires. In fact, words that connote intensity and emotion seem inappropriate to describe his inner life. That life is bland. The infant has interests rather than desires or impulses. A child without fixed and powerful intentions can easily be handled should he begin some undesirable practice. It is necessary only to distract his attention. As Wolfenstein continues:

. . . [In contrast to 1914] we find in 1942–45 [in *Infant Care*] that the baby has been transformed into almost complete harmlessness. The intense and concentrated impulses of the past have disappeared. Drives toward erotic pleasure (and also toward domination, which was stressed in the [1929–1938 editions]) have become weak and incidental. Instead we find impulses of a more diffuse and moderate character. The baby is interested in exploring his world. If he happens to put his thumb in his mouth, or to touch his genitals, these are merely incidents, and unimportant ones at that, in his over-all exploratory progress. The erogenous zones do not have the focal attraction which they did in 1914, and the baby easily passes beyond them to other areas of presumably equal interest. "The baby will not spend much time handling his genitals if he has other interesting things to do." . . . Everything amuses him, nothing is excessively exciting.

The mother in this recent period is told how to regard autoerotic incidents: "Babies want to handle and investigate everything that they can see and reach. When a baby discovers his genital organs he will play with them. . . . A wise mother will not be concerned about this . . . See that he has a toy to play with and he will not need to use his body as a plaything." . . . Similarly with thumb-sucking: "A baby explores everything within his reach. He looks at a new object, feels it, squeezes it, and almost always puts it in his mouth." Thus again what was formerly a "fierce" pleasure has become an unimportant incident in the exploration of the world. . . . "As he grows older other interests will take the place of sucking." . . .

American Child Training—Old and New **19**

In [1914] there is a clear-cut distinction between what the baby "needs," his legitimate requirements, whatever is essential to his health and well-being, on the one hand, and what the baby "wants," his illegitimate pleasure strivings, on the other. This is illustrated, for instance, in the question of whether to pick the baby up when he cries. In 1914, it was essential to determine whether he really needs something or whether he only wants something. Crying is listed as a bad way of expressing his "needs"; if he is expressing a need, the mother should respond. "But when the baby cries simply because he has learned from experience that this brings him what he wants, it is one of the worst habits he can learn." . . .

In 1942–45, wants and needs are explicitly equated. "A baby sometimes cries because he wants a little more attention. He probably needs a little extra attention under some circumstances just as he sometimes needs a little extra food and water." . . . What the baby wants for pleasure has thus become as legitimate a demand as what he needs for his physical well-being and is to be treated in the same way. . . .

. . . .

. . . in 1914, playing with the baby was regarded as dangerous, it produced unwholesome pleasure and ruined the baby's nerves. . . .

The mother of 1914 was told: "The rule that parents should not play with the baby may seem hard, but it is without doubt a safe one. A young, delicate, and nervous baby needs rest and quiet, and however robust the child, much of the play that is indulged in is more or less harmful. It is a great pleasure to hear the baby laugh and crow in apparent delight, but often the means used to produce the laughter, such as tickling, punching, or tossing, makes him irritable and restless.

In the recent period (1942–1945) play . . . has been . . . dissociated from unhealthy excitement and nervous debilitation and has become associated with muscular development, necessary exercise, strength, and control . . . (27).

There is a kind of calmness and reasonableness to the child. Frustrated with one thing, he turns to another—or can be guided to some alternative. He acquires desires through learning just as he acquires the skills of walking and talking and of eating with utensils. Parents and teachers can guide this process. But, should they?

For many American parents of that period, the answer was affirmative, but with qualifications. They found their thoughts well stated by John Dewey and the progressive educators. In a changing world, it is important that children be as flexible and creative with new situations as possible. Existing knowledge has a way of becoming outdated in the course of scientific advance. The most important thing the child can learn is not this goal or that skill, but the technique of solving problems—any problems that an ever-new world presents to him. A method of handling life's problems, not a preconstructed set of solutions for them, is the heritage each generation should pass to the next. Now, since the infant comes already possessed of flexible, exploring tendencies, the thing to do is to keep these free and operating. They can be crushed if he is given all the answers or if he is forced to learn skills that have no bearing on his interests. Let the child set the pace. Let his elders provide opportunities for him to explore. Let them introduce information he will need as an adult as it becomes relevant for his childish interests. Does he want to build things? Then he must learn to read and write in order to follow plans and order supplies. In a continuing experience with meeting and overcoming hindrances to his interests, the child will become a rational, creative person. *Infant Care*, as we have seen, reflects this view of the baby in urging that he be allowed to explore the environment, including his own body. His wants become his needs when he is directed toward an adulthood in which he must carve out his own way in an unstable social world. He must learn how to shape the environment to his interests and his interests to the environment. No one can tell him what will be in his interest or what he will need to know tomorrow, for the world will be different then. Only one thing is certain. His interests will be better served if he pays attention to reality as he tries to solve the problems life presents.

1945 to the Present

But we may ask, is this still the current trend in American child rearing? In part it is. The baby still explores, and exploration is encouraged. He is sexually innocent. Nevertheless we feel that some new trends are emerging. As before, we cannot cite detailed and conclusive evidence for our impressions, but we can report what they are and then, in our own study, provide some test of their accuracy.

The flavor of much current opinion in the popular women's magazines and in the newspapers gives us a number of impressions. In particular, it seems to stress the following themes:

1. Although the child loves to explore, and should be encouraged, he needs limits and will come to recognize this if the benefits of limits are provided.

2. Although a baby is sexually innocent, he behaves as if he had unlimited desires for immediate satisfaction of his wants (whether inherent or learned). Should this pattern continue, he becomes dominating and, when blocked, aggressive.

3. All wants and desires may be acquired through learning, but this

American Child Training—Old and New **21**

fact does not prevent their being intense and persistent. Sometimes they cannot be distracted. Sterner measures must be taken.

4. The world does not change as rapidly as was supposed. Some things persist for long periods if not forever. The fundamental relations the child must expect to establish with other people, if they are to tolerate him, are much the same as they ever were in human history. And he will have to live most of his life with other people. He must be responsible as well as creative. He must be a good member of the groups in which he participates.

5. A relaxed, leisurely pace is something the child wants and needs a good part of the time. He does not want to be "racing the motor" all the time, solving problems and exploiting opportunities. Often he enjoys lying back and letting a flood of sense impressions or of fantasy pour over him, or he may enjoy finding a quiet place and a quiet day.

Referring once more to Wolfenstein's analysis of *Infant Care*, we find a number of these notions repeated in the summary of the bulletin's comments in 1951 (28):

. . . The infant now may suffer from boredom. And this has become the main reason for autoerotic activities. The baby may suck his thumb out of "loneliness or boredom." He may rock or bang his head because of "boredom." In toilet training the baby the mother must take care that it does not become a "hateful bore" for him. . . .

The exploratory impulse of the baby continues to be stressed. We have interpreted this as an attempt to conceive the child's impulsive endowment in harmless terms. But . . . condemnation of impulses seems to be catching up with this displacement. Bounds must now be set to the baby's exploration. "We know that if we leave him free to creep everywhere he'd get into trouble."

There are still more striking signs that the belief in the dangerousness of impulses is breaking through the defenses that have been erected against it. In 1942–1945 the view was advanced that the early gratification of the baby's demands led to the subsequent moderation of demands. There is now a conflict on this point. In some areas the precept is maintained, notably in relation to sucking and food preferences. But in respect to the impulse to dominate it has been reversed. . . . The baby may get the parents "at his mercy by unreasonable demands for attention."

Here are repeated the dangers of failing to teach the child the limits on his behavior as set by reality. The child may get into trouble if he is unwary or too demanding.

Here, too, is a new theme. The infant can get bored. Dangers lie in boredom. Implied is the notion that children are active, restless little creatures and that they are certain to be doing something. If more desirable ventures are not at hand, the child sucks his thumb or bangs his head. Presumably these activities are less interesting as well as less desirable than something else.

Just as we find *Infant Care*'s early advice akin to that given by the Holts, Watson, and many others, so we find its more recent suggestions much like those given by that exceedingly popular book on the subject by Dr. Benjamin Spock, perhaps best known in its paper-bound edition as the *Pocket Book of Baby and Child Care* (29). And, of course, Spock is only one of the more conspicuous of the host of contemporary writers giving similar counsel.

Again, we find some similarities between our own impressions and those recorded by Riesman and his collaborators in their speculative book on modern American life. They speak (30) of an increasing emphasis on teaching children to be other-directed, to be consumption oriented, and to compete through becoming somewhat unique personalities rather than by possessing unusual technical skills.

Other-direction is based on an expectation that the individual will not be able to know what he wants, to determine his own course of action, or to make independent choices. As a result he must get guidance by paying attention to other people and their preferences for his conduct. However, this is not the full meaning of other-direction. Riesman seems to have in mind a situation in which people acquire their standards and decisions from others because, first, they have none themselves, and, second, because their way of life must satisfy their fellows. This situation should be distinguished from adapting one's behavior to the expectations of others out of necessity because other people will punish the individual for nonconformity. Riesman feels that the modern child is trained in such a way that he often lacks any strong desires of his own, desires that he will try to pursue in the face of obstacles.

Something also should be said about Riesman's idea of training children in consumption orientation. Riesman provides no rigorous description of consumption orientation. The closest we have been able to come to one is to say that it represents an ability to enjoy things here and now for their own sake rather than forever postponing enjoyment until some later time "when one's work is all done." The pattern of postponement is what Riesman calls "production orientation." It would seem that parents who are oriented toward consumption should train their children to accept a more relaxed and leisurely pace for life and a kind of passive enjoyment.

At this point we might look back over the course we have traced. The relations of parents and children in the United States have changed again and again. The changes appear in the treatment of the child in the first weeks and months of his life as he is fed and washed and fondled and taught, and thence throughout his upbringing and in the contacts with his parents after he has established his own home and family. These changes have not stopped. In Wolfenstein's sensitive account of advice given for rearing the infant, we can distinguish some of the most recent and important developments. In her study, in Riesman's reflections, and in our own impressions, we find some clues about the present and future.

But we suggested near this chapter's beginning that there is a difference between the older and newer authors on infant care that goes beyond the specific things they recommend. They come to their task with a different spirit, a different point of view. We shall have more to say about these differences as we go along, but this seems a good place at which to give point to this change in attitude.

The most recent advice on child training appears always to ask two questions in deciding what desirable practice would be. It asks, "What is 'natural' for mother and child?" It also asks, "Is the child old enough?"

Spock puts the matter of naturalness at the very beginning of his book. He tells parents that there have been many conflicting opinions about caring for babies. He prophesies that others will appear. The parent is to trust himself. Why?

. . . We know for a fact that the natural loving care that kindly parents give to their children is a hundred times more valuable than their knowing how to pin a diaper on just right, or making a formula expertly. Every time you pick your baby up, even if you do it a little awkwardly at first, every time you change him, bathe him, feed him, smile at him, he's getting a feeling that he belongs to you and that you belong to him. Nobody else in the world, no matter how skillful, can give that to him. It may surprise you to hear that the more people have studied different methods of bringing up children the more they have come to the conclusion that what good mothers and fathers instinctively feel like doing for the babies is usually best after all . . . (31).

But this says both much and little. What do kind parents think they should do? Susannah Wesley and the others we have mentioned felt they were being kind and good. Watson felt that cuddling the infant was the unkindest deed of all. Kindliness is not simply an immediate response of sympathy for the infant's plight in the here and now, but a judgment of what will benefit him in the future as well. When Spock and the others speak of "instinctive" ways of handling babies, they usually refer to acts of tenderness, to the indulgence of infants within the parents' ability to tolerate their demands. We can probably say, then, that the newer advice is less concerned about the consequences for the child's future, not because that future is unimportant, but for two other reasons. First, a successful future requires the child to have confidence in himself and to be confident of others' regard for him. Sympathy in infancy is believed to build such confidence. Second, the child, and the parents as well, are thought healthier if they allow themselves the expression of their feelings and the satisfaction of sensuous and loving appetites when this is possible without serious consequences.

There also is that second question, "Is the child old enough?" Its meaning seems closely related to the idea of naturalness.

The spirit of modern advice is like that of the middle and late nineteenth century in challenging the authoritarian parent, denying mothers and fathers the right to force the child to conform to their aspirations or to demand impossible achievements of him. It is different from that of the reformers of the nineteenth and early twentieth centuries in saying that, even though the child wants and needs to be independent, he is not able to learn to stand by himself if he finds the world of infancy and early childhood too cold, impersonal, and dispassionate. It warns parents that the young will reach out to explore and direct their worlds only if they can have a breathing space to digest and integrate the new experiences presented by earlier explorations. Otherwise the child is overwhelmed. He becomes disorganized and fearful and uncertain. And, crucial in that digestion and integration of new experiences, is steady support, help, and encouragement from his parents. They must accept the child when he fails as well as when he succeeds, in order that failures are not so dreaded that he is unwilling to risk trying new behaviors or learning new skills. Further, the newer advice suggests that the child reared without concern for his ability to take and manage the demands made on him will become asocial, babyish, cold, unfriendly, and unsupportive of others. Continued courage requires success and support, and the experiences children have with their peers and with others outside the family do not provide these things in sufficient quantity or degree. Parents must make up some of the difference.

American Child Training—Old and New **25**

In describing the psychoanalytic position on habit training, Hartmann, Kris, and Loewenstein (32) present many features of the modern approach. They say that effective parents make four types of judgments. First, they decide if the child is mature enough to perform the required acts. If he cannot sit up, for example, he should not be required to begin toilet training. Secondly, they evaluate the extent to which he can tolerate deprivation. Even if he can sit up, he may not be emotionally ready to tolerate the parental pressure without becoming unduly anxious or despondent. Third, the parents give the child enough love to motivate his efforts. As these authors say, "There can be little doubt that the better assured the child is that indulgence will follow the postponement of demands, the more easily will the deprivation be tolerated." In commenting on the regulation of hostility, they add that "friendly restraint tends to reduce aggressive responses." A child is best distracted by loving attention. Finally, consistency of parental requests is imperative in getting the child to comply. If the parents disagree with each other or are so uncertain that they vacillate in their requests, the child becomes confused and his habit training suffers accordingly.

But, say many contemporary writers, the child needs not only love and sympathy. He needs encouragement. He is not old enough to supply this support for himself. True, as the late nineteenth and early twentieth century taught, he has great curiosity. But if he is often hurt or discouraged, he becomes fearful and withdraws from his explorations. He suffers from ennui, hopelessness, boredom, and loss of a desire to live.

At times, though less frequently than is the case for the foregoing, there are suggestions that children need stimulation as well as encouragement. This theory seems to mean that curiosity is not enough to guarantee that the world will seem interesting and worth mastering. The child also needs the help of expressions of interest and worth by parents if his amorphous, vacillating curiosity is to settle upon some things and if, consequently, considerable skill in, and understanding for, any pattern of behavior are to develop.

We see the lessened demands being made on American children as symptoms, at least to an important degree, of these broader currents. When Spock and other popular advisers tell parents not to rush the weaning or toilet training of their children, or when contemporary writers take a tolerant view of thumb-sucking and masturbation, or when they do any of the things we have discussed as leading away from an emphasis on stern self-control and an actively manipulative orientation in the rearing of children, we take their remarks as being, in good measure, signs of the more general trends we have just presented. This means that we shall not try to understand changes in each particular method of rearing children by means of an explanation peculiar to it. Instead, our approach to understanding the newer developments in child training will be one that seeks to identify the sources of the broad currents described above and to explain the changes in particular methods of training youngsters as symptoms of those more general tendencies.

. . . . . *CONCLUSION*

Our search for an understanding of recent changes in American child care has led us back over two centuries of history. What have we learned about the present by comparing it with the past? Our results seem to fall into two clusters. First, we can see that present-day changes in child rearing are only the most recent of a long series of such modifications. Second, we are better able to say what is distinctive about the current scene.

Our history of change in American child rearing began with the decline of practices which "broke" the youngster's will. It appears that such practices were almost extinct by the time of the Civil War. Then, beginning early in the last century, there occurred the struggle against parental domination of their children's lives. The child was to have a life of his own; his parents could not live it for him. When this campaign was won by the reform movement at the turn of the century, it was followed by vigorous new measures to teach the child to be self-sufficient and independent; to adapt skillfully to the new demands of a shifting society. Finally, and especially since the end of the Second World War, we saw the growth of yet another change. We have summarized its spirit in the slogans, "Do what seems 'natural' in training your child" and "Be sure the child is ready before you urge him to acquire new skills."

Such evidence as we could muster suggests that middle-class Americans shifted from nursing at the breast to bottle feeding at the same time that they were giving their children more freedom for self-determination. Similarly, they seem to have accepted the idea that corporal punishment was to be minimized to avoid crushing the child's spirit and independence. The use of rigid schedules for feeding appears to have risen after these other developments—probably reaching its peak of acceptance during the 1920's and the early 1930's.

By contrast, many techniques of child care seem to have persisted

American Child Training—Old and New **27**

from the early 1800's on, changing only toward the end of World War II. The age at which infants were weaned completely from breast or bottle appears to have been approximately 12 months. Then, in the middle of the 1940's, the feeling grew that it would not hurt the child if he nursed still longer. In like manner, the custom of beginning toilet training by six months of age was practiced with little variation over some 150 years. Like the age of weaning, the approved age for toilet training was increased substantially around 1945. That same date seems the approximate point at which there was a softening of other long-time practices such as the rigorous prohibition of thumb-sucking and genital exploration and of the firm insistence that children should be put on their own as soon as possible.

How may these recent developments be explained? What accounts for the practices which preceded them? Some answers to these questions are the subject of the next chapter.

NOTES

[1] Robert Sunley, "Early Nineteenth-Century American Literature on Child Rearing," in Margaret Mead and Martha Wolfenstein (eds.), *Childhood in Contemporary Cultures* (Chicago: The University of Chicago Press, 1955), 150–167.

[2] *The Mother's Magazine*—a periodical written from the Calvinist point of view.

[3] *Ibid.*, 160.

[4] Quoted in Arnold Gesell, *The Guidance of Mental Growth in Infant and Child* (New York: The Macmillan Co., 1930), 20–33.

[5] Frances Trollope, *Domestic Manners of the Americans* (New York: Alfred A. Knopf, 1949), 213.

[6] Anthony Trollope, *North America* (New York: Alfred A. Knopf, 1951), 142.

[7] John G. Brooks, *As Others See Us* (New York: The Macmillan Co., 1910).

[8] See: *Ibid.*, and Katherine G. Busbey, *Home Life in America* (London: Methuen and Co., Ltd., 1910).

[9] *Poole's Index* covers the years 1802 through 1907. *The Nineteenth Century Readers' Guide to Periodical Literature* indexes references from 1890 through 1899.

[10] May Belle, "Hasty Mothers," *The Ladies' Home Journal*, 1 (June, 1884), 2. Some trends in this period have been summarized in Celia B. Stendler, "Sixty Years of Child Training Practices," *The Journal of Pediatrics*, 36 (January, 1950), 122–134.

[11] Barnetta Brown, "Mothers' Mistakes and Fathers' Failures," *The Ladies' Home Journal*, 17 (December, 1899), 36; (January, 1900), 30; (February, 1900), 32.

[12] An American Mother, "The Modern Son and Daughter," *The Ladies' Home Journal*, 17 (March, 1900), 17.

[13] Elizabeth R. Scovil, "The Child and Its Mother," *The Ladies' Home Journal*, 17 (March, 1900), 36.

[14] Luther E. Holt, Jr., *The Care and Feeding of Children: A Catechism for the Use of Mothers and Children's Nurses* (New York: D. Appleton and Co., 1929), 183–184.

[15] *Ibid.*, 52.

[16] See, for example: Louise F. Bryson, "The Artificial Feeding of Infants," *The Outlook*, 51 (February 16, 1895), 270–271.

[17] Holt, *op. cit.*, 186.

[18] John B. Watson, *Psychological Care of Infant and Child* (New York: W. W. Norton and Co., 1928).

[19] *Ibid.*, 3.

[20] *Ibid.*, 80.

[21] *Ibid.*, 81–82.

[22] *Ibid.*, 121–122.

[23] *Ibid.*, 126.

[24] *Ibid.*, 150–151.

[25] Martha Wolfenstein, "The Emergence of Fun Morality," *The Journal of Social Issues*, 7, No. 4 (1951), 15–25.

[26] *Ibid.*, 16.

[27] *Ibid.*, 17–20.

[28] *Ibid.*, 24–25.

[29] Benjamin M. Spock, *The Pocket Book of Baby and Child Care* (New York: Pocket Books, Inc., 1954). For the original edition, see: *The Common Sense Book of Baby and Child Care* (New York: Duell, Sloan and Pearce, 1946).

[30] David Riesman and others, *The Lonely Crowd: A Study of the Changing American Character* (New Haven: Yale University Press, 1950).

[31] Spock, *op. cit.* (1954), 3–4.

[32] H. Hartmann, E. Kris, and A. L. Loewenstein, "Comments on the Formation of Psychic Structure," *The Psychoanalytic Study of the Child*, 2 (1946), 11–38.

CHAPTER TWO

. . . . *C*HANGES IN SOCIETY

AND CHILD TRAINING

IN THE UNITED STATES

Distinctive features of child training in the recent American past and in the emerging future are now spread before us. How can the differences between the past and that developing future be explained?

The methods of child care of the first forty years of this century closely resemble the broad spirit and meaning of a style of life long associated with the older kinds of middle-class families in this country. Many of those methods can be found in use by middle-class parents over the last two hundred years. On the other hand, the parental practices that we believe are becoming conspicuous since 1940 look as if they were peculiarly in harmony with the values and ideas—with the way of life—of a new kind of middle-class person whose numbers are rapidly increasing.

We do not distinguish the "older" and "newer" middle classes by the age of their members. They differ in that the occupations in which the older middle classes are found have existed for a long time, whereas the occupations of the newer middle classes have opened up for large numbers of persons only within the past fifty years or so. These older and newer classes also differ in the opportunities and problems afforded by the occupations they hold.

In this chapter we want to describe the older and the newer middle-class occupations, the way of living associated with them, and how it is that each produces a distinctive pattern for the training of children. Reflecting what we believe is the most important difference between them, we shall call these two types of middle classes "individuated-entrepreneurial" and "welfare-bureaucratic"—or, for brevity, entrepreneurial and bureaucratic. We do not say that the differences between them account for all the recent changes in child care found in Chapter One. We do want to claim that their differences are one important source of those changes.

The explanations for trends in child rearing which we develop here and in succeeding chapters require us to make many judgments and interpretations. Not all of these can be firmly substantiated with data from our study.

Fortunately, we can draw upon some fifty years of work by historians and social scientists as we try to picture recent historical changes in America. Our footnotes reflect only a small portion of our indebtedness to this previous scholarship. We have, however, projected explanations for differences in child care which cannot always be verified by referring to earlier studies. As a result, both our explanations and our findings should be considered as only suggestive of the reasons behind historical changes in methods of rearing youngsters. Predictions implied by our explanations find support in our results. Beyond that, as in any scientific enterprise, we must look to further research if the plausible is to become increasingly definitive. It will be for the sake of an uncluttered presentation, and not because we are insensitive to the preliminary state of our work, that we speak in this chapter and the next without constant qualifications and counter-arguments. Later chapters examine some explanations other than those we give here.

..... THE MIDDLE CLASSES IN AN INDIVIDUATED AND ENTREPRENEURIAL SOCIETY

The way of life of the older middle classes in the United States is best understood if we see it as growing out of the opportunities and difficulties such people experience. The way children are trained is partly set by that style of life and springs from the same sources. We shall try to explain methods of child rearing in such terms.

From their beginning, the middle classes were creatures of the rise of commerce and industry and of the cities burgeoning with these new methods of enterprise. Their fate was bound up with the classes above and below them. Middle-class persons—both older and newer— who operate a business are generally distinguished from the upper classes, by the fact that middle-class enterprises are local rather than regional or national in scope. Further, as compared with upper-class families, middle-class households do not have enough surplus income to save more than they spend. Their incomes are more likely to be in the form of salaries, wages, or profits rather than from dividends on investments. As a group, they are more likely than the upper classes to have a high school rather than a college education. Their skills are those of coordinating and recording and of providing specialized advice, but not those of controlling large organizations.

It is useful to distinguish between upper and lower middles. Upper middles are typically the owners or the managers of considerable enterprises. Or they may be persons with special skills, usually achieved through the completion of training at a college level, that enable them to take part in the planning and designing of work on which others will pass at a policy level. Or, as in the case of such independent professions as law and medicine, they have skills that enable them to deal, as no one with lesser training can, with the complexities of problems that are recurrent and most severe for the larger part of the population. As a result of the continuous demand for their skills, whether administrative or professional, such people have considerable job security and sufficient income to enable appreciable savings, while maintaining a level of life that assures plentiful food, home ownership, extended education for the children, and the maintenance of these benefits into the years after the husband has retired from active participation in the economy.

The lower middles are in much less favorable positions. They may have ownership or administrative duties in small enterprises. They may be the communicators and recorders of events—the secretaries and bookkeepers, accountants, clerks, and salesmen—in large concerns, working at a skill level requiring perhaps a high school education. Or, they may be the teachers in the public schools having, at best, an education directed toward producing very specific skills but lacking in the provision of any profound understanding of the philosophical and scientific bases of the tasks performed. Income is most likely to be in the form of salaries. They can save, but this has to be done at the expense of the current standard of living. Furthermore, that standard probably cannot be preserved after retirement. One child in the family might be given a college education or staked to a beginning in business, but most of the children would have to make their own way in life. Finally, since the skill levels of lower middles are modest and the number of such people often is large in relation to demand, their job security is not great.

We can better understand the middle-class family's life if we compare its position with that of the lower classes. Since we will include information about lower class families when we present the findings of our study, these few remarks will serve as background for that later discussion as well as for our immediate purpose of highlighting the characteristics of middles by comparing them with other social classes.

The lower classes are typically distinguished from the middle by working in occupations in which the contribution of the worker comes from manual skills or the use of muscle power. Income is in the form of wages, often on a piecework basis, but rarely on a plan like that of the annual salary which gives some guarantee of the amount that will be earned if the job continues.

The upper lower is the skilled laborer. His training in the schools may vary somewhat, but there is almost certainly a training for the job in an apprentice capacity that involves from two to four years of supervised experience. Until the period of the Second World War, the incomes of upper lowers as a group were usually somewhat lower than those for lower middles. The job security of upper lowers was comparable to that of lower middles if they worked for someone else. Their chances for moving into the upper middle or upper classes were significantly less.

This last point is often overlooked when, as we find in Detroit today, the incomes of upper lowers are slightly higher than those of lower middles. The top positions of power in our society require conceptual and administrative skills. These are not simple to acquire. The individual, usually his family as well, must come to value them and to practice them constantly so that he becomes thoroughly familiar with their uses. Further, this practice requires special education and the postponement of immediate opportunities to earn a living at jobs which, in the beginning, often afford a higher rate of pay. The individual and his family must have some incentive for that kind of sacrifice and some resources to permit its being made instead of devoting their energies to helping support the family. This is why it seems to take at least two generations for a lower-class family to shift into the middle classes with enough stability so that it becomes unlikely that it will return again to a manual labor type of job.

Along with this greater possibility for lower middles rather than upper lowers to advance to the topmost positions of the society, go at least three related advantages. First, there is the greater likelihood of being in a position to meet upper middles and upper-class persons and, having attracted their attention, to gain their help in further advancement, if not for themselves, then for their children. A second advantage of the lower middle over the upper lower is that he has developed a style of life that enables him to capitalize on such contacts and other opportunities that may open up a higher status for him. Finally, the kind of work he does is such that individual advancement, rather than the kind of collective advance that comes through the negotiations of the employee group, is more likely. These advantages have been somewhat lessened by the developments discussed under bureaucratization in the next section of this chapter, but they are still potent.

The lower lowers are the semiskilled and unskilled laborers. Their training is minimal, often requiring but a few hours on the job to equip them for work. When there is a downward trend in the business cycle or an over-supply of labor, theirs are the first jobs to be stripped of security. Such hopes as they have for advancement tend, even more than for upper lowers, to depend on political action or on worker organizations. However, since lower lowers have considerably less in the way of resources and since the road to security through these means is long and involved, they often have little incentive either for the union or for politics.

We have been highlighting the characteristics of all middle-class people by comparing them with the lower and upper classes. Now we turn to consider some features distinctive of the *older* middle classes.

In addition to having the characteristics just described, the older middle classes are entrepreneurial. This is the case not because all their members are businessmen, but because, whether owner, manager, or employee, most of their members' jobs are sharply affected by the risks and vicissitudes of the market place. The entrepreneur is a man who gages how well a product or service will sell and what resources must be spent to produce and market it. His income depends on the accuracy of these judgments. Other occupations become entrepreneurial as they too are affected by these risks and dependent on the accuracy of these judgments. Such effects and dependencies were heightened for most white-collar workers by several aspects of business and industry more prevalent in the nineteenth and early twentieth centuries than today.

First, we must remember that most white-collar employees in that earlier period worked in small establishments. It is true that great enterprises could be found. It is also true, however, that they required relatively few middle-class workers. They were commanded and coordinated by a small corps of white-collar employees at the top, and manned primarily by large numbers of unskilled laborers on the production lines. The elaborate and vast clerical, managerial, engineering, sales, and accounting staffs of present-day corporations are a later development. Far larger proportions of middle-class workers found employment in small stores and workshops than is presently the case. Retailing and the "service" occupations, like manufacture, were more often on a small scale. Large department stores and chain stores did not appear in an important way until the early 1900's.

The small enterprise is highly susceptible to market fluctuations. It lacks resources to tide it over the declines of the business cycle or the difficulties created by the misjudgment of its operators. Its employees, like its managers, become very sensitive to risk and to the impact of the current success of the business on their income.

The second sense in which the older middle classes are entrepreneurial is that risk taking and the creation of enterprise is valued as the highest of economic activities. Financial success as well as financial failure is always possible. Their children prize entrepreneurship as the ideal occupation. Home and school praise and train for it. The heroes of fiction succeed through it. Religion commends it to man as the will of God.

But we say these older middle classes are individuated as well as entrepreneurial. What does that mean?

Individuated people lack close and continuing contacts with each other. They are like the heroes and heroines of so much of recent American fiction, who walk alone through a world crowded with other wanderers. What they have of the world's goods they win for themselves. If they have nothing, it means they have not been able to

Changes in American Society and Child Care **35**

appropriate what they desired. Increasingly, they lack friends and firmly held convictions and a sense of common humanity with their fellows. They are isolated and lonely.

To be individuated is not to be individualistic. The individualistic person has a personal, private life that he cherishes. Like that notable individualist, Thomas Jefferson, he pursues his own interests with zest, convinced of their importance. He sees other people as like himself in possessing personal interests. He believes that they should be encouraged to develop those interests, to pursue those interests, and to be protected and supported in what they choose to do. To him, each person is important as a living, creative being, sharing with him a common human condition.

City life makes people individuated. The very size of cities makes it difficult for them to know most of those whom they see on the streets. At the same time, urban conditions sap the strength of kinship ties. The urban worker depends on his wage or salary from a job that does not put him to work with his relatives. He must, in a dynamic economy, be ready to move his residence to obtain work. Each child must find his own way without the secure reserve or the patrimony of the family farm. Urbanites become impersonal with relatives as well as with strangers.

The diversity of people and values drawn to, and produced by, city life makes it still more difficult for people to meet one another in close relations. Diversity, like size, isolates people from one another.

Wirth (1) gives an admirable sketch of the individuating results of urban conditions:

Characteristically, urbanites meet one another in highly segmental roles. They are, to be sure, dependent upon more people for the satisfactions of their life-needs than are rural people and thus are associated with a greater number of organized groups, but they are less dependent upon particular persons, and their dependence upon others is confined to a highly fractionalized aspect of the other's round of activity. . . . The contacts of the city may indeed be face to face, but they are nevertheless impersonal, superficial, transitory, and segmental. The reserve, the indifference, and the blasé outlook which urbanites manifest in their relationships may thus be regarded as devices for immunizing themselves against the personal claims and expectations of others.

The superficiality, the anonymity, and the transitory character of urban social relations make intelligible, also, the sophistication and the rationality generally ascribed to city-dwellers. Our acquaintances tend to stand in a relationship of utility to us in the sense that the role which each one plays in our life is overwhelmingly regarded as a means for the achievement of our own ends. Whereas, therefore, the individual gains, on the one hand, a certain degree of emancipation or freedom from the personal and emotional controls of intimate groups, he loses, on the other hand, the spontaneous self-expression, the morale, and the sense of participation that comes with living in an integrated society.

. . . .

In a community composed of a larger number of individuals than can know one another intimately and can be assembled in one spot, it becomes necessary to communicate through indirect mediums and to articulate interests by a process of delegation. . . . The individual counts for little, but the voice of the representative is heard with a deference roughly proportional to the numbers for whom he speaks.

. . . .

. . . as Simmel has suggested, the close physical contact of numerous individuals necessarily produces a shift in the mediums through which we orient ourselves to the urban milieu, especially to our fellow men. Typically, our physical contacts are close but our social contacts are distant. . . .

. . . The competition for space is great, so that each area generally tends to be put to the use which yields the greatest economic return. Place of work tends to become dissociated from place of residence.

. . . persons of homogeneous status and needs unwittingly drift into, consciously select, or are forced by circumstances into, the same area. The different parts of the city thus acquire specialized functions. The city consequently tends to resemble a mosaic of social worlds in which the transition from one to the other is abrupt. The juxtaposition of divergent personalities and modes of life tends to produce a relativistic perspective and a sense of toleration of differences which may be regarded as prerequisites for rationality and which lead toward the secularization of life.

The close living together and working together of individuals who have no sentimental and emotional ties foster a spirit of competition, aggrandizement, and mutual exploitation. To counteract irresponsibility and potential disorder, formal controls tend to be resorted to. Without rigid adherence to predictable routines a large compact society would hardly be able to maintain itself. The clock and the traffic signal are symbolic of the basis of our social order in the urban world. Frequent close physical contact, coupled with great social distance, accentuates the reserve of unattached individuals toward one another and, unless compensated for by other opportunities for response, gives rise to loneliness. The necessary frequent movement of great numbers of individuals in a congested habitat gives occasion to friction and irritation. . . .

. . . The heightened mobility of the individual, which brings him within the range of stimulation by a great number of diverse individuals and subjects him to fluctuating status in the differentiated social groups that compose the social structure of the city, tends toward the acceptance of instability and insecurity in the world at large as a norm. This fact helps to

Changes in American Society and Child Care **37**

account, too, for the sophistication and cosmopolitanism of the urbanite. . . .

. . . .

. . . There is little opportunity for the individual to obtain a conception of the city as a whole or to survey his place in the total scheme. Consequently he finds it difficult to determine what is to his own "best interests". . . .

These individuating experiences can be intensified by two additional conditions. The first is the absence, in the city, of active and effective institutions that bind people together. The second is the fact of coming to urban ways from the small town or countryside as a stranger who must learn to live in this new and difficult world. The American experience has included both of these conditions. The second still persists for many city dwellers.

As cities grew, the old institutions of government and religion, of education and charity had neither the ability nor the experience to function with such large and diverse populations, to bind them together for effective joint action or to give them common purpose. It took time for these organizations and others such as trade associations, unions, service clubs, and political parties to grow sufficiently in resources and skill to undertake the job. And, as they did, the narrow and isolated experiences of urban life were reduced in number and importance. Of course they were not obliterated, only diminished in scope and frequency.

Again, even today, some citizens find urban life especially trying because they or their parents have come from the farm and have different expectations from those appropriate for the city. The industrial cities of the United States were fed by migrations of people from the small towns and the countryside. In they came by thousands and tens of thousands. The ties of kinship were broken. The familiar world of town and country was left behind. Bonds to fellow workers or employers were weak. And, with all this, the vastness and strangeness and impersonality of the city made it seem a wilderness. In 1906 Upton Sinclair, speaking for the immigrant to the city, could call his life history "The Jungle." Over and over run the themes: Men come to fear each other. They are strangers. The common law and the common morality corrode. People treat each other as means, not ends. A man in trouble is isolated from the help of kin or clergy or friend. This kind of society in which people live near each other, compete with each other, work with, for, and against each other, yet do not get to know each other with close, sympathetic understanding, as in the smaller community, is a shocking experience to many newcomers within its labyrinth of streets.

When we speak of individuated-entrepreneurial experiences, we refer to a characteristic way in which people are integrated with others in their society. Social classes are said to represent the way people are ranked in a hierarchy of power—are stratified—in a society. We may speak of a particular social class as a man's "stratification position." Correspondingly, we shall want to speak of an entrepreneurial or bureaucratic setting as a man's "integration position" or "integration setting."

. . . . . ENTREPRENEURIAL ORGANIZATION AND CHILD TRAINING

If the foregoing are the sources of individuated and entrepreneurial experiences, how do such experiences affect the way middle-class families rear their children? The answer, though speculative, is probably twofold. First, they are an important part of the kind of world in which those children will have to live. Only foolish or irresponsible parents will fail to train them for it. Second, they determine many of the values and hopes and expectations of the parents with the result that they treat their children, as they treat themselves and most other people, in terms of those values and expectations. Thus, both purposely and unwittingly, these individuated and entrepreneurial experiences are involved in the socialization of the child.

Just how do such middle-class parents find the world? We must look at several features of their experience.

To begin with, there is the matter of self-control. A person with some prospects for personal advancement, or, at least, for maintaining such of the good things of life as he has, but with limited resources, has to learn wise management. In the present, he has to be ever-conscious of his future, husbanding his time and contacts and savings and skills for use at the most propitious moment. His behavior, like his money, is capital for investment. Doing and saying the right things at the correct places can hold or improve his social position. Slender resources of prestige as of money do not permit many bad investments without a loss of status. Such conditions put a premium on controlled, rational behavior, on ignoring the impulse of the moment in the interest of long-range prospects.

But there are other features of the older middle's position that are conducive to the same pattern of behavior. He has to look out for

Changes in American Society and Child Care **39**

himself. No longer can the close ties of kinship hold security for him. He has to rely on his own profits or salary to take care of his wife and children. In the metropolis, friends on whom he might call in time of stress are scarce. Individuation as well as entrepreneurship places a premium on self-control.

Despite their differences, one continuing theme from Susannah Wesley to the time of John Watson is that the child must be taught self-denial, rationality, and a firm control over his current impulses. This is precisely the theme we have just sketched as a product of the experiences of the older middle classes and we want to suggest that it is as their numbers decrease that this theme declines in manuals of advice on child care.

A mother can begin to train her child in self-control and self-denial at a tender age if she will. She can require him to stop nursing before he desires to do so. She can ignore his wails when he is thwarted and upset, leaving him, in crying himself to sleep, to start toward the discovery that all that he wants cannot be had. In feeding him on a schedule which she sets and in putting him on the toilet and rewarding him for having his bowel movements when and as she chooses, she lays a foundation for teaching him that giving up immediate pleasures can lead to future gains. By punishing him when she herself is calm and controlled, she sets an example on which his own conduct can be modeled. By comparing his misconduct to objective standards of goodness, by threatening future punishment for misbehavior that is not amended, by providing deprivations that extend over several hours or days—by any of these instead of through an immediate spanking or slapping, painful at the moment but also something with which she and the child are over in a short time, the mother can underscore the importance of the child's directing himself, counting the costs in the future, and guiding his behavior accordingly.

There is, however, still another individuated-entrepreneurial theme concerning the way to point a child. It runs through the course of more than two hundred years. It is the notion that a youngster must be able independently to go out into the urban world, to capitalize on such opportunities as it may present, to carve out a life for himself which, in a rapidly changing society, may well require different tasks to be performed than were required of his parents. His is to be an active, manipulative approach to people and things. He must learn, as we see in the preceding discussion of urban life, that what he wants he will have to get for himself. Watson closes his book on that note (2).

. . . I believe that the internal structure of our American civilization is changing from top to bottom more rapidly and more fundamentally than most of us dream of. Consequently today less than ever before, is it expedient to bring up a child in accordance with the fixed molds that our parents imposed upon us.

We have tried to sketch . . . *a child as free as possible of sensitivities to people* and one who, almost from birth, *is relatively independent of the family situation.*

Above all, we have tried to create a problem-solving child. We believe that *a problem-solving technique* (which can be trained) *plus boundless absorption in activity* (which can also be trained) are behavioristic factors which have worked in many civilizations of the past and which, so far as we can judge, will work equally well in most types of civilizations that are likely to confront us in the future. [Italics supplied.]

How might such an emphasis on active, independent behavior actually appear in training the child? We feel that it could appear very early in a prohibition of activities in which the child would learn to get satisfactions from his own body or from passive behaviors that did not require him to march upon his world and shape the environment to his own needs. This, we feel, is why such autoerotic activities as thumb-sucking and masturbation have been looked upon with genuine horror and disgust in previous times. We must not underestimate the violence of that disgust. It is not simply from considerations of the care of the teeth or the dangers of infection that children were prohibited from sucking their fingers. Such objective matters might be phrased in terms of dangers to health, but hardly in words like "odious habit," "disgusting practice," and the others that were commonly used. Violent adjectives suggest strong feelings, and our judgment is that those feelings represent, in part, a revulsion at the passivity of these pleasures of the child.

Although touching the genitals may be prohibited in order to prevent the child from becoming sexually stimulated (and we shall have more to say of that later), such prohibitions also prevent his gaining satisfaction from his own body. We believe the older middle classes find it an important element in their indictment of masturbation.

There are, of course, many other kinds of evidence of training the child to be active and independent. Such training appears in purposely breaking the ties to the parents by exposing the child early to other children and to the care of strange adults, and deliberately confronting the child with problems to be solved on his own and without parental assistance.

Under these two themes of child care—training for self-control and the teaching of active and independent behavior—are subsumed many of the specific methods of training youngsters that now are undergoing change. Why are those changes occurring?

Changes in American Society and Child Care **41**

One source of an individuated society, and of techniques of rearing children related to it, lay in the conditions of urban living. Surely the proportion of urbanites has not declined. More people than ever live in cities and metropolitan areas and the movement from the farms proceeds at a rapid pace. Further, even those families still living in small towns and in rural areas increasingly find their experiences set by the urban centers that dominate the American scene.

It is true that urbanism continues and swells in importance, and that many of its salient features as already outlined persist up to the present. It is also true, however, that city life has been modified and the entrepreneurial experiences known to the older middle classes—the uncertainties of the man of modest resources who must use them with care and caution—have been altered in drastic ways. We cannot be certain that these modifications in the form of the bureaucratization of American life are the only source of the newer styles of rearing children, but we feel they are an important source of the newer developments and quite consistent with the results in child and adult behavior that those styles seem to produce. It is to the origins and nature of this modification that we now turn. First, we describe the sources and characteristics of welfare bureaucracy. Then we examine its impact on the way parents train their children.

. . . . . THE MIDDLE CLASSES AND WELFARE BUREAUCRACY

Toward the end of the nineteenth century and the beginning of the twentieth, new organizational trends appeared that were to transform much of the life of all Americans and to produce a new kind of middle class. These new trends are modifying the older and more individuated society of the United States just as the latter took the place of village and rural ways of life. For this emerging pattern of social life, we shall use the term "welfare bureaucracy." This new pattern of life is bureaucratic because it is characterized by large organizations employing many kinds of specialists and coordinating their activities by supervisors who follow a codified set of rules of practice. Its flavor is that of "welfare" bureaucracy because it can and must provide a large measure of security for its participants. Since the white-collar workers—the middle classes—are more likely to be highly specialized than the blue-collar employees, they are also more likely to be the first to feel the impact of these new conditions. Our purpose here is to describe these conditions, to contrast them with those of a more individuated period, and to show some of their effects on parents and children.

As we see it, four essential conditions are bringing about the change from individuated-entrepreneurial to welfare-bureaucratic (or, as we shall speak of it, bureaucratic) organization. These are: (*a*) the increase in the size of the organization of production, (*b*) the growth of specialization in organizations, (*c*) the great increase in the real incomes of the population, and (*d*) the enlarged power in the hands of lower-middle and lower-class workers (3).

The increase in the size of organizations and in the proportion of their personnel who are specialists of some kind are the two defining characteristics of bureaucracy. Organizations are bureaucratic to the extent that they exhibit these features. Much that we shall have to say about the newer methods of child care will be explained as flowing from the experiences which parents encounter in a bureaucratized society.

We feel that American prosperity and the enlarged power of the lower middle and lower classes are important for our story because these two developments provide crucial aspects of the setting in which we expect bureaucratic influences to modify techniques of rearing children. These two conditions underlie our conception of welfare bureaucracy. Prosperity not only represents greater income, but it means, in our day, that there is a considerable shortage of workers. That shortage, in turn, forces employers to give active attention to the problem of keeping their personnel happy and satisfied. We shall try to show how this makes an important modification in the amount of impersonality and insecurity experienced by bureaucratic employees.

The political strength of the American people, like prosperity, seems to us to affect the consequences of bureaucratization. It has forced the creation of governmental welfare measures which, like prosperity, enhance the economic security of the labor force. And, like prosperity, it provides a measure of freedom for employees that enables them to make demands of the organizations for which they work to the end that mutual respect and satisfaction are underwritten between employer and worker.

Each of these four conditions of welfare bureaucracy will now be discussed. Then we shall turn to the way of life and the methods of rearing children we believe to be consistent with them.

Increased Organizational Size

The decline of small business in all fields of endeavor and the shift toward larger and larger units have many sources. The population has been growing. Larger scale manufacturing and commerce can serve that population with greater economies on each unit sold than can small concerns. Because such large-scale concerns are working over vast regional, national, and international markets, they are not so susceptible to the ill effects of purely local drops in purchasing power; their profits are more stable. Not only can they compete successfully for existing markets, but they can create new ones through their ability to sponsor research, conduct massive advertising campaigns, and produce a greater variety of goods and services tailored to the desires of small, but significant, groups of purchasers. All of these potential advantages have been helped on their way to reality by the continuing development of machinery that increases the amount that can be produced and by such organizational inventions as assembly-line production, the corporation, and the holding company. By breaking production into small parts, the assembly line permits a considerable increase in the volume of work turned out. The corporation, owned by large numbers of investors, with each liable for its debts only to the extent of his investment, allows for gigantic increases in the amount of capital available to start and expand production.

We have spoken of the growth of factories before the twentieth century as a growth of large organizations. In relative terms this is true. It was experienced as such by the people at the time. Yet, in a modern sense, most of these factories would not be considered large. The difference may be illustrated this way. It is estimated that the typical American urban manufacturing concern in the first half of the nineteenth century employed from fifty to one hundred persons. We may contrast this situation with estimates for 1948. Based on reports from establishments paying wages taxable under the Old-Age and Survivor's Insurance plan, a program covering the vast majority of employees in manufacturing concerns, we find that 75 per cent of all employees in manufacturing were employed in firms having 100 or more persons. Some 47.5 per cent worked in firms numbering 500 or more employees, and 34.9 per cent were in establishments of 1000 or more workers (4). For manufacturing, Table 2–1 (5) is a summary of increases in organizational size since the turn of the century (6).

Table 2–1

PERCENTAGE OF WAGE WORKERS IN MANUFACTURING INDUSTRIES BY SIZE OF ORGANIZATION

Number of Wage Workers in Reporting Unit	Year			
	1909	1919	1929	1939
1–50	26.0	19.4	19.8	19.2
51–100	11.8	9.8	10.3	10.8
101–250	19.0	17.4	18.1	18.7
251–1000	27.9	27.0	27.9	29.1
1001 or more	15.3	26.4	24.0	22.4
Total	100.0%	100.0%	100.1%	100.2%
Number	6,615,046	9,096,372	8,369,705	7,886,567

Number of Wage Workers in Reporting Unit*	Year	
	1947	1951
1–49	15.9	
50–99	9.1	38.6†
100–249	15.6	
250–999	26.6	27.0
1000 or more	32.8	34.4
Total	100.0%	100.0%
Number	14,294,304	15,612,619

* The published groupings of the Census of Manufactures changed for 1947 and 1951. So slight is the change, that it will hardly account for the major shifts described in this table.

† The published report of the 1951 *Annual Survey of Manufactures* gives only this summary figure for firms employing from 1 to 249 wage workers.

45

Table 2–2

NON-FARM LABOR FORCE: SOCIAL-ECONOMIC GROUP OF THE EMPLOYED CIVILIAN LABOR FORCE FOR 1950, OF THE EXPERIENCED LABOR FORCE FOR 1940, AND OF GAINFUL WORKERS FOR 1870 TO 1930

(FOR PERSONS FOURTEEN YEARS OLD AND OVER)*

Socio-economic Group	Year					
	1870	1910	1920	1930	1940	1950
Professional persons	6.2	6.3	6.6	7.7	7.8	8.6
Wholesale and retail dealers	⎤ 8.7	4.8	4.5	4.6	4.7	⎤ 12.4
Other proprietors, managers, and officials	⎦	4.7	4.5	4.9	4.5	⎦
Clerks and kindred workers	4.7	14.8	18.3	20.7	20.7	22.4
Skilled workers and foremen	⎤ 50.3	17.0	18.0	16.4	14.2	14.5
Semiskilled workers		21.3	21.4	20.8	25.4	32.3
Laborers	⎦	21.2	19.4	16.3	12.9	6.1
Servant classes	14.7	9.8	7.2	8.7	9.7	3.7
Total	84.6%	99.9%	99.9%	100.1%	99.9%	100.0%
Number	6,578,156	25,731,890	30,990,994	38,395,379	43,037,126	51,648,000

* The data for 1870 do not add to 100 per cent since the basic tables include a group numbering 15.3 per cent of the labor force that is called "unclassified."

Growth of Specialization

Luther Gulick has given a succinct statement of the causes of specialization (7):

1. . . . men differ in nature, capacity, and skill.
2. . . . no man can be in two places at the same time.
3. . . . no man can do two things at the same time.
4. . . . no man knows everything.

Most of the jobs that have become specialized did so for one of the first three reasons listed by Gulick. The classic illustration is the establishment of assembly-line procedures.

Specialization has made important changes in the characteristics of the labor force. Table 2–2 (8) shows the major differences. Several important trends have appeared since the 1890's. Especially striking are the decline of laborers and the steady rise of semiskilled workers and of "clerks and kindred" types of employees. The percentage of professional and semiprofessional persons increased steadily but slowly in the non-farm labor force. Skilled workers and foremen showed a decline of similar proportions (9). Servants and the broad group of proprietors, managers, and officials held relatively steady positions over these years.

These changes sharpen our picture of the results of a growth in the size and specialization of economic enterprise. Increasingly, machines have provided skills that in an earlier period would have been found in the talents of workmen. The machine tender, a semiskilled worker, does not have the kind of technical knowledge that he can take with him from job to job. His skill lies in "his ability to adjust quickly to the sequence and timing of his operation and to the attainment of an acceptable volume and quality of output" (10). Simultaneously, however, technological development has opened new jobs for skilled workers, and the demand for their services has shown only a slow decline.

Greater size and specialization of organizations have meant somewhat different things for white-collar employees. First, the proportion of white-collar workers has risen sharply. Second, although their numbers are small in relation to the total work force, increased demands for specialized skills have produced a rise in the proportion of professional workers in the population. In Table 2–3 (11) we find, similarly, that there has been an increase in the percentage of salaried corporation officers and a decline in the proportion of proprietors and

Changes in American Society and Child Care **47**

members of firms in the total labor force. This last pair of tendencies reflects the larger requirements of big organizations for specially trained management. This growing separation of ownership and administration has been dramatized as the "managerial revolution."

Broad data from the census mask some of the sharpness of the increase in managerial and other professionals as a proportion of the labor force. If, for example, we look only at some professions most closely connected with economic production, the change is clearer. Thus, from 1890 to 1940 the number of gainful workers per college-trained engineer employed in manufacturing, mining, construction, transportation, and public utilities dropped from about 300 to less than 100 (12).

Table 2–3

PERCENTAGE OF PERSONS EMPLOYED IN MANUFACTURING ESTABLISHMENTS, BY OCCUPATION

Occupation	Year*						
	1899	1904	1909	1919	1929	1939	1947
Proprietors and members of the firm		3.6	3.6	2.5	1.4	1.2	
Salaried officers of corporations	7.7†	1.0	1.1	1.2	1.6	1.3	16.5‡
All other salaried employees		7.4	9.2	12.2	11.6	14.2	
Wage earners	92.3	88.0	86.1	84.1	85.5	82.4	82.5
Total	100.0%	100.0%	100.0%	100.0%	100.1%	100.1%	99.0%

* The data for 1899 through 1919 include reports for establishments with products valued between $500 and $5000. More recent data do not include these small manufacturers.

† Information for 1899 grouped salaried persons together and did not include statistics for proprietors and members of the firm.

‡ Information for 1947 grouped together all administrative, supervisory, sales, technical, office, and all other clerical personnel. It is not clear whether it does or does not include information for proprietors and members of the firm.

Increase in Real Income

One of the phenomenal differences between the lot of most Americans in the nineteenth and those of the twentieth centuries is the rise in income, not only in terms of dollars, but of buying power. Despite a great depression and the inflation that accompanied two global wars, there has been a steady rise in the buying power of the American people at about the rate of 2 per cent a year (13). Even over shorter periods, the rise in real income is most impressive. From 1929 to 1951, real income rose 131 per cent (14). Another way to see the size of American prosperity is to compare real income in the United States with that in other Western, industrial countries. In 1949 (15) real income was $1450 *per capita* in the United States. By contrast, it was $870 in Canada, $780 in Sweden, $770 in the United Kingdom, and $230 in Italy. Asian and African peoples fared even less well by comparison. For example, the estimated figure for Korea is $35, for Japan, $100, for Communist China, $30, and for Ethiopia, Kenya, Liberia, and Northern Rhodesia, $40.

Again, it is impressive that in recent years the percentage increase in American incomes has been greatest for those in the lower income groups. On every hand are signs that there has been a progressive equalization of income within the population through the rise in the amount of money in the hands of the least well paid (16).

Enlarged Power of the Lower-Middle and Lower Classes

The final condition that has led to what we call welfare bureaucracy is the increased power in the hands of lower-middle and lower-class people in the United States (17). The sources of this trend are complex, but its presence is reflected in the progressive enfranchisement of all the American people, and in the greater sensitivity of the Federal government to their needs and wishes. The trend is also mirrored in the success of such organizations as the labor unions which (whether or not actually providing the forces responsible for the rise in workers' incomes) seem to have gained greater job security for their members, to have helped them mobilize for political action, and to have represented them as effective pressure groups in the nation's councils.

We have been looking at the changes from an individuated-entrepreneurial to a welfare-bureaucratic society as if they happened in smooth transitions without overlap or conflict. This is not the case. An English economic historian (18) could say that his country at the turn of the century embodied most of the previous economic systems of her history with sizable portions of the population employed in each organizational setting. It is easy to find examples of such a variety of economic patterns in contemporary America. The small businessman still exists. The unorganized worker in fields oversupplied with labor can be found. The employee in the small establishment, depending on his employer's good will and clinging precariously to the uncertain fortunes of the little store or shop lives in the same towns as do the employees of welfare bureaucracies. Sons and daughters from both backgrounds often work in the same establishments and,

Changes in American Society and Child Care **49**

with their very different expectations of the future and interpretations of the present, find it difficult to understand one another (19). We shall find integrations of both the entrepreneurial and bureaucratic varieties in the Detroit area.

..... *THE DEMANDS OF BUREAUCRATIC
ORGANIZATIONS*

The whole development of welfare bureaucracy changes the world for the middle-class citizens who join its ranks. No longer need they struggle and strive so hard. They must still be circumspect and respectable, but their incomes do not depend on manipulating a host of risks and investments.

The early picture that observers had of the likely consequences of bureaucratization for the middle classes took its cues primarily from the educational and governmental bureaucracies of Europe and the United States where this form of organization first matured. The employee in a bureaucratic situation should, it was felt, be more secure than his fellow in an individuated situation. The large organization had resources enabling it to continue operation without becoming disorganized through the minor ups and downs of the business cycle. Therefore it could provide job security.

Bureaucracies also embodied other sources of employee security. It takes time to train a man for a specialized type of work. To lose trained men costs money. They are hard to replace. Large organizations could keep their employees by providing them with tenure and pension plans and by guaranteeing them advancement on the basis of seniority.

Seniority not only worked to keep employees with a particular company, but it solved another problem of bureaucracies as well. A large, complex organization requires the continued, faithful performance of duties. Payrolls must come out. A product must flow from the production lines. A sales force has to be advised, stimulated, and coordinated. And these functions must be performed on an hourly and daily basis. They do not allow for drastic or continuous tampering. Steady morale must underlie steady performance. An employee with unusual imagination and energy who tries to institute drastic changes can cause the whole complex machine to grind to a halt. Such enterprising efforts are desirable, but need to be kept under control. To retain a high level of staff morale and to discourage excessive drive and ambition, a regular system of promotion through seniority provides an answer.

Just as size and complexity of organization can lead to employee security, they also exact a price from their personnel. The ideal worker must be precise and conscientious in performance. He must keep to his assigned task and not stray off into the provinces of others even if he has some new ideas for the performance of their work. He must always "clear" ideas and problems "through channels" with his superiors. Because he may leave the company or die, his work and plans must be reported on paper so that someone else may take his place and continue where he left off. He must, like the individuated middle-class worker, be rational, looking to the consequences of his action and curbing momentary desires until their consequences can be examined and evaluated. He must not be aggressive or too ambitious for these qualities disturb the organization's course.

Thus it is clear, even though entrepreneurial and bureaucratic organizations make some similar demands of their personnel, they also differ in critical ways. In particular, bureaucratic organizations find unnecessary or undesirable the rather extreme self-control and self-denial and the active, manipulative, ambition that entrepreneurial organizations exalt. This difference is one that we expect to find influential in determining how children are reared.

This takes us a little ahead of our story. There is one feature of bureaucracy as described by the early writers on European and American developments that we feel has undergone considerable modification in the contemporary United States. Because the interpretation of this feature of bureaucracy makes a difference in the account of how the newer middle classes rear their children, we shall take it up in some detail. It is the stress in the earlier accounts on the theme that bureaucratic organizations force people to deal impersonally with one another (20).

Those accounts say that the size and complexity of bureaucratic organizations force employees to see each other, the organization's clients, and themselves as parts of an organization, not as people. Bureaucratic personnel, these descriptions asserted, must learn to treat each other, not as living, feeling flesh that might make demands for special treatment or that might have idiosyncratic needs, but as human machines who might legitimately require only those things necessary for playing their parts in the organization. Each participant, these accounts continued, has a job to do, with limited but compulsory responsibilities and requirements. Other considerations must not be allowed to interfere with this impersonal order.

Changes in American Society and Child Care **51**

If these early descriptions of bureaucracy were correct about the unadulterated impersonality of the human relations in such organizations, we would have to conclude that bureaucracy exacerbates rather than relieves the individuating tendencies of urban life. In its impersonality it would be yet another way of isolating people from one another and should promote a wary self-control. However accurate these early accounts may have been as descriptions of the governmental and military bureaucracies on which they are based, we feel that they do not describe the growing spirit of large organizations in the United States today. This is the reason that we speak not simply of "bureaucracy" but of "welfare bureaucracy" as characterizing our place and time.

What difference does that adjective "welfare" make? We use it to represent developments having the effect of reducing impersonality; of doing much toward transforming the relation of employees to their employers and to each other from one based on a formal job contract to one based on a shared moral relationship. All of this has consequences for the interpretation we want to make of the newer developments in child care, so we shall elaborate our meaning before presenting that interpretation.

The language of employer-employee relations tells much of the story. In the entrepreneurial organization and in the earlier and more authoritarian bureaucracy, management defined its relations to the work force in terms of employee discipline. It was assumed that the worker came haltingly to his tasks. He was seen as resisting or lazy or stubborn and the problem of the supervisor was that of providing him with direct and effective rewards and deprivations which would force him, in his own self-interest, to behave as desired. It was also implicit that supervisors had the power to perform such a task. One magazine much favored among entrepreneurs still describes its model for labor relations with the telling analogy of the donkey that can be persuaded only by the proper, but minimal, rewards of the carrot and, simultaneously, proper and judicious prods from the master's stick. But even *Time* is not always timely. The day of forcing the worker to his desk or machine passed. The day of fitting him to the job took its place.

Shortly before the First World War, a student of industrial management, Frederick J. Taylor, published his epochal *The Principles of Scientific Management* (21). He pointed out that workers "soldiering" on the job hurt their company's competitive position. Labor discontent was costly. Taylor urged on management the adoption of procedures that would minimize such discontent. If unruly impulses could not be eliminated, they could be managed. The way to do it was to fit the worker's needs to his job by a program of determining the demands the job would make, by simplifying jobs through breaking them into tasks "anyone" could perform, and by hiring employees who would find these jobs congenial. This theory became a great modern impetus for the personnel man—a man defined as one who could analyze jobs and administer tests to find workers whose personalities and skills fitted the work situation.

However, even Taylor's scientific management was not adequate to the newer problems of contemporary organization. It assumed a degree of managerial dominance that was already passing in his time. The latest step has been the adaptation of the job to the worker. Pressures for such a move were inherent in welfare bureaucracy. They were, as we remarked earlier, enhanced by the growing political power of employees and by their prosperity. From the assumptions of the disciplining of labor, the social relations of management moved to adapting the worker to his tasks, and from that to the maintenance of his morale. This last step needs some elaboration.

A concern with worker morale suggests that managerial skills are now directed toward enlisting worker desires and aspirations. But it also assumes that it is in the worker's power to grant or to refuse such enlistment. If he refuses, management will have to continue trying to gain his support. Within the limitations set by technology, the worker's loyalty can be had by adjusting the conditions of work to his desires. The word "loyalty" is central. He must be prevented from disturbing the routines of production by transferring to another company. If he is highly specialized in tasks such as those of business operation or design or sales or any of the pyramiding number of others in which there is no clear and rapid index available by which his performance may be judged, supervision is extremely difficult. He must be self-supervised. He must want to perform with high proficiency. An essential part of that performance is set by the way he gets along with other people. For many reasons the older conceptions of control and decision-making in giant organizations have broken down (22). Again, there is required a devotion to the welfare of the enterprise and a satisfaction with its procedures if the irritations of human interaction are to be minimized. No known techniques of supervision could compel such behavior (23).

This kind of natural loyalty and devotion does not come solely from good pay and a feeling of dominance over one's employer. It represents the experience of a fundamentally moral relationship. Morals, in turn, are the code of social rules that grow up to preserve a situation in which people find each other's presence to be so mutually rewarding and, simultaneously, so lacking in threat, that they feel wholly comfortable and spontaneous and seek to preserve their happy and productive state. The problem of management is to establish such a moral relationship with its workers without losing its authority over them. There has been a persistent and analogous problem for parents in dealing with their children—how to be both authority and benefactor. The management solution, like that of many parents, is one of seeking avidly for benefits it can give without jeopardizing control. The pastel-colored washrooms, the coffee breaks, the use of first names on the job, the company banquet, the employee picnic, the practice of consultation with employees on those decisions where a crucial management position will not be compromised are examples of the important devices to be used. The change of the personnel man and the vice-president in charge of employee relations from, respectively, giving tests and settling disputes on a legal, contractual basis to the roles of counselors and liaison men is part of the same movement. What once was accomplished in small informal groups in the little communities and in the countryside now is the subject of planning and of the construction of elaborate formal organizational devices. Moral relations in large institutions, like the daily quota of parts produced, must be planned.

The benefits, not the planning, must be the conspicuous thing in the worker's experience. He must feel that what was done occurred because management was genuinely interested in his welfare, not because the benefits would result in higher productivity. Since there are always suspicions of management's motives, there are persistent tests of the genuineness of the employer's concern. The limits of his willingness to fraternize and spend time on non-productive employee interests are sought. Walkouts that seem irrational to workers, union leaders, and supervisors alike may occur to determine whether management will be punitive or understanding. Morale may be the overt subject of discussion, but morality is its central object.

These paragraphs on the moral nature of relations in a welfare bureaucracy have been broad and descriptive. They have sought, in the absence of more systematically gathered evidence, to bring together a picture of a new and potent and, in good measure, incipient style of life. They emphasize our view that the competitive and amoral world of the individuating metropolis is being changed. The consequence, we believe, is yet another force that makes striving and extreme and rigid self-control less necessary than before. Further, it seems to us that the reestablishment of moral relations makes such striving and self-control less desirable than formerly for they interfere with the development of supportive and moral relations among employees. Now we must examine some of the effects of moralization and the other features of welfare bureaucracy on the training of children.

. . . . . BUREAUCRACY AND CHILD TRAINING

Bureaucratized parents train their children for this new world and treat them in terms of its values. For most parents, this will not be a matter of self-conscious planning. Their methods of child care will simply reflect the values these mothers and fathers have learned from living in a bureaucratized society.

In the previous chapter we summarized some of those values in the questions, "Is it natural?" and "Is the child old enough?" In the more relaxed and secure atmosphere of a society whose tone is set importantly by welfare bureaucracy, the child, like the adult, is free to enjoy the present, to express his feelings. Not only is he free, but the confident, smooth social relations of the great organizations of which he must become a part will require him to get along well with other people and to take their feelings as well as his own into account with skill and confidence.

This child will need to be taught that superiors are not hateful figures to be challenged, but men of skill and feeling, whom he should emulate, and with whom he can cooperate. As William Henry (24) puts it in his study of workers who win high executive appointments:

> The successful executive posits authority as a controlling but helpful relationship to superiors. He looks to his superiors as persons of more advanced training and experience, whom he can consult on special problems and who issue to him certain guiding directives. He does not see the authorities in his environment as destructive or prohibiting forces.
>
> . . . .
>
> In general the mobile and successful executive looks to his superiors with a feeling of personal attachment and tends to identify himself with them. . . .

The adult, as the child, must be warm, friendly, and supportive of others. The child will not develop in this way if his family provides too little nurturance or too cold and objective and difficult an environment for him. It is a plea for just such high and continued nurturance that characterizes the advice to parents by Spock and other "authorities" on child care in our time. The powerful ambitions and desires for independence cherished by our middle classes for two centuries would unfit a youngster for participation in a society that requires him to be relaxed and cooperative—a willing subordinate to the policies of a great organization. Such passive enjoyments as thumb-sucking not only fail to incapacitate the child for future independence, but may actually be one way of teaching him valuable skills. They may give him practice in an accommodative approach to life. They may teach him to relax and be content when under pressure rather than to make demands on other people for a change in his environment.

By contrast, teaching the child self-control and self-denial at a very early age through such devices as bowel training in the first six months of life, or requiring him to give up the breast or bottle at such an age, or refusing to pay attention to him if he cries "just to get attention" not only is made unnecessary by the lesser demands of bureaucratic life but may actually disturb the baby's confidence in people. It may shake his firm sense that, as Spock puts it, he belongs to them and they to him.

The bureaucratization of adult experience does not lead to a lack of discipline in training children. It does not mean that highly "passive" or "dependent" persons are desired. It means that discipline takes "external" forms such as spanking rather than "internal" forms such as appeals to conscience, and that more passivity and dependence are tolerated and, on occasion, encouraged than would have been true under individuated conditions.

When parents expected that their children would be relatively unsupervised and isolated from others as they moved into adult activities, they needed to train their youngsters by means which would insure that strong consciences were acquired. Armored with a powerful conscience, a man might be expected to obey the social codes even when surrounded by the opportunities and temptations afforded by the anonymity and heterogeneity of an entrepreneurial society. However, when parents can feel that their children will grow up in a closely knit and moral society in which, as members of great organizations, their behavior will be guided and supervised through daily contacts with others, there is less need for fathers and mothers to provide the child with a stern, self-propelling conscience. For reasons we elaborate as we present our finding, such external punishments as spankings may be expected to occur more frequently under bureaucratic than under entrepreneurial conditions, whereas entrepreneurial families, to develop and reinforce a vigorous conscience in the child, will be more likely to make use of such disciplines as deprivation of privileges and parental lectures that make the child feel he is responsible for his own misdeeds and that make him feel guilty when he disobeys.

Thus we expect that two themes of child care emphasized under entrepreneurial conditions—the themes of self-control and of an actively manipulative orientation toward the world—will receive less stress in a bureaucratic society. We have argued, further, that greater dependence is placed on continuing and external controls exercised on the individual by his fellows and his superiors in the bureaucratic situation while a more accommodative orientation toward the world is actually encouraged.

Intrigued by the seeming consistencies and affinities between the values of the newer middle classes and the methods now being advocated for rearing children, we have concluded that the bureaucratization of the American people is an important source of the recent emphases in child care. Although the picture given in this chapter pays special attention to those whose involvement in that change is best understood, the middle classes, lower-class Americans and their children certainly are affected by these same trends. We will describe the social situation of lower-class families as we present findings about them as well as about the middle-class parents in our study. The next chapter tells how we obtained information about child rearing in order to test our ideas.

..... *SUMMARY*

At this point we bring together some of the observations in this chapter. We have described two types of integration setting, the entrepreneurial and bureaucratic, and have associated them with certain methods of child care.

The term entrepreneurial has referred to organizations having these features: small size, a simple division of labor, a relatively small capitalization, and provision for mobility and income through risk taking and competition. Social situations were called individuated if they isolate people from one another and from the controlling influence of shared cultural norms. Children reared in individuated and entrepreneurial homes will be encouraged to be highly rational, to exercise great self-control, to be self-reliant, and to assume an active, manipulative stance toward their environment.

The term bureaucratic has referred to organizations which are large and which employ many different kinds of specialists. It is typical that the capitalization of such enterprises is substantial and that participants' incomes are in the form of wages or salary. Mobility comes through specialized training for a particular position rather than through success in taking risks once on the job. A welfare bureaucracy is one in which the organization provides considerable support to the participants in meeting their personal crises and offers the security of continuity of employment and income despite some fluctuations of the business cycle. Children reared in welfare-bureaucratic homes will be encouraged to be accommodative, to allow their impulses some spontaneous expression, and to seek direction from the organizational programs in which they participate.

NOTES

[1] Louis Wirth, "Urbanism as a Way of Life," *The American Journal of Sociology*, 44 (July, 1938), 1–24.

[2] John B. Watson, *Psychological Care of Infant and Child* (New York: W. W. Norton and Co., 1928), 186–187.

[3] The development of automation may have as profound effects on the organization of American life as any of these, but its role is in the future and has no consequences for our present study.

[4] Wladimir S. Woytinsky and others, *Employment and Wages in the United States* (New York: The Twentieth Century Fund, 1953).

[5] The sources of the data in this table are the volumes of the United States *Census of Manufactures*. The respective years reported in the table and the dates of publication of the census reports in which they are found are:

1909—*Census of Manufactures*, 1913, Vol. 3, 185.
1919—*Census of Manufactures*, 1923, 85.
1929—and 1939—*Census of Manufactures*, 1942, Vol. 1, 120.
1947—*Census of Manufactures*, 1950, 97.
1951—*Annual Survey of Manufactures: 1951*, 1953, 126.

The use of evidence here and elsewhere for manufacturing establishments as symptoms of bureaucratization should not be taken to mean that this trend fails to appear elsewhere in the economy. Data for manufacturing happen to be more complete on many points than are those from other enterprises.

[6] The argument is sometimes advanced that, since the percentage of the American labor force employed in service occupations is growing more rapidly than the proportions engaged in agriculture and manufacturing, it is likely that the number of small enterprises and the proportion of persons employed by them will evidence a sharp increase. If this trend is in the making it has not yet appeared in any dramatic fashion in the official government statistics. An examination of the United States *Census of Business* for the years 1929 through 1948, and including retail, wholesale, and service occupations as the data for each become available, shows that there has been an increase in the average number of employees working for each of these types of enterprise. Although it is true that, among retail stores, fewer outlets are centrally controlled by the managements of the very

largest grocery chains, it also is true that the total number of persons employed by chain stores has increased over the period for which data exist. In the face of a somewhat declining number of stores operated by chain management, this means that the size of each remaining store under such control is larger than before.

Even if future studies show that there is an increase in the number of small enterprises in the retail, wholesale, and service fields, it may well be that the character of such enterprise will be substantially different from that which we have considered typical of an entrepreneurial society. These small businesses will operate in a society in which bureaucratized manufacturing provides a kind of security and stability that should serve to reduce the risks and isolation of the small shopkeeper and other minor businessmen even as it has that effect on its own employees.

[7] Luther Gulick, "Notes on the Theory of Organization," in Luther Gulick and L. Urwick (eds.), *Papers on the Science of Administration* (New York: Institute of Public Administration, Columbia University, 1937), 3.

[8] Data for 1870 are adapted from Wladimir S. Woytinsky, *Labor in the United States: Basic Statistics for Social Security* (Washington, D. C.: Social Science Research Council, 1938), 270. Statistics for the years 1910 through 1940 were computed from a report in: United States Bureau of the Census, *Historical Statistics of the United States: 1789–1945* (Washington, D. C.: United States Government Printing Office, 1949), 65. The information for 1950 was taken from A. J. Jaffe and Charles D. Stewart, *Manpower Resources and Utilization: Principles of Working Force Analysis* (New York: John Wiley and Sons, Inc., 1951), 146.

[9] Because of the nature of the categorization of data by the United States Census, it is likely that this trend should not be applied to skilled laborers. There is evidence that the proportion of skilled laborers in the urban labor force is rising.

[10] Harry Ober, "The Worker and His Job," *Monthly Labor Review*, 71 (July, 1950), 15.

[11] Data for the years 1899 through 1939 were obtained from United States Bureau of the Census, *Census of Manufactures*, Vol. 1 (Washington, D. C.: United States Government Printing Office, 1942), 67. Data for 1947 come from the *Census of Manufactures* for that year and published in 1950. See page 69 of that report.

[12] "Employment Outlook for Engineers," *Monthly Labor Review*, 69. (July, 1949), 15.

[13] See, for example, Elizabeth E. Hoyt and others, *American Income and Its Use* (New York: Harper and Bros., Publishers, 1954), 87–91; and William F. Ogburn, "Technology and the Standard of Living in the United States," *The American Journal of Sociology*, 60 (January, 1955) 380–386.

[14] Hoyt, *op. cit.*, xvi.

[15] *Ibid.*, xii.

[16] *Ibid.*, 132–135.

[17] For the story of this change see Richard Hofstadter's *The American Political Tradition and the Men Who Made It* (New York: Alfred Knopf, Inc., 1948). Also useful are: Charles A. and Mary R. Beard, *The Rise of American Civilization* (New York: The Macmillan Company, 1930) and their *America in Midpassage* (New York: The Macmillan Co., 1939).

[18] George Unwin, *Industrial Organization in the Sixteenth and Seventeenth Centuries* (Oxford: The Clarendon Press, 1904), 1–15.

Changes in American Society and Child Care **59**

[19] David Riesman and others, *The Lonely Crowd: A Study of the Changing American Character* (New Haven: Yale University Press, 1950), 3–35.

[20] For a convenient summary of the literature describing bureaucratic characteristics, see: Robert K. Merton and others (eds.), *Reader in Bureaucracy* (Glencoe, Illinois: The Free Press, 1952).

[21] *The Principles of Scientific Management* (New York: Harper and Brothers, 1911).

[22] A book written largely in the course of attempts to identify the newer problems of organizational functioning is Herbert A. Simon and others, *Public Administration* (New York: Alfred A. Knopf, Inc., 1950).

[23] A summary of many studies of the relation of the newer attempts at supervision to overcome this problem appears in Edward A. Shils' article "The Study of the Primary Group," in Daniel Lerner and Harold D. Lasswell (eds.), *The Policy Sciences: Recent Developments in Scope and Method* (Stanford University Press, 1951), 44–69. See also: Riesman and others, *op. cit.*

[24] William E. Henry, "The Business Executive: The Psychodynamics of a Social Role," *The American Journal of Sociology*, 54 (January, 1949), 288, 290.

THE FINDINGS . . . .

CHAPTER THREE

Interviewing Mothers in the Detroit Area

Testing one's ideas against the facts is never a direct and perfect affair. The limitations of funds and facilities, and of methods for observing what one needs to see, force many compromises while they permit some gains in knowledge. We now want to report some of those gains and compromises. For any reader, this review of the methods used in our study will help in understanding the findings we obtained. For the professional social scientist, it may aid in judging what should be done to improve our work.

The facilities available to us were those of

the Detroit Area Study (DAS) of the University of Michigan (1). Supported by a grant from the Ford Foundation, the DAS conducts a large scale study in the Detroit metropolitan area once each year. A number of reasons, principally the desire to obtain samples of basic social data on a large urban area for several consecutive years, dictated that the form taken by the first few studies using DAS resources would involve random samples of the adults in the area's households. Each year, in addition to collecting information on such questions as family income, age and occupational distributions, length of residence in the area, and educational level, the DAS gathers information of special interest to the one or more participating faculty members of the University. In 1953, interview length was planned to average an hour. Of that time, we were given about thirty-five minutes for our questions. Approximately ten additional minutes were used to gather the social data to be compared with that for other years, and the fifteen minutes remaining in the interview hour were given over to questions for another faculty research project.

The larger part of the task of constructing an interview and of testing the clarity and validity of the questions must be completed within the four-month period from October through mid-January. Difficulties still apparent in the interview form by that time cannot be removed. The reason for this schedule is that the DAS is also a facility for training graduate students in research methods. Students, usually working for master's degrees in sociology, psychology, or political science, are involved in planning the study and in its execution. The actual conduct of DAS research is determined in part by this fact. Students entering the program in September must be able to collect the bulk of the data for the year's research during the two-week period in February that comes between the fall and spring semesters. This is necessary because it is the only large block of completely free time they have for such work and because the spring semester must be used for processing the data and for the writing of student reports on selected portions of its contents.

. . . . . *INTERVIEWERS*

In 1953, this time schedule allowed for the testing of most of our questionnaire items in interviews with mothers at least twice before the final period of interviewing began. Some questions were given three such preliminary tests. As a result, most problems of unclear phrasing were eliminated.

All student participants were given thorough supervised practice in methods of interviewing by the DAS staff and the Field Staff Section of the University's Survey Research Center, an organization with long experience in conducting public opinion surveys. The students collected two-thirds of the interviews on which our study is based. Professional interviewers from the Survey Research Center's field staff gathered the remainder.

. . . . . *THE SAMPLE*

The methods for choosing the people who were interviewed are described in a 1953 report of the DAS (2).

Interviews were taken in a representative cross-section of 1157 Detroit Area homes between January 21 and April 1, 1953. These interviews contain information about a representative cross-section of 2556 individual adults. . . . Approximately two-thirds of the interviews were taken in the City of Detroit. One-third were taken outside of Detroit in the cities, villages, and unincorporated parts of the suburban area. The area covered in our survey does not coincide completely with the official Detroit Standard Metropolitan Area used by the U. S. Census Bureau. The Census Area includes all of Wayne, Macomb, and Oakland Counties. Our definition of the area excludes those outlying points of the three counties which are not divided into census tracts. In addition to the City of Detroit, the area represented by our sample includes the following communities: Allen Park, Berkley, Birmingham, Dearborn, East Detroit, Ecorse, Ferndale, Garden City, Grosse Pointe Park, Grosse Pointe Woods, Hamtramck, Hazel Park, Highland Park, Huntington Woods, Inkster, Lincoln Park, Livonia, Melvindale, Oak Park, Pleasant Ridge, River Rouge, Roseville, Royal Oak, St. Clair Shores, Trenton, Wayne, and Wyandotte, as well as the remaining tracted area in the three-county area.

Since the survey was restricted to private households, those people residing in military establishments, hospitals, religious and educational institutions, hotels, and large rooming houses were excluded from the sample. These excluded groups probably comprise less than 5 per cent of the adult population of Detroit.

The sample was selected by the method known as "area sampling." By this method every member of the population had a known chance of being selected. . . .

In general, the sampling procedure involved: 1) selecting a sample of blocks, and 2) within these blocks making a random selection of households.

Interviews were taken in 282 blocks. If the individual to be interviewed was not at home, from one to ten call-back visits were made in an attempt to reach her. However, even after repeated calls, a small portion of the

Interviewing Mothers in the Detroit Area **65**

individuals to be interviewed were not found at home, and a few refused to be interviewed. Interviews were completed in 92.6 per cent of the homes on the original interview list.

In this year's study there were two kinds of interviews:

(1) "Mother Interviews." In all households in which there was a mother with a child under 19, an interview was taken with the mother. It consisted of (*a*) one part dealing with family activities and (*b*) census-type questions about the social and economic characteristics (e.g., occupation, age, etc.) of all adults (persons 21 years of age or over) in the household. These latter questions were asked directly of each adult if the mother was unable to give the information. There were 582 interviews with mothers.

(2) "Census-type Interviews." In all other households only the census-type information was obtained—in this case from any adult who had the information. There were 575 such interviews.

A more technical report on sampling procedures appears in Appendix Two. It shows that the sample gives findings which compare closely with the 1950 U. S. Census returns for the Detroit metropolitan area on the number of persons living in dwelling units, the proportion of renter-occupied to owner-occupied dwelling units, the percentages of workers in the various occupational groups, and on several other indices.

The 582 interviews with mothers having one or more children under nineteen years of age living in the household provided a representative cross-section of such parents for the Detroit area.

. . . To make certain that we would also have information about a representative cross-section of children of various ages, the interviewers first obtained a complete list of the children in the household, then used a . . . [special selection table] to select one child randomly in each household as the one about whom the interview was taken. So in some households the mother talked about the youngest child, in others about a middle child, in others about an oldest child . . . (3).

The final distinctive feature of our sampling was determined by the bare thirty-five minutes available for our part of the interview. We found it impossible in that time to ask what we considered a minimum number of questions, so we decided not to ask all the questions of all the mothers. Instead we devised a procedure of asking some questions of *all* mothers and of dividing the remainder of our schedule items into two groups requiring approximately equal interviewing time, *each* group to be asked of a randomly chosen *half* of the mothers seen. The questions asked of all the mothers were those expected to show important differences for only restricted portions of the sample, especially those cases in which we were confident of our predictions only for differences between the entrepreneurial and bureaucratic middle classes.

The professional social scientist will understand our pleasure at having a well-selected, random sample of mothers and children for study. He will also appreciate that, given a set of hypotheses and hunches about relations to be found between certain social positions and the methods of child training used in each, we regretted not being able to use a sampling design that would give us a greater number of cases to represent each of those social positions than can be gotten from a random sample of the community at large. For example, as we noted in Chapter Two, a number of our ideas applied especially to upper middle-class mothers. The number of such persons in the Detroit area is small compared with those in lower middle- and lower-class positions. It is unfortunate, but inescapable, that they could not have been oversampled to increase the numbers of such women available for statistical processing.

. . . . . HOW THE PRINCIPAL SOCIAL POSITIONS WERE DEFINED

We shall refer to many social positions in telling the story of mothers and children in the Detroit area, but some positions—the integrative positions we have called entrepreneurial and bureaucratic, and the stratification positions represented by the social classes—will be used so often that the way we defined them in our results must be explained at this point. They were defined both conceptually and with respect to the operations that would represent those concepts, *before* they were used in the analysis of our results.

The Definition of Entrepreneurial Organization

Entrepreneurial organization has been described earlier in this report. When the time came to be specific about the people who would be considered as living in such an organizational pattern, we had to face some problems of which we have not spoken up to this point. These problems arose because we had not foreseen how central and important a place we would want to give to the ideas of bureaucratic and entrepreneurial integration when the interviews were taken and because we had provided ways for determining the integration settings of only upper middle- and upper-class families. But this is getting ahead of the story. Suppose we start back where we actually began in our planning.

For some time we had been working together on quite a different problem from the one of concern in this book (4). This earlier study included interviews with the mothers of about 250 adolescent boys in the Detroit public schools. From the things they told us of the way they trained their sons, we tried to predict some aspects of their boys' behavior.

The mothers and sons included in this previous study were not chosen to be representative of all the parents and children in the Detroit area. However, our interest gradually focused on the question: How typical are these mothers in the way they handle their children? At that point, the directors of the DAS asked if we would like to ask a representative sample of all mothers in the metropolitan area the same questions we had put to our first group of 250 mothers. We accepted their invitation.

As we chose questions from our original interviewing forms to be asked by the DAS, we decided to see if we could also pick up the kind of differences in child rearing which we believed might be related to the rise of the new middle classes and which we have already summarized in Chapter Two. At that time, we were especially confident of finding these new methods in use by the part of the middle class—the upper middles—who we felt were experiencing the impact of bureaucratic conditions first and most strongly. For that reason we sought ways of distinguishing entrepreneurial and bureaucratic integration settings for upper middle-class people. (The upper classes are a very small part of the population of a metropolitan area, so we planned to group them with the upper middles and apply the same criteria to uppers as to upper middles in determining integration settings.)

What we did was quite simple. We sought to separate those families which would have more risk taking, individuating, and isolating experiences from those in whose lives these entrepreneurial experiences were relatively absent. Following the reasoning given in Chapter Two, we classified a family as entrepreneurial if *any one* of the following characteristics was met by the husband: if he (*a*) was self-employed; (*b*) gained at least half of his income in the form of profits, fees, or commissions; or if he (*c*) worked in an organization having only two levels of supervision, a small-scale organization. Having one or more such experiences certainly would not mean that the family's integration was exclusively entrepreneurial, but, we felt, families confronting such conditions would be more entrepreneurial than those in whose experience they were lacking.

The remaining upper middle- and upper-class families we said were, relative to the ones we have just defined, bureaucratic in their experiences. It is important to observe that they are not being called "bureaucratic" by default or because they are not entrepreneurial. Instead, they are families in which the husband has the kind of occupational experiences we have specified as bureaucratic in Chapter Two. He works for someone else in an organization of at least moderate complexity (three or more supervisory levels) and gets most of his income from a salary or wage. His income and job security do not depend in as large a measure as those we call entrepreneurial on his taking frequent risks. It must be remembered that as the size of the concern for which a man works increases, so does the probability that it has enough resources to protect his job and his income from at least the lesser declines in the business cycle.

But, it may be protested, what of cases such as that of the man who works for a giant bureaucratic corporation like one of the automobile companies, yet gets half or more of his income from profits, fees, or commissions? Is his integration primarily bureaucratized or entrepreneurial? We agreed that he has important bureaucratic experiences provided by his job in the bureaucratic organization. We reasoned, however, that because of the conditions under which much of his income is obtained he also has a greater likelihood of having entrepreneurial experiences than does a man who works for the same corporation and receives income only in the form of a salary. We were looking for *relative, not absolute, differences* in the integration of the families in our sample. We expected to find that the styles of child training we have called entrepreneurial would appear with greater frequency among those families encountering at least some entrepreneurial conditions than among families encountering only bureaucratic conditions. Our findings justify that expectation.

As the interviews came in and their results were summarized and entered on Hollerith punch cards, we set an assistant to work on an exploratory tabulation. His results surprised us and forced us to reconsider our thinking.

The tabulation he prepared was simple in conception. Previous research by other social scientists had shown that middle-class mothers differed from lower-class mothers in the way they trained their children. It suggested, for example, that middle-class mothers were more likely to wean and toilet train their youngsters earlier than lower-

Interviewing Mothers in the Detroit Area 69

class mothers. Our assistant was asked to tabulate the results obtained from our sample of Detroit area mothers by the social class position assigned those mothers. Few significant differences of the kind reported by the earlier studies appeared. Further, few significant differences of any kind were to be found between mothers of middle- and lower-class status.

There was, however, another finding from the assistant's tabulations that qualified this picture. Many of the differences in child training practices that we had expected to appear between entrepreneurial and bureaucratic mothers were evident. Those results are given and discussed in the next chapter. At this point we want to outline the effects they had on our conception of our study and on the way in which we finally defined and used the distinction between bureaucratic and entrepreneurial families.

We decided that it was illogical to confine the use of this distinction to upper middle- and upper-class families. We felt that, although there was less information available about the extent to which lower middle-class families were experiencing the impact of bureaucratic conditions, differences between such families in entrepreneurial and bureaucratic integration settings should be appearing along the same lines as those for higher status families.

Similarly, we decided to use the distinction of integration settings with lower- as well as middle-class families. For reasons that we will elaborate as we present our results, we were far less certain that differences in child rearing would appear when entrepreneurial and bureaucratic lower-class families were compared and, as we will show, we found it hard to anticipate just what those differences would be. Despite these difficulties in prediction, all families at all class levels were to be classified as entrepreneurial or bureaucratic.

That decision required another. We had to find a way to make the classification.

The three entrepreneurial conditions—self-employment, employment in a small organization, and considerable income from profits, fees, or commissions—seemed appropriate for selecting those upper middle- and upper-class people with relatively individuated experiences. These conditions were equally appropriate for that purpose when they were applicable to families of lower status. The difficulty lay in the fact that most families of lower status work for someone else in fairly large enterprises and gain all of their incomes in the form of wages or salary. Were there other individuating experiences that some such families might have that we had overlooked when we considered only upper middles and uppers? We concluded that there were and decided to classify a family as relatively entrepreneurial in its integration setting if the wife or her husband were (*d*) born on a farm, or were (*e*) born outside the United States. Added to the three earlier individuating conditions, this made a total of five. A family meeting *any one* of these five was called entrepreneurial. Just as the three previous conditions now were applied to lower middle- and lower-class families, these two new conditions were applied to upper middle- and upper-class families.

To recapitulate:

1. We had anticipated that middle- and lower-class mothers would differ in several respects in the rearing of their children. We also expected certain differences to appear between the patterns of child care found among entrepreneurial upper middles and those found among bureaucratic upper middles.

2. The first expectation received weak support. The second showed promise.

3. Therefore, we decided to extend our hypotheses about integration setting and child care to lower middles and, although unable to make predictions for them, to examine the relation of integration setting and child training in the lower classes as well.

4. This third step required that we find some criteria for classifying lower middle- and lower-class respondents by integration setting.

5. All of these steps were taken *before* the data for lower middles and lower-class respondents were analyzed by integration setting. Indeed, they were a necessary prerequisite for such an analysis.

But what reasoning underlies the addition of these new criteria? There were two reasons for saying that, *relatively speaking*, persons born on the farm (*5*) were more likely than those born in towns or cities to have had entrepreneurial experiences and to have developed values and expectations appropriate to such experiences. First, since we studied these farm-born parents in and around the city of Detroit, they were migrants from the countryside to the urban area. From the large number of studies made of such migrants, we concluded that they and their families would require at least a generation or two before they became thoroughly at home in this strange urban world and incorporated in, and adjusted to, its institutions. Prior to that point of great familiarity and ease in an urban environment, they would have the relatively isolating and individuating experiences of strangers to the city.

Second, most migrants from the farm are people reared in, and adapted to, the life of a small, independent business. (All our white

Interviewing Mothers in the Detroit Area **71**

respondents with rural backgrounds say their parents were farm owners, not farm laborers.) The farmer, like the small urban businessman, must be a taker of risks—an entrepreneur—and may be expected to share the small businessman's point of view and way of life in important respects. This may be especially true in the United States where farmers live, not in a little village from which they go to till their fields, but in the midst of their acreage, relatively isolated from their neighbors.

As we stated in Chapter Two, the small businessman, whether on the farm or in the city, is likely to have a very limited understanding of the organization of a complex society such as ours. His occupational contacts tend to acquaint him with a small part of the economy. He is unlikely to have an occasion for coming to understand its larger organization and his place in it. He knows something of a small part of a city's patterns, but has little appreciation of its more embracive structures. Thus, even in a rural setting, and despite the development of intimate relations in his family and with near neighbors, the small entrepreneur is likely to find the larger society a vast, unclear, confusing environment, with respect to which he feels isolated and a stranger. It is from judgments of our respondents' experiences in the larger society that we seek to predict their methods of rearing children.

Since some of the foreign-born certainly came from rural backgrounds, and since almost all of them might be assumed to come from countries that were strikingly less patterned as welfare-bureaucracies than is the social structure of the United States, we could make assumptions for their experiences in the Detroit area similar to those used with the farm-born. Hence we called foreign birth a sign of entrepreneurial experiences and expectations.

This classification of the foreign-born as entrepreneurial may be challenged at once on the grounds that many European countries have long been "welfare" states, providing many kinds of social security for their citizens. Our reasoning has been as follows: Although a number of countries have had substantial and effective welfare programs, this situation is much less true for those nations from which most of our foreign-born respondents originate, in particular, Poland and the countries of Eastern and Southern Europe. Second, national welfare programs and a large governmental bureaucracy can, and do, exist in countries whose economies have the features we call entrepreneurial. Since most of the economic security of the individual comes from his occupation, not from health or retirement benefits, it would be quite possible that most citizens in such countries will have an entrepreneurial outlook.

On the other hand, we must acknowledge that our assignment of the foreign-born to an entrepreneurial classification is speculative. It is probably more speculative than the similar assignment we have given to those born on the farm or to those with certain occupational characteristics. Although our study does not provide information which can definitively support or invalidate these assignments, we shall present data in later chapters suggesting that our classifications are plausible enough to warrant continued, and more searching, investigation.

The reasoning in the last half dozen paragraphs allows us to underscore a crucial point which we made earlier and which must be grasped to understand the way we interpret our findings. When we speak of entrepreneurs in this book we do not have in mind only persons who are self-employed or whose incomes depend heavily on the outcome of the risks they take. Our conception is much broader. We want to include under the label of entrepreneur all persons who, *relatively more than the population at large,* may be expected to have their lives strongly affected by individuated-entrepreneurial values. Relative to persons born in towns and cities, those born on the farm are more likely to have the outlook of small businessmen because most farms from which our respondents might have come were small businesses. Further, we believed such persons would, relative to persons in towns and cities, have individuated experiences in the Detroit area. This would be true because, as relative strangers to city life, they would be more likely to lack a large number of close, personal contacts in the city. It would be true also because, in a society in which urban ways set the pace and form of rural events, persons living on farms should, like small businessmen in the city, find the vast and impersonal national economy a confusing environment. In such an environment, farmers must often make important decisions without any clear knowledge of, or control over, the conditions that determine the results of their choices. Rural Americans have faced such dilemmas with increasing frequency since the Civil War. Government subsidies and programs of crop control do something to ameliorate these confusions and uncertainties, but do not eliminate them. In addition, in the period in which most of the farm-born parents in our study would have been reared—the period around the end of the First World War—many of these governmental protections were not in effect. To summarize, we call people "entrepreneurial" when they are more likely than others in our sample to have had experiences that lead them to have what we describe as entrepreneurial values.

We recognize, of course, that people like the farm-born and foreign-born will gradually lose those values as they come to work in, and participate in, welfare-bureaucratic organizations and to live in a society which, increasingly, promotes the values of such organizations. This is happening to many respondents whom we call entrepreneurial. To the extent that it does happen, it works against our finding the differences we expect when we compare our "entrepreneurs" with respondents who seem to have more uniformly bureaucratic experiences. It can hardly explain the differences we do find.

We appreciate that the successes we report in predicting differences in methods of child care between entrepreneurial and bureaucratic families may have occurred for reasons other than the ones we give. It may be, for example, that there is something about being born on a farm or in a foreign land, other than the individuated-entrepreneurial outlook we judge to be associated with these backgrounds, that makes such persons rear children differently than do people in our bureaucratized population. By exercising a large number of controls, we have done what we could to minimize this possibility. These controls are described in Chapter Seven. As a matter of personal judgment, we also have concluded that the explanations we have offered provide a more plausible, comprehensive, and parsimonious account of our findings than do others we have examined. However, this is a matter of personal judgment. The final test of our ideas must come from continued research. It would be especially desirable to have direct evidence that the economic, political, and other values of persons born abroad or on the farm are more entrepreneurial than those of the urban-born, native Americans beside whom they now work in Detroit. Until these data are available, we must acknowledge that the explanations employed in this study are suggestive but far from the last word. Our present views are a point of departure for such investigations. With these points clarified we shall go on to the definition of another criterion of entrepreneurial experience—organizational size.

It probably is obvious that direct and simple questions are enough for finding out whether the parents in a family were born on a farm or outside the United States, and whether the husband is self-employed or the family gets half or more of its income in the form of profits, fees, or commissions. Perhaps, however, a more detailed picture should be given of the way in which we determined organizational size.

At first we thought of asking the wife to estimate the number of employees in the husband's place of work. That, however, was not practical. Many wives cannot make the faintest guess. Further, as indicated in Chapter Two, an organization can have several employees and still not take on bureaucratic features. What we needed was some question that wives could answer accurately and that would indicate the number of specialists and the corresponding problems of coordination that an organization would exhibit. We decided to inquire whether anyone worked above or below the husband—whether he had a boss or subordinate—and, if so, if someone worked above the husband's superiors or below his subordinates (6). We chose to call organizations with three or more supervisory levels "bureaucratic" after looking at a tabulation of the number of such levels encountered by the whole sample. We found that, whereas there were a number of husbands working in two-level organizations and steadily increasing numbers of bread-winners employed in organizations with four or more supervisory levels, there were almost no cases of men in three-level occupations. Of course, any choice in this matter is somewhat arbitrary.

About half of the white and unbroken (defined below) families in the sample fell into the entrepreneurial integration setting. Of these, the largest number get that classification by reason of being born on the farm or by being born outside the United States. Table 3–1 gives a detailed summary. For interested readers, Table 3–2 shows the national origin of the fathers of foreign-born husbands. Information was not obtained for the ethnic origin of fathers of foreign-born wives.

As Table 3–1 shows, there were 105 families in which either the husband or wife was born on a farm and neither was born outside the United States. In another 85 cases, either the husband or wife was foreign-born. Unfortunately, we cannot be certain from our data whether any of these were or were not born on a farm in a foreign country. Families classified as entrepreneurial for other reasons than the farm or foreign birth of one or both of the parents are 51 in number.

As a final stage in this part of our work, we divided our entrepreneurial organization cases into the three groups just mentioned. Then, dividing each of these again into the four social classes—upper middle and higher, lower middle, upper lower, and lower lower, we examined the way in which their answers to our questions on child training were distributed. Since we could find no significant number of differences among the three entrepreneurial subgroups, and since the differences that did appear evidenced no particular common themes, we put these subgroups together and treated them as one population for comparison with those people we classified as bureaucratic (7). Some readers will want to look at Table 3–3 which gives the number of differences at various levels of probability among these three subgroups on their answers to the questions about training children (8).

Table 3–1

NUMBER OF FAMILIES CLASSIFIED AS ENTREPRENEURIAL BY
THE FIVE CONDITIONS USED AND THEIR COMBINATIONS

	Condition	Number of Families
1	Husband born on a farm	48
2	Wife born on a farm	24
3	Husband born outside the United States	17
4	Wife born outside the United States	21
5	Husband self-employed	8
6	Husband employed in a two-level organization	21
7	Family gets half or more of its income from profits, fees, or commissions	0
8	Combination of conditions 1, 2, and 5	1
9	Combination of conditions 1, 2, 5, and 6	3
10	Combination of conditions 1, 2, and 6	25
11	Combination of conditions 1, 4, and 6	4
12	Combination of conditions 1, 5, and 6	2
13	Combination of conditions 2 and 3	2
14	Combination of conditions 2 and 6	2
15	Combination of conditions 3 and 4	23
16	Combination of conditions 3, 4, 5, and 6	4
17	Combination of conditions 3, 4, and 6	1
18	Combination of conditions 3 and 5	1
19	Combination of conditions 3, 5, and 6	3
20	Combination of conditions 3 and 6	4
21	Combination of conditions 3 and 7	1
22	Combination of conditions 4, 5, and 6	3
23	Combination of conditions 4, 6, and 7	1
24	Combination of conditions 5 and 6	16
25	Combination of conditions 6 and 7	6
	Total	241

Before leaving the consideration of Table 3–3 certain other points should be made about the evidence on which we combined the three entrepreneurial subtypes into a single group. First, it must not be thought that the division of our sample into so many categories reduced the number of respondents falling in each social class and integration classification to the point at which it would be impossible to obtain significant differences among the subtypes in their answers to our questions. Table 3–3 shows that a slightly greater number of significant differences than would be expected by chance were actually found.

Table 3–2

NATIONAL ORIGIN OF HUSBAND'S FAMILY ON HIS FATHER'S
SIDE WHEN HUSBAND IS FOREIGN-BORN

Nation of Origin	Number of Husbands
England	2
Scotland	4
Ireland	4
France	1
Germany	5
Other countries of Northwest Europe	3
Poland	12
Other countries of Central Europe	5
Italy	5
Countries of Eastern Europe	4
Canada	4
Other	6
Total	55

Second, an inspection of the tabulations from which Table 3–3 was calculated does not reveal signs of a persistent though non-significant difference in the distributions of answers by respondents in any pair of the three entrepreneurial subtypes.

Third, and finally, there is not a single instance in which one of the differences at or beyond the .10 level of probability in Table 3–3 occurs in connection with responses to a question for which we report a significant difference between entrepreneurs and bureaucrats in the succeeding chapters of this book. Each of these three considerations supported our decision to combine the three entrepreneurial subtypes in a single group. In Chapter Seven there will be more evidence bearing on the appropriateness of this decision.

Interviewing Mothers in the Detroit Area **77**

Table 3–3

NUMBER OF DIFFERENCES AMONG THE THREE ENTREPRENEURIAL
SUBGROUPS BY LEVEL OF PROBABILITY (8)

Level of Probability	Number of Differences When Each Subgroup Is Divided into	
	Four Social Classes*	Two Social Classes†
1.00	1	0
.99	1	0
.98	2	0
.95	2	1
.90	7	7
.80	12	7
.70	15	21
.50	15	17
.30	10	11
.20	5	8
.10	7	5
.05	2	1
.02	1	1
.01	2	3
.001	0	0
Total	82	82

* Upper middle, lower middle, upper lower, and lower lower.
† Middle and lower.

The Definition of Bureaucratic Organization

Having defined the participants in entrepreneurial organization, we treated the remainder of our mothers as bureaucratic participants. Again, it is important to note that they fall, not into some vaguely defined residual classification, but into a specific conceptual and historical position. They are persons who, together with their husbands, were born in towns or cities in the United States. Their husbands work for someone else in organizations with three or more supervisory levels. Their income is primarily in the form of wages or salary. They are not taking entrepreneurial risks. Nor do most of them have entrepreneurial opportunities. They are, in short, the people who may be expected to have had the most experience in the non-entrepreneurial roles in welfare-bureaucratic relations.

It is clear, of course, that the lines drawn between entrepreneurial and bureaucratic participants do not separate them as cleanly as might be possible, given the descriptive precision of these two concepts. The limitations of our planning and of the method of sampling prevented our using more rigorous methods for locating these people in the Detroit area.

We wondered, of course, whether the people we called entrepreneurial and those we classified as bureaucratic would differ from one another in other respects. Would bureaucratic families tend to come from ethnic backgrounds different from those of entrepreneurial families? Would there be a larger proportion of Protestants in one of these integrations than the other? Somewhat to our surprise, very few such differences appeared.

Bureaucratic and entrepreneurial families do not differ significantly in the proportion of their members in the four social classes. They are very much alike, when social class is held constant, with respect to ethnic origins, to the income of the breadwinner of the family and the total income of the family, or to the proportion of husbands who have a type of occupation more or less prestigeful than that of their fathers. When social class is controlled, families in our two integrations do not differ significantly in their judgment of the social class to which they belong. They are alike in the length of time they have lived at their present address, in the type of occupation held by the husband's father, and in the proportions in which they live in neighborhoods heavily populated by people of a similar or a different social class level from their own. They are not distinguished by the frequency with which they say they attend religious services. When one looks at those husbands and wives in both groups who were born in towns or cities, he does not find any differences between entrepreneurial and bureaucratic families with respect to the proportions of spouses born in communities of various sizes.

Only on the four social characteristics that follow were we able to find entrepreneurial and bureaucratic families diverging from one another.

1. In all social classes, a higher proportion of bureaucratic husbands and wives have had more years of formal schooling than is the case in entrepreneurial families ($p = <.001$).

2. In the middle classes, more bureaucratic husbands are in professional and clerical occupations while more entrepreneurial husbands work as managers, owners, and proprietors of establishments or as salesmen ($p = <.01$).

3. In the lower classes, more of those entrepreneurial fathers who

were born in the United States came to the Detroit area from the South rather than from other parts of the country and fewer were reared in the Detroit area itself ($p = <.001$).

4. In the lower classes, more entrepreneurial families are Protestants ($p = <.01$).

Since many of our entrepreneurial husbands and wives were born on a farm or outside the United States, it is not too surprising to find that they have fewer years in school than their bureaucratic counterparts. The larger number of entrepreneurial fathers from the American South may be explained by our use of farm birth as a basis for classifying a family as entrepreneurial. Rural and Southern origins may also explain the larger proportion of Protestants among entrepreneurial homes. Finally, and, again, not unexpectedly, we discover that our middle-class entrepreneurial families are more likely to be found in such risk-taking occupations as managing organizations or selling their products while middle-class bureaucratic families appear more frequently in professional and clerical work—work more commonly found in bureaucratic organizations. Interested readers will find many social characteristics of our respondents tabulated in Appendix One. Later on, and after presenting our findings, we will discuss the possibility that it is something connected with these differences in type of occupation, religion, or in amount of schooling rather than the broad divergences between entrepreneurial and bureaucratic conditions that should be thought of as producing the results we obtain.

The Definitions of the Social Classes

There is a large and contentious literature on methods for determining the existence of social classes, their nature, and the points at which to draw the boundaries between them. We have already given our reasons for feeling that they exist and have described our ideas of what, for this study, the term "social class" shall represent. That done, many controversies can be side-stepped and we can go directly to the way we set boundaries between the classes.

While saying that there are persuasive reasons for treating the classes as if there were boundaries between them—as if the distinctions, say between upper middles and lower middles or lower middles and upper lowers were not merely arbitrary divisions of an essentially continuous distribution of social power—we feel there are no existing studies adequate to establish this. Our hypotheses and explanations are couched as if this were indeed the established case. The methods used for dividing the classes reflect this judgment. If it is wrong, if the power structure is shown to be continuous rather than made up of discrete segments, no great harm will be done. Our dividing lines between the classes will then be seen as arbitrary and the differences in child training corresponding to the social class differences separated by our divisions will then be understood as attached to different points on a single line rather than to discrete though ordered attributes.

The social class placement of the families began with the assignment of the occupation of the husband to one of the occupational categories used by the U. S. Bureau of the Census. This code provides a set of broad labels under which more special job titles can be arranged. It distinguishes between blue- and white-collar occupations, farm and non-farm types of work, and among several degrees and types of skill and authority on the job. Figure 3–1 shows how social class was tentatively assigned, with exceptions that are noted below:

Figure 3–1

OCCUPATIONS BY SOCIAL CLASS

Social Class	U. S. Census Occupation Categories
Upper middle	Professional, technical, and kindred workers
	Managers, officials, and proprietors except farm
Lower middle	Clerical and kindred workers
	Sales workers
Upper lower	Craftsmen, foremen, and kindred workers
Lower lower	Operatives and kindred workers
	Service workers
	Laborers, except farm and mine
Class not ascertained	Farmers and farm managers
	Farm laborers and foremen
	Occupation not ascertained

Although the assignment of social class by the Census occupation categories seemed generally fitting, we felt it necessary to change some of the occupations to other classes for these reasons:

(1) The prestige of some occupations differs markedly from that of others in the same census classification (9). This finding is based on the results of a national sample of the white population made by the National Opinion Research Center (NORC) in the mid-1940's. NORC asked its respondents to rate the prestige of a sample of jobs. The NORC finding is important for our purposes since we treat prestige as representing a kind of summary judgment of the amount, stability, and legitimacy of power. Hence, it is, when based on an

Interviewing Mothers in the Detroit Area **81**

accurate judgment of the facts, a potent index of social class. Although we cannot be certain of the accuracy of the ratings by respondents in the NORC study, it is unlikely that, in the rough groupings we have used, there are major errors.

(2) The incomes of individuals in some occupations differ considerably from those for others in the same census classification. Although it is commonly believed that occupation is a somewhat more accurate basis for judging the relative power position a man has in his society than is income, the combination of the two is generally felt to be superior to the use of either by itself (10). Certainly any sharp discrepancy between them suggests that the family is moving up or down in the power levels.

(3) For the analysis of parts of the interview containing data for another faculty member's study (11) in relation to our own, it was desired to keep some correspondence between the social classes and the groups of occupations employed in our colleague's work.

On these three grounds, the following changes were made, guided principally by the prestige of the husband's occupation and his income:

From professional, technical, and kindred workers, the following occupations were removed and put into the lower middle class: public school teachers, nurses, draftsmen, and laboratory technicians, and also those engineers and accountants not having college degrees.

From managers, officials, and proprietors, except farm, the following occupations were removed and put into the lower middle class: owners of small businesses (i.e., having any *one* of the following characteristics: capital investment less than approximately $25,000, income less than $10,000, or five or fewer employees), managers of small offices who were not in executive positions.

There were no changes from clerical and kindred workers.

From sales workers we removed salesmen making more than $10,000 and put them into the upper middle class.

There were no changes from craftsmen, foremen, and kindred workers.

There were no changes from operatives and kindred workers.

From service workers, the following occupations were removed and put into the lower middle class: city firemen, policemen, investigators, sheriffs.

There were no changes from the category laborers, except farm and mine.

Other occasional changes were made, using the same criteria of prestige and income discrepancies from occupation, where the coders agreed that the occupation was different from others in the same census classification.

It will be seen that we have defined as upper middle class all subjects judged as superior to lower middles in power and prestige. There are, of course, some upper-class persons among them. It should be remembered, then, that our brief designation "upper middle" really means "upper middle and higher."

Three people participated in the assignment of social class ratings. Discussions were held before the coding began, at which time the general criteria to decide social class placement were agreed upon. Each coder rated a group of interviews for social class, and each wrote down the interview number and the kind of change made for all cases in which the Census occupation code was not converted directly to social class as given in Figure 3–1. All the interviews were coded again by a second coder, using the procedures just described. In the 5 per cent of the cases in which the two coders disagreed in their assignment of a family to a particular social class, they jointly reached a final decision.

. . . . . *SOME CONTROLS*

There were some conditions that might confuse the interpretation of our findings. We tried to rid our work of their influence from the very beginning.

As would be expected, the vast majority (94.6 per cent) of the mothers interviewed were living with their husbands. Likewise, the preponderance (94.1 per cent) of the children were their parents' own rather than stepchildren or adopted children. Since their numbers were too small for separate study and since their presence would complicate our interpretations, we eliminated cases in which the wife was, for some reason, not living with her husband and the cases in which the child in our sample was a stepchild or adopted child.

Finally, the number of Negroes in our sample proved very small. Since we were less certain about the nature of their involvement in the society's organization than we were for the whites, and since their numbers were not large enough to allow a detailed analysis, we eliminated them from most of the analyses. A report presenting such comparisons as we could make between white and Negro mothers is included in Chapter Six.

The controls already mentioned involved eliminating cases. Our original sample had had 582 respondents. After applying the foregoing controls, our sample numbered 479. We were quite aware that further difficulties could enter into our interpretations if the ages of the mothers or children or the sex of the children were not randomly distributed among the social positions under investigation. We have checked on this possibility and can report that it is not the case except for the ages

Interviewing Mothers in the Detroit Area **83**

of lower-class mothers. Entrepreneurial lower-class mothers tend to be older than those of bureaucratic integration. We find, however, that the difference of age does not affect the direction of our findings. As a result, none of our interpretations of differences between these social positions are made uncertain by being associated with these factors (12).

. . . . . SELECTING THE QUESTIONS ABOUT CHILD REARING

Because we did not foresee that we would become interested in classifying all our respondents by their integration settings, we did not foresee that we would want to make the recent change in American methods of training children so central in our work. This means that we were forced, to some extent, to "make do" with questions about children that were written for other purposes.

We had several objectives in mind when we first came to write the questions that the interviewers would ask. There was the hope that we could locate upper middle- and upper-class families living within the entrepreneurial and bureaucratic settings and that we would find the kind of differences in their ways of handling children that we have associated with their social positions in Chapter Two. We also wanted to test some ideas about differences in child training that we felt should be associated with middle- as against lower-class status in our society. We wanted, further, to get information that would allow us to place the results of some of our earlier studies—already mentioned in this chapter—in the context of the whole community, thus helping us to estimate how far they could be generalized. Finally, we appreciated how little was known about the relation of social positions to child training and feared that, if we asked only about those features of the rearing of children which occurred to us on theoretical grounds or as simple extensions of other people's research, we would overlook important connections that previously had not been imagined. We wanted to provide enough of a range of information about the training of the child to enable such new results to appear and be explored.

This diversity of objectives is fairly common in research. Sometimes it presents impossible problems. Adequate work cannot be done on some objectives if the others must also be met. We tried to find a compromise approach that would satisfy our strongest interest along with those of others connected with the project.

Two additional criteria guided our choice of questions related to each of these objectives. We tried to choose those training practices which are believed to have an important effect on the child's personality. In addition, we inquired about some types of child care designed to solve problems faced by parents in all societies. These two criteria gave us additional reasons for asking about such practices as those connected with weaning and bowel training, reward and punishment, the restriction of thumb-sucking and masturbation, the extent to which parents supervise children at different ages, and the ages at which the child is expected to assume responsibility for various tasks.

There is some disagreement among scholars about the effects of such practices on the child's later development (13), and even more disagreement about the nature of the possible effects. At the same time, these features of child training appear frequently in studies of socialization.

The scholarly disagreements can be illustrated by references to any of these practices. Weaning is a good instance. There is evidence that time of weaning is related to several personality characteristics in children. But how are we to interpret the relation? Some specialists feel that, by itself, the timing of weaning provides an index of the extent to which the child is later to be orally fixated. Thus, if he is weaned too harshly, he may later tend to overeat as a consolation for unpleasant events, he may be unduly inclined to seek passive relations, or he may be more likely to become angry at people because they do not do more things for him. By contrast, other specialists feel that the timing of weaning can have many different kinds of effects depending on the other practices which accompany it and on the cultural setting in which the weaning occurs. From this point of view, early weaning, by itself, may not create passivity if the weaning is not experienced by the child as a punishment and if he is given much love for accepting this limitation on his behavior. Still other specialists, however, regard weaning as important mostly because of the incidental lessons which it provides. If it occurs early, it may do something toward teaching the child that he is to take responsibility for performing certain acts as soon as possible, or it may teach him that adults are harsh and unloving.

Since we were not studying the relations between child rearing and later personality, we did not have to take a particular position about these disagreements. We were inclined, nevertheless, to take a position between the second and the third of those mentioned above: that weaning practices do teach some lessons and that we can infer those lessons if we know the social context in which the training occurs.

Some readers may want to examine the questionnaire which emerged from our objectives and criteria. It appears in Appendix Three.

. . . . . *HOW VALID ARE THE RESPONSES TO*
OUR INTERVIEWS

Any scientist prefers a large and representative sample of cases to study when he does research. He wants information about those cases to be gathered with care. But he also wants some assurance that the information is valid: that it faithfully represents the facts he seeks to study.

This problem of validity in research appears with particular force in our study. How do we know that the answers mothers give our interviewers are faithful reports of how they do, or did, feel and of how they behaved toward their children? We can make only an estimate of their accuracy, but we feel that this estimate is conservative and reassuring.

As the story of our findings unfolds, it develops that we asked some questions that mothers should be able and willing to answer accurately. Those we phrased in a perfectly straight-forward fashion.

There are other questions that mothers might reasonably be expected to be able to answer correctly, but which they might be unwilling to answer. When we could foresee such a difficulty, we tried to get information through a phrasing that made a reliable answer easier to give. For example, we wanted to know if certain mothers found less satisfaction in having a new baby in the home than did others. It would be hard for a mother to be honest with herself or with an interviewer if she disliked having a young infant in the house. For that reason, we asked mothers to tell us the things they most liked and disliked about having a new baby about the home. Then, paying little attention to their answers, we simply counted the number of likes and dislikes a mother gave. We assumed that women listing more "dislikes" and fewer "likes" than others in our sample would unwittingly be revealing stronger negative feelings about the presence of an infant.

Again, there were times when we felt our respondents would be willing to give accurate answers to a question, but might find it hard to express themselves. We tried to help them say what they probably were willing to tell us. There was such a problem in getting mothers to tell us how large were the firms in which their husbands were employed. Most wives could not tell us how many persons were employed by those firms. Consequently, we asked each woman whether her husband had a superior in the organization and whether there was someone over her husband's boss. Similarly, we asked whether her husband had subordinates and whether those subordinates, in turn, had persons working under them.

When possible, within the limits set by having only thirty-five minutes of interviewing time available, we asked more than one question to get at a particular point. In this way we sometimes are able to gain assurance about the meaning of answers to one question by checking them against the answers to another question.

But there is one especially difficult problem about the validity of answers to the questions we asked in this study—as compared with those used in many other pieces of research. How accurate were the mothers' memories? We talked with a random sample of mothers having one or more of their children eighteen years or younger living at home. When we inquired about the age at which a particular child was weaned, some mothers had just completed that job and presumably could recall the exact time with high accuracy. Others had to say that the child under discussion was still nursing. (These last were not a problem, since we were able to restrict our tabulations only to cases in which weaning is completed.) But some mothers had to think back ten years or more in order to give us the date. How accurate were their answers?

We cannot be certain of the answer to such a question. Perhaps most mothers find the age at which a child is weaned so important that they can report it with little error even after the passage of many years. Perhaps they are accurate within a month or two of the actual time. Perhaps they are quite inaccurate.

The importance of possible inaccuracy on such matters varies from one part of our findings to another. When we make a prediction that mothers in the older middle classes will wean their children earlier than those in the newer middle classes, inaccuracies that are large and random work against our finding the difference that we expect between these groups. If the difference appears as predicted, it is less likely that these mothers were wildly inaccurate. On the other hand, when, as in a later chapter, we give the average age at which Detroit children are weaned, we must be more cautious. Errors in our respondents' memories may well mean that such a result has a considerable margin of error.

In another sense, however, there is no certainty of the validity of these responses to an interview. It may be that entrepreneurial mothers, bureaucratic mothers, or both differ in their ideas of when a child should be weaned but, in fact, complete the weaning of their babies at the same time. Perhaps they remember and report what they think an ideal practice would be, not what they actually did. To the extent that we asked more than one question about a particular topic and got similar answers, the likelihood of such distortion probably lessened, but it never disappeared. This is a matter that can be settled only by observations of what mothers do and by matching those findings with their reports of how they behave. To the extent that this source of fallible results is important, we must treat our conclusions with caution.

. . . . . *THE NEXT CHAPTERS*

Our plan is to discuss the importance and interpretation of each of the questions we asked as we present findings from its use. For example, in the next chapter, we are going to bring together those questions most closely related to the older and newer methods of child training and test the hypothesis that they will be related to a family's placement as entrepreneurial or bureaucratic in integration. Or, again, in Chapter Five we present those questions for which we felt there would be different answers according to the social class to which the family belonged. We now are ready to go on to Chapter Four and its test of the importance of our families' integration in the society for the way they rear children.

NOTES

[1] For a description of this program see: Ronald Freedman, "The Detroit Area Study: A Training and Research Laboratory in the Community," *The American Journal of Sociology*, 59 (July, 1953), 30–33.

[2] Detroit Area Study of the University of Michigan, *A Social Profile of Detroit: 1953* (Ann Arbor, Michigan: The University of Michigan Press, 1953), 2–4.

[3] *Ibid.*, 25.

[4] Daniel R. Miller and Guy E. Swanson, *Inner Conflict and Defense*, to be published by Henry Holt and Co. in 1958.

[5] We had a choice of using the fact of being born on a farm or of having had farm experience as the index of rural experience. We chose the former because there were relatively few people with farm experience who had not been born on a farm and because we felt place of birth was, generally, a better indicator of the person's values than a transitory experience in farming at some point in the occupational career.

[6] In computing number of supervisory levels, that of the husband is always

counted as one. Thus a man with no subordinates and working under a superior who, in turn, has no one over him is in a two-level organization.

[7] We recognize that the absence of significant differences is not, in itself, proof of the homogeneity of these three groups. We used it here as but a gross criterion to check our expectations. Chapter Seven presents other data bearing on homogeneity—data which became available after we had tested our hypotheses.

[8] Variance attributable to social class was partialed out in these computations. The method of partialing is described in Milton J. Rosenberg, "The Experimental Investigation of a Value Theory of Attitude Structure," unpublished doctoral dissertation, Doctoral Program in Social Psychology, University of Michigan, 1954, 118–123.

[9] See: National Opinion Research Center, *National Opinion on Occupations* (Denver: University of Denver, 1947). Especially relevant material appears in Table I, pages 15–17.

[10] See, for example: W. Lloyd Warner and others, *Social Class in America, A Manual of Procedure for the Measurement of Social Status* (Chicago: Science Research Associates, Inc., 1949), 163–185; Genevieve Knupfer, "Indices of Socio-Economic Status, A Study of Some Problems of Measurement," unpublished doctoral dissertation, Department of Sociology, Columbia University, 1946.

[11] By Theodore M. Newcomb.

[12] We cannot, of course, completely rule out the existence of interaction effects between age or sex and a family's integration and stratification positions.

[13] Irvin Child has recently summarized the literature on this and related topics. See his: "Socialization," in Gardner Lindzey (ed.), *Handbook of Social Psychology*, Vol. 2 (Cambridge, Mass.: Addison-Wesley Publishing Co., Inc., 1954), 655–692.

CHAPTER FOUR

. . . . *C*HILD TRAINING

IN ENTREPRENEURIAL AND

BUREAUCRATIC FAMILIES

Children are many things to many people. Some parents find children a fulfillment; some, a millstone. There are mothers who see their youngsters as did one whom we interviewed: "Children are like flowers. You should have lots of them." But another finds her growing daughters "clocks that tick off the years and remind you that your time is passing and theirs is coming."

Although the parents themselves may think of the child as an insurance policy that will mature when they are old, or as a realization of their own frustrated aspirations, or as a companion that amuses and is amused, or as countless other things, the society outside the family also finds in the child a charge and a future. He must be watched, encouraged, curbed, and guided. He must be trained to be a mature and knowledgeable adult. In a time when there is much talk of "permissive" child training, the fact may be obscured that permissiveness is never complete, that it is, in itself, a particular way of teaching children how to live in a specific kind of world, and that, at no time in history—including present-day America—do families or societies allow youngsters to develop as they will.

In this chapter we shall present evidence that the old and new middle-class families in the Detroit area differ in their methods of rearing children. We were not at all certain that they are conscious of their techniques or of the effects those techniques are likely to have on children's conduct. We had some confidence, however, that we could forecast at least a portion of the differences in child care to be found between entrepreneurial and bureaucratic parents—a portion of the influence of a family's integration setting on the methods by which it shapes its children's behavior.

When our interviewers knocked on the doors of a sample of mothers in the Detroit area, they carried a set of questions designed to obtain information that would test some predictions we had developed. We were forecasting the behaviors that entrepreneurial families, as contrasted with bureaucratic families of upper middle-class status, would encourage in their children. Chapter Three told how we came to feel that these different integration settings should produce the same kind of contrasts among lower middle-class families as well. As we suggest there and in Chapter Two, we felt that too little was known about the experiences of the bureaucratic lower classes to predict how their methods of training children might differ from those of the entrepreneurial lower classes.

In this chapter we give our predictions about the methods mothers in older and newer middle-class families would use in rearing their youngsters. Beside these predictions appear the findings from our interviews. The chapter ends with a report of the differences in child training which we found between lower-class mothers in the two integration settings.

Except where it is said to be otherwise, all the predictions and findings mentioned in this chapter and throughout this book refer to white families. A section on the small number of Negro families in our sample appears in this chapter. Again, unless stated otherwise, all our findings refer to families in which the parents were living together at the time of the interview and in which, as far as we know, the child on whom the interview focuses was the natural son or daughter of those parents.

. . . . . PREDICTIONS

Following the reasoning already presented in Chapter Two, we predicted that, among whites, entrepreneurial middle-class mothers would be more likely than those with a bureaucratic integration to emphasize the child's development of strong self-control. Several of our questions relate to that emphasis. We call them Internalization Indices.

Similarly, we predicted in Chapter Two that entrepreneurial middle-class mothers would train their children to take a more active and independent approach to the world than would their bureaucratic counterparts. We said that bureaucratic middle-class mothers should encourage children to adopt a more accommodating and adjustive way of life. A number of our questions seem related to this theme. We call them Activity Indices.

We discuss Internalization and Activity Indices in that order.

Internalization Indices

In Chapter Two we suggested some of the ways a mother might treat a child in order to encourage in him a habit of self-control and self-denial. We pointed out that this encouragement could well begin when he was an infant. Here (in Figure 4–1) are the questions that we felt would give us evidence of the extent to which mothers in our sample taught their children self-control.

The sense in which each of these questions might reveal that the mother did or did not emphasize the child's acquiring self-control can now be summarized. We chose some items because they would refer to demands that the child give up present bodily pleasures for the mother's love or for other rewards in the future. These demands teach the youngster to curb the immediate expression of his desires in the interest of satisfying his long-range needs. The questions that we felt might refer to such training are those asking for the ages of weaning and of bowel and bladder training, and those inquiring about the use of scheduled as against demand feeding in infancy.

Figure 4–1

INTERNALIZATION INDICES

Item Number	Item
3	Mothers have different ways of handling a crying child of five months. Suppose that you were busy preparing the family dinner and the baby was cranky and crying—if you thought nothing was wrong with him (her), and he (she) only wanted attention, what would you do?
5, 5a	We'd like to know (name's) age at different times when you made changes in feeding. When did he (she) stop breast feeding as the main way of feeding at meal time?
5c, 6b	When did he (she) give up using the bottle entirely?
5d	When did he (she) give up breast feeding entirely?
5e, 6c	Did you feed him (her) at special times when he (she) was a baby, or when he (she) seemed to want to eat?
14	How old (in months) was he (she) when you began bowel training?
17	How old was your child when you began to train him (her) not to wet himself (herself)?
19, 19a	Think about a time when (name) will be (was) ten years old. He (she) has just done something that you feel is very good, or he (she) has been particularly good. What would you do at those times? Can you give me an example?
20, 20a	Now, please think about that same time when (name) will be (was) ten years old. He (she) has just done something that you feel is very wrong, something that you have warned him (her) against ever doing. What would you do at such times? Can you give me an example?

Types of reward and punishment that would use and reinforce the internal controls the child has acquired would be in keeping with such training in self-control. Thus, we expected that entrepreneurial middle-class parents would be more likely than their bureaucratic counterparts to praise the child or to let his virtue be its own reward instead of giving him some directly rewarding experience such as a piece of candy, or some money, or permission to stay out later than usual. We shall speak of this distinction as being one between symbolic and direct rewards.

Similarly, we can point to symbolic and direct types of punishment. We thought entrepreneurial middles would more probably use the symbolic disciplines of blame, appeals to guilt, and restriction of movement (for example, sending the child to his room to "think it over")

Entrepreneurial and Bureaucratic Families **93**

instead of more direct punishments such as spanking. Items 19, 19*a*, 20, and 20*a*, in Figure 4–1 get at these matters.

In connection with Item 3, we judged that the mother who is successful in teaching the child to control his immediate desires must be somewhat less warm and empathic toward her child, other things being equal, than mothers using less stringent and persistent measures, or she would be unable to bring herself to carry through with the task. Perhaps what is necessary is that, though she is equally warm, the entrepreneurial mother must be able to control the immediate expression of her sympathy for the child in distress. In any case, she must not be too completely gratifying to the child. She must not do what he would like without a price, or he will not learn strict self-control. Consequently, we expected that entrepreneurial middles would be less likely than bureaucratic mothers to give immediate care to an infant who cried for attention.

We did not try to predict whether differences would exist between the older and newer middle classes with respect to the time at which they completed the bowel or urinary training of their children. Evidence from earlier studies (1) suggested that such differences were unlikely.

Up to this point, we have spoken as if we were confident that these methods of rearing children would produce self-control, and as if we were equally confident that each of them would lead to that end. Actually, that gives far too simple a picture of the state of our thinking. We had several kinds of qualms and uncertainties. At the same time, we had serious reasons for thinking that early weaning and bowel training and symbolic rewards and the rest might lead a child to control his own behavior. We must say something about these conflicting thoughts so that our interpretation of the findings we are about to present will be clear.

First, then, consider the reasons we felt to be important in connecting these methods of training children with the mother's task of encouraging youngsters to examine their desires and modify or inhibit some of them. An important source of those reasons is found in the psychoanalytic idea of internalized controls.

"Controls" are standards the individual learns—standards like eating three meals a day or keeping clean or being honest—and which, once acquired, make it difficult for him to behave in alternative ways. Internalized controls are not simply those that are well learned or that are learned without contradiction. They are learned in ways that give them the characteristics of what, following Freud, is often called the superego. Where ways of behaving are well learned, but not internalized, they change if new conditions make them inappropriate. The change may be slow. The individual may be very unhappy and uncomfortable, but he does not blame himself for changing. He does not feel a guilt he cannot shake.

Ways of behaving that are internalized may also change under such special conditions as those provided in therapy. But the change is made especially difficult because the individual feels great guilt: an anxiety about forces within himself that are about to punish him. It is not simply that the outside world is upsetting and, perhaps, frightening. Silent, faceless threats within him make him pause.

Present knowledge of personality development suggests that there is a connection between learning a socially required pattern of conduct at a very early age and the internalization of that pattern. This is believed to be a significant feature of early weaning and toilet training. The child learns to give up pleasures. He is too young to understand why the parents force this deprivation on him. He needs their love. Therefore he must obey. They insist and persist. Thus a foundation is laid for his postponing immediate gratifications for future gains. In short, to the extent that the child does not understand why the demands that are put upon him are made, and to the extent that he finds that refusal to conform to seemingly irrational requirements leads to severe and persistent deprivations, whereas conformity brings reward and peace, he does conform. Since he may find obedience distasteful, he may have to control rebellious thoughts by denying their existence, by convincing himself that he always wanted to do what his parents now require. In later years, he still conforms even when there is not the faintest threat for nonconformity from the real world outside, or even when that world no longer demands that he continue behaving as he has. And he feels compelled to teach his children to behave as he does and is shocked and irrationally alarmed if they do not. It is believed that the person with internalized behavior patterns acts this way because he has learned those patterns under conditions (2) that make it impossible for him to think about their rationality or irrationality or to expect anything but great deprivation from nonconformity. As a result, he cannot control and change his conduct when new external conditions make it appropriate. Thus if he has internalized the standard of washing his face in the morning, he feels very uneasy and uncomfortable, and, possibly, guilty and depressed, if something interferes with this habit, even if his face is quite clean (3). Such reasoning supports our belief that these early body regimens train children in self-control.

In describing the coming of the bureaucratic order, we have stressed

Entrepreneurial and Bureaucratic Families **95**

the greater stability of the community and its larger potential for supervising and controlling its members. Once again parents may rely with some assurance on the ability of the groups the child meets to provide adequate controls and checks on his behavior. As a consequence, the need for his internalizing as extensive a set of controls in order to grow into a responsible adult is not so great.

We found the psychoanalytic picture of the internalization of some controls—of a special kind of learning of self-control and self-denial —highly suggestive. We recognize, however, that future research may modify it in whole or in part. The evidence in its favor resides in very suggestive reports from clinical records of therapy with children and adults, but these do not provide anything like conclusive evidence. Further, our own study contains no findings about the actual effects of early weaning or bowel training or the rest of these methods on the behavior of children. How, then, shall we interpret any findings obtained from the use of our Internalization Indices?

Our essential assumption is that these indices can reflect differences in the extent to which mothers use controlled and rationalized behavior with their children and that evidence of more extensive self-control in behavior will be found among entrepreneurial middle-class mothers than among bureaucratic mothers of the same social status. Our data enable us to test the existence of this connection between social positions and methods of child care. The data do not provide any evidence of the extent to which children adopt a pattern of conduct like that of their elders. The findings certainly give no evidence on the subject of whether, if children do acquire differences in self-control from their parents, those differences are learned through internalization or in some other fashion.

It is our personal judgment that children do learn a relatively impersonal and self-controlled style of behavior if parents set such a model for them and reward them for adopting it. We shall feel free to speak of our indices as reflecting themes that are taught to children. Yet, in strictest logic, we must admit that this way of speaking will represent what we believe to be the case, but not something that our data can establish or disprove.

Now, however, we come to a different problem. Were we certain that each of our questions was an equally good sample of the extent to which mothers practiced or taught self-control?

We were not. We appreciated that mothers might use any one of these techniques for reasons quite unconnected with exhibiting self-control in their own conduct or with teaching it to the child. Some women may wean or toilet train a child at an early age because they are ill and must simplify their housework. Perhaps the mother has a large family or plans to return to a job outside the home and must socialize the baby as rapidly as possible. It may be that the family's income has to be a certain size before parents will be likely to use many direct rewards such as giving the children candy or toys when they behave well. And these reasons can be multiplied manifold times.

What we did conclude was that some of these reasons, like that of a possible relation between family income and the use of direct rewards, would be less important when we controlled social class while comparing families with entrepreneurial and bureaucratic integrations. Other reasons, such as ill health, did not seem likely to be more frequent for mothers in one integration than the other. Finally, we judged that though we might be in error about the extent to which any particular technique of training children would reflect the theme of self-control, it was less likely that we were wrong about all of them or a significant number of them. It was also less likely that mothers who used several of these techniques would fail to be entrepreneurial in integration than would those who happened to use only one or two of them.

Findings. With the uncertainties just mentioned, but with several reasons for believing that our predictions about internalization practices had a solid foundation, we proceeded to test their accuracy. Table 4–1 summarizes the results of that test. Table AI–1 in Appendix One presents those results in more detail.

The findings in Table 4–1 confirm most of our expectations. We find that entrepreneurial mothers among the middle classes are significantly more likely than bureaucratic mothers of similar social status to feed babies on a schedule, to begin urinary training before the baby is eleven months old, and to use symbolic rather than direct punishments. They also are more likely to give a baby who cries when "nothing is wrong with him" some attention only after he sobs for a while or, in some cases, to pay no attention to him at all. Although it is not quite large enough to meet our standard for significance [a confidence level of .05 or beyond (4)], we find that the difference between entrepreneurial and bureaucratic mothers with respect to the age at which bowel training is begun is in the direction we expected. Entrepreneurial mothers are more likely to begin such training with their youngsters before the baby is ten months old.

We find, however, that there is no difference of note between entrepreneurial and bureaucratic mothers with respect to two of our seven indices of training for self-control. These have to do with the age at which the baby is weaned and the use of symbolic as against direct rewards. We can only guess as to the reasons why significant differences do not appear for the answers to these questions. It may be, for example, that mothers do not usually think of praise or a pat on the head when trying to remember how they reward children. Perhaps, although they give these rewards, they fail to report them, thus confounding our prediction. It may be, however, that age of weaning and type of reward do not reflect the theme of self-control to the same extent as do the other five questions. They may be inappropriate for other reasons. We cannot be certain.

What is of more immediate interest is whether, despite these two failures of prediction, we have obtained enough evidence at a high enough level of significance to conclude that our expectation of large differences between entrepreneurial and bureaucratic mothers with respect to this set of seven questions is fulfilled. There are many technical and statistical problems involved in making such a judgment. Interested readers may consult Appendix Two where we consider those problems and describe how we arrived at an answer. At this place, the important point to make is that we consider it correct and conservative to conclude that our prediction is upheld. Entrepreneurial middle-class mothers are more likely than those in a bureaucratic integration to use practices which emphasize self-control in training children.

Table 4–1 shows something else of interest. It shows that there are far more significant differences in the expected direction on these Internalization Indices between mothers of lower middle-class status than between upper middle-class mothers in the two integration settings. The reason for this trend is quite unexpected. Contrary to our earlier beliefs, we find that the older and newer upper middles are rather like each other in being more strict than lower middles in their training on these Internalization Indices.

We said earlier that upper middles, whether entrepreneurial or bureaucratic, have considerable economic security. We observed that they occupy positions in society that give upper middles some appreciation of the whole complex organization of modern life and of their place in it. From these facts we expected upper middles, generally, to strive and struggle less than lower middles; to have fewer experiences of being lost and confused in an urban society.

Now, however, we must revise our judgment. It may be that we have underestimated the extent to which American upper middles, whether of the older or newer type, still have reason to stress self-control in training their children. Perhaps the pressures of the kinds of work they do—work in which the individual has considerable responsibility even in the framework of a large enterprise—forces an emphasis on the control of impulses. Perhaps there are subtle but important pressures on upper middles as a consequence of their relatively superior social positions; that is, it may be that they feel called upon to behave as elites and with a corresponding gravity and self-restraint. Our present data do not allow us to decide among these and other possibilities.

Table 4–1

SIGNIFICANCE AND DIRECTION OF FINDINGS THROUGH THE USE
OF THE INTERNALIZATION INDICES*

Item Numbers	Prediction: Entrepreneurial Mothers Are More Likely Than Bureaucratic Mothers to:	Among Upper Middles p	Among Lower Middles p	Among All Middles p
3	Give delayed attention to crying baby or give no attention.	$+ <.01$	$+ <.005$	$+ <.0005$
5c, 5d, 6b	Wean the baby by the end of twelve months.	$<.90$	$<.95$	$<.90$
5e, 6c	Feed the baby on a schedule.	$+ <.05$	$<.70$	$+ <.03$
14	Begin bowel training before the baby is ten months old.	$<.95$	$+ <.10$	$+ <.10$
17	Begin urinary training before the baby is eleven months old.	$<.70$	$+ <.03$	$+ <.03$
19	Use symbolic rewards.	$<.95$	$<.80$	$<.70$
20	Use symbolic punishments.	$<.80$	$+ <.03$	$+ <.03$

* The notation in this table gives a symbol for the direction of the findings followed by the level of probability. The direction symbols are as follows: a plus (+) means the results show the direction predicted; the absence of a symbol indicates that the p value is greater than .50, making hazardous any statement about trends. All p values reaching the .20 level or beyond and having the predicted direction, are presented using one tail of the probability distribution. The degrees of freedom in each χ^2 computation are one.

Table 4–2 gives the answer to a different question. Is it true that mothers who answer several of the Internalization Indices in a way that we feel leads to training the child in self-control are more likely to be entrepreneurial than are other mothers? Table 4–2 supports an affirmative answer. To understand that answer, however, we must describe how it was obtained. (A discussion of some of the more technical considerations involved appears in Appendix Two.)

Entrepreneurial and Bureaucratic Families **99**

Table 4-2

SIGNIFICANCE OF ENTREPRENEURIAL-BUREAUCRATIC COMPARISONS
IN CUMULATIVE INTERNALIZATION SCORES

Schedule Form	Groups Compared	χ^2	df	One-tailed p
A	Upper middles	.33	1	$<.35$
A	Lower middles	3.76	1	$<.05$
A	All middles	6.17	1	$<.01$
B	Upper middles	.54	1	$<.25$
B	Lower middles	8.03	1	$<.005$
B	All middles	8.26	1	$<.005$

In the preceding chapter we described how, in order to increase the number of questions we could ask mothers in our sample, we asked some questions of only a random half of that sample and still other questions of the remaining mothers. Three groups of items from our Internalization Indices (Items 3, 5c and 5d and 6b, and 5e and 6c) were asked of the half of the sample who answered the questions on Schedule Form A. The remaining four groups of items (Items 14, 17, 19, and 20) were asked of the half of the respondents who were interviewed by means of Schedule Form B. (The reader will find these two Schedule Forms reproduced as Appendix Three.)

Our procedure for obtaining the results in Table 4-2 was quite simple. Let us take the case of mothers answering Schedule Form A. For each of the three groups of questions in that form that were included among our Internalization Indices, mothers' responses were categorized as likely or less likely to train a child in self-control or as "uncodable." For example, beginning to teach the child to urinate in the toilet before he was 11 months old was considered as likely to train him in self-control, while teaching him this skill at 11 months of age or later was considered less likely to train him in self-control. Mothers who said they could not remember when they began this training were classified as uncodable. Mothers responding to Schedule Form A could have answered as many as three questions in such a way as to suggest that they were interested in teaching the child to control himself. But they might have answered in that fashion with respect to two, one, or none of the three possible opportunities. When the same approach is applied to mothers answering the questions from Schedule Form B, we find that there were four questions in our Internalization Indices in that form. Hence, these mothers may have responded in ways we feel indicative of an interest in teaching self-control to their youngsters on four, three, two, one, or none of those questions. Our prediction is that the larger the number of questions to which a mother responds with an answer indicative of an effort to train the child to control himself, the more likely it is that mother is entrepreneurial.

Table 4–2 reports the findings from mothers responding to each of the schedule forms. The results support our prediction. They also repeat a finding we discovered in Table 4–1, namely, that our prediction holds more clearly for lower middle-class mothers than for upper middles. Table AI–5 in Appendix One gives these results in more detail.

Activity Indices

At the beginning of this chapter we predicted that the same pattern of socio-economic conditions that leads to an emphasis on self-control pushes the entrepreneurial middle classes toward activity instead of toward an accommodative style of behavior. As we see it, the individual in the older middle classes is taught to change himself if he must, but, when possible, to impose his will on the world rather than simply to adapt to his environment. This should be especially true for entrepreneurial males, since they are expected to be the risk takers and to lead in winning higher status for their families. There actually are pressures against a woman becoming as independent and manipulatory as her husband. Parsons has observed (5) that, when the economic system emphasizes extreme competition and involves comparisons of the relative success and superiority of the competitors, the stability of the marriage relation is enhanced if only the husband participates in the economy. In that circumstance, he does not compete with his wife, nor she with him. His is the active, aggressive, independent role. Hers is the more integrative, passive, accommodative one. Because these roles are complementary, they gain in stability.

That long-time Detroit resident and poet of America's entrepreneurial middles, Edgar A. Guest, once spoke of the need for active mastery of one's future in these terms (6):

> So long as men shall be on earth
> There will be tasks for them to do,
> Some for them to show their worth;
> Each day shall bring its problems new.
> And men shall dream of mightier deeds
> Than ever have done before:
> There always shall be human needs
> For men to work and struggle for.

And the kind of man who can grasp opportunity (7):

> A man doesn't whine at his losses.
> A man doesn't whimper and fret,
> Or rail at the weight of his crosses
> And ask life to rear him a pet.
> A man doesn't grudgingly labor
> Or look upon toil as a blight;
> A man doesn't sneer at his neighbor
>
> . . . .
>
> A man looks on woman as tender
> And gentle, and stands at her side
> At all times to guard and defend her,
> And never to scorn or deride.
> A man looks on life as a mission.
> To serve, just so far as he can;
> A man holds his noblest ambition
> On earth is to live as a man.

As we have seen, the bureaucratic situation strips from the worker much of his potentiality for striving and achievement and for the active shaping of his own future through planning and risk taking. It becomes, then, increasingly possible for women to participate in the economy without as serious a threat to the marital relationship (8). Together with the previously mentioned increase in the number of clerical jobs, the declining requirements for heavy muscular skills in industry, the freeing of women from many older household duties, and the decline of striving and competition lead to greater similarity of participation by men and women in the economy, and in the home.

We concluded that, relatively speaking, the entrepreneurial middle classes would show greater devotion to activity and independence and mastery than would bureaucrats of the same social classes, and that they would also prefer sharper differences between masculine and feminine roles. It is these differences in emphasis that the Activity Indices listed in Figure 4–2 were grouped to expose.

Among these Activity Indices, Items 11 and 35 and their subparts are efforts to catch the sharpness of the distinction between the sex roles, with its implication for the greater mastery required of male behavior. Items 2 and 7 reflect the efforts of the parents to prevent a child from finding pleasures in a passive manipulation of his own body instead of in control of the world outside himself. It may be objected that the major reason parents try to prevent children's explorations of their genitals is their fear that the child will become too interested in sex as such. This objection seems doubtful, since we do find

Figure 4–2

Item Number	Item
2	Did (child's name) ever suck his (her) thumb, or arm, or hand, or something like that?
2a	(IF YES) Have you thought it necessary to do anything about it?
2b	(IF YES) What was that?
7	Have you or your husband done anything at any time when (name) was five years old or younger and he (she) touched his (her) sex organs?
7a	(IF NO) Did he (she) ever do that?
9	Suppose a mother has a very good woman who will stay with her three-year-old boy two afternoons a week while she goes shopping and visiting. She decides not to do this because she feels three year olds are too young to be away from their mothers so often. How do you feel about this?
9a	Why would that be?
10	We hear a lot these days about different ways to bring up children. Some people think children should be on their own as early as possible to work out their own problems. Do you agree or disagree?
11	Here are some things that might be done by a boy or a girl. Suppose the person were about thirteen years old. As I read each of these to you, I would like you to tell me if it should be done as a regular task by a boy, by a girl, or by both.
11a	Shoveling walks.
11b	Washing the car.
11c	Dusting furniture.
11d	Fixing light cords.
11e	Making beds.
35	Here are some things that might be done by a husband or wife. As I read each of these to you, I would like you to tell me if, in your home, it is usually done by you, by your husband, or by both of you.
35a	Painting rooms in the house.
35b	Getting up at night to take care of the children if they cry.
35c	Deciding where to go for a holiday or celebration.
35d	Punishing the children, if necessary.
35e	Picking out more expensive things like furniture or a car.
35f	Washing dishes.

significant differences by social position in their answers to Item 7, but no differences by those positions in their responses to a question (9) asking if they permit the child to follow the parent of opposite sex into the bathroom. It is improbable that the latter item has no connotations relating to a stimulation of the child's interest in sex.

It may be wondered why we did not include length of nursing as well as items on thumb-sucking and genital exploration among these questions assembled to reflect the parents' toleration of passivity in their children. We cannot exclude the possibility that some parents who wean their children late are more tolerant of passivity. However, we do find that there is not a significant relation between the age at which a child is weaned and his parents' answers to these questions on what they did if he touched his sex organs or sucked some part of his own body. It may also be useful to give our original reason for excluding age of weaning from the Activity Indices. We felt that most parents would consider nursing to be an activity the child carries on in relation to the environment. In this sense, as contrasted with thumb-sucking or genital exploration, nursing involves gaining satisfactions through manipulating the environment in the service of the infant's needs, not getting satisfactions without making efforts to control the outer world.

The reasons for including Item 10 seem clear without explanation. Item 9 was not added for the direct answers which respondents gave to the question it posed. On reading the interviews, we discovered that the vast majority of mothers added a comment to their answers. Almost all mothers told the interviewer *why* they agreed or disagreed with the hypothetical mother in the question. Of course, a mother might agree or disagree and we still would have no basis for predicting whether she would feel that her child should be active or accommodative. However, if she said that she disagreed because it would be good for the mother to get away from the child, we felt this was a plausible reflection that she felt somewhat detached from, and independent of, the child. We assumed that the child, in turn, would have to become independent of a mother with such an attitude; that he would not become overly attached to any single adult on whom he would then be dependent.

Findings. Table 4–3 summarizes the findings we got from using the Activity Indices. In Appendix One, Table AI–2 gives these results in more detail.

Of the twelve Activity Indices reported in Table 4–3, nine show trends in the direction predicted. Six of these trends are strong

Table 4–3

SIGNIFICANCE AND DIRECTION OF FINDINGS OBTAINED THROUGH THE USE
OF THE ACTIVITY INDICES*

Item Numbers	Prediction: Entrepreneurial Mothers Are More Likely Than Bureaucratic Mothers to:	Among Upper Middles	Among Lower Middles	Among All Middles
2	Say the child never sucked parts of his body.	+ <.50	<.95	+ <.50
2a	Say the parents felt it necessary to do something about the child sucking his body if he did so.	†	1.00	+ <.50
2b	Use harsh means (mechanical and chemical) to stop the child who sucked his body.	†	+ <.05	+ <.05
7	Say the child did not touch his sex organs.	+ <.30	+ <.005	+ <.005
7a	Say the parents felt it necessary to do something when the child touched his sex organs.	†	+ <.05	+ <.03
7	Use harsh means (spankings, threats) if they did something when the child touched his sex organs.	†	<.80	<.70
9a	Feel it is good to leave a child at home frequently with a competent woman while the mother shops or visits because the mother benefits.	+ <.005	<.90	+ <.05
10	Agree that a child should be on his own as soon as possible to solve his own problems.	<.70	+ <.03	+ <.005
11a, b, d	Feel that only males should perform activities traditionally associated with their sex among adolescents.	+ <.30	+ <.10	+ <.03
11c, e	Feel that only females should perform activities traditionally associated with their sex among adolescents.	<.95	<.80	+ <.50
35a	Feel that only males should perform activities traditionally associated with their sex among adults.	<.70	<.70	<.99
35b, f	Feel that only females should perform activities traditionally associated with their sex among adults.	+ <.03	<.80	<.70

* The notation in this table gives a symbol for the direction of the findings followed by the level of probability. The direction symbols are as follows: a plus (+) means the results show the direction predicted; the absence of a symbol indicates that the p value is greater than .50, making hazardous any statement about trends. All p values reaching the .20 level or beyond, and having the predicted direction, are presented using one tail of the probability distribution. The degrees of freedom in each χ^2 computation are one.
† The number of cases is too small to warrant computation.

enough to make it improbable that they occurred merely by chance. These significant differences show that entrepreneurial middle-class mothers are more likely than bureaucratic mothers of the same social class to use harsh means to stop a child from sucking his body, to declare that their children did not touch their sex organs, and to say that they took measures to stop a child who touched his sex organs. Mothers in the older middle classes are also more likely to feel that it is desirable for his mother's sake that a child frequently be left at home with a competent woman while the mother shops, and to say that children should be put on their own as soon as possible to solve their own problems. Finally, the entrepreneurial mothers more often state that, among adolescents, only males should perform activities traditionally associated with their sex, like washing the family car and shoveling sidewalks.

Three trends occur as we expected except that they are not significantly large. Thus entrepreneurial mothers are less likely than those of bureaucratic integration to say that their children ever sucked any part of their bodies. Moreover, among entrepreneurial and bureaucratic respondents who report that their children were seen sucking their fingers or arms or feet, the mothers in the older middle classes frequently declare that they did something to stop the child's sucking. This older type of middle-class mother is also more likely to feel that, among adolescents, girls and only girls should perform activities traditionally associated with their sex—activities such as making beds and dusting furniture.

Whether as a result of widespread teaching, or because of a growing tolerance for sexual exploration, or for some other reason, we do not find differences of any note between mothers in the old and new middle classes with respect to the use of harsh means to stop the child who touches his sex organs. Almost no middle-class mother uses spanking or threats in such situations.

Another point at which a prediction failed deserves attention. It may well be that the absence of any important difference between the integration settings with regard to the degree to which adult sex roles are sharply separated is due to the way Item 35 is written. In retrospect, it seems like a question that is badly designed for the purpose to which it was put. Too many of the activities listed in its six subparts are performed jointly by husbands and wives. This is conspicuously true for such matters as deciding where to go on a holiday or choosing expensive purchases. As a result, these items may be insensitive to the definitiveness with which male and female behaviors are distinguished from each other. On the other hand, we cannot discount the possibility that Item 35 is valid and our prediction was incorrect. Deciding between these accounts will require further research.

If the reader compares Figure 4–2 and Table 4–3, he will find the former listing several subparts for questions 11 and 35, whereas the latter does not. What happened was that the individual parts of these two Items did not generally show sharp entrepreneurial-bureaucratic differences by themselves and we combined them into single indices. For example, in connection with Item 11, we assumed that shoveling walks, washing the car, and fixing light cords are traditionally thought to be activities for men and boys, whereas making beds and dusting furniture have traditionally been considered the work of women and girls. Mothers were rated as saying that three, two, one, or none of the traditional masculine tasks should be performed only by boys or that two, one, or neither of the traditional feminine tasks should be performed only by girls. We used a similar method to make up combined indices for Item 35. This is reported in more detail in Table AI-2 in Appendix One.

There is yet another interesting finding from the material of Table AI–2 in Appendix One that should be reported before going on to other matters. That table shows entrepreneurial middle-class mothers as more likely than those of bureaucratic experience to say that only boys can do tasks traditionally considered suitable for males. Curiously, however, these mothers do not show a parallel tendency to prohibit boys from performing girls' tasks. We have more to say about the possible meaning of the changing conception of the sex roles and about this particular finding in Chapter Eight, where we discuss the evolution of a new kind of American family.

We assumed that a further prediction would be supported by our data from the Activity Indices. This is a prediction that the larger the number of the indices that a middle-class mother answers in a manner we believe indicative of an emphasis on an active, manipulative orientation, the greater is the likelihood that the respondent is classified as entrepreneurial. Following the procedures already

Table 4–4

CUMULATIVE SCORES ON ACTIVITY ITEMS ON SCHEDULE FORM A

Cumulative Score	Entrepreneurial Upper Middles	Bureaucratic Upper Middles	Entrepreneurial Lower Middles	Bureaucratic Lower Middles	Entrepreneurial Middles	Bureaucratic Middles
High (6–9)	3	3	16	9	19	12
Low (1–5)	1	10	10	9	11	19
χ^2	1.70*		.20*		3.70	
df	1		1		1	
One-tailed p	<.10		<.35		<.05	

* Chi-square corrected for continuity.

Entrepreneurial and Bureaucratic Families **107**

described for obtaining cumulative scores for the Internalization Indices, such cumulative ratings were computed for the Activity Indices. (A more detailed description is found in Appendix Two.) Table 4–4 supports our prediction. Its findings also show that the trend predicted is present in about equal degree for upper middles and lower middles.

The reader may wonder whether the activity items are really another set of measures of internalization. Certainly some writers have looked upon the rigid forbidding of thumb-sucking and masturbation in early life as practices that produce internalization. The following points are relevant to our position:

1. Cumulative scores obtained by respondents on these Activity Indices have only a very insignificant relationship (the product-moment coefficient is $.10 \pm .09$) to their cumulative scores on the three Internalization Index items (3, $5c$–$5d$–$6b$, and $5e$–$6c$) that also appear on the same form of the interview schedule. Furthermore, we still find this lack of a significant relation when we examine only entrepreneurial respondents or only bureaucratic respondents. It could scarcely be otherwise. If the reader will consult Appendix Two, he will find that the reliabilities of the Internalization and Activity Indices, although adequate when they are used singly, are so low that they make it impossible to obtain significant correlations between them with the number of respondents in our study.

What we do find, nevertheless, is that entrepreneurial middle-class respondents are significantly more likely than bureaucratic middle-class respondents to have high cumulative scores on *both* of these indices ($p = <.03$). This means that, while we do not find any significant relation between these two indices in the whole population under study, our prediction of a greater likelihood of entrepreneurial middles having higher scores on *both* indices than do bureaucratic middles is supported.

2. It is still possible that one of the indices reflects emphasis on training in self-control and the other does not. It is even possible that both reflect such an emphasis to some extent but that mothers differ in the areas of behavior with respect to which they try to implant controls in the child. It is also possible that the two indices reflect the same emphasis in child care. We do not have information to determine which of these possibilities is correct. The reliability of our indices must be improved before we can say whether the child-training theme of Activity is distinctive from the theme reflected in what we call the Internalization Indices.

With these materials on Internalization and Activity Indices, we complete the review of the principal points at which we predicted differences in child training between the older and newer middle classes. There were, however, some other questions included in our interviews with an eye to the possibility that mothers would answer them in different ways depending on the integration setting to which they belonged. These questions were inspired by our reading of that remarkable book, *The Lonely Crowd* (10), by David Riesman and his collaborators.

We have already made passing mention of Riesman's ideas in Chapter One, where he is named as among those who recently have pointed to a revolution in American life and in the rearing of American children. Something may be said of the relation of our work to his.

We had determined on the importance of the distinction between the old and new middle classes and on the central role of bureaucratization in producing the shift from one to the other when we read *The Lonely Crowd*. Riesman seemed to be getting at many of the things we had sensed up to that point in our own work and had gone far in formulating some of the specific characteristics of child training that we considered to be related to the new developments in the middle classes. In addition, he had some original insights from which we decided to borrow. These are found in his concepts of other-direction, consumption orientation, and parental responsibility. We shall describe each of these in somewhat more detail than was suitable in Chapter One, and give findings from our efforts to obtain information about them. It must be remembered that, since Riesman does not use the entrepreneurial-bureaucratic distinction to explain his observations, we are not testing his account of these three trends. We shall see if the differences in integration will help to explain his observations.

Other-Direction

Riesman, like ourselves and many others, tries to distinguish between the old and new middle classes. He too hits upon the emphasis of the older middles on self-control and self-denial as of central importance. In *The Lonely Crowd*, he speaks of the self-controlled man as "inner-directed." By this he means that such a man judges the world by a set of standards which he seeks to impose on the environment. In this way, the inner-directed person is like a ship or an airplane with its course already set. It may veer to avoid obstacles but its general direction does not change (11).

We have interpreted this pattern of behavior as a product of entrepreneurial conditions. As we have seen it, the entrepreneurial middle-class child, like his parents, struggles to maintain or to improve his social position with little help from others. He must be taught to behave properly and responsibly without direct supervision. He must learn the difference between the knock of opportunity and the call of temptation. He must learn to control and restrain himself.

The meaning Riesman wants to give to other-direction is not completely clear, though such clarity is not to be expected when an idea is new and developing. It seems reasonable, however, to say that Riesman pictures the newer middle classes as relatively lacking in fixed standards learned from childhood on and, consequently, paying close attention to other people in order to learn how to behave. Since others are also seeking such guidance, social life becomes a matter of the confused looking to the confused for direction.

We share Riesman's feeling that such a period of confusion once appeared in American life, but we feel it was brief and transitory, that the new middle classes have a different spirit and problem. In a later chapter we compare the confused period of the 1920's and 1930's with the present. For our immediate purposes, however, the important point is that we do not see bureaucratic conditions as lacking standards, but as producing standards under such circumstances that they can be learned without severe internalization. We feel that internalization was not so extensive an aspect of most personalities in pre-entrepreneurial times as it later became. The child's conduct was supervised by the gossip, the constant surveillance, and the quick reporting of the small town. It was not necessary that he learn all the standards of his group so that they became internalized, that they would guide his behavior even in the face of continued and contrary influences. If he learned a way of life approved in the small community, his conformity would be reinforced by his daily round of contacts. As we have seen, entrepreneurial conditions changed this pattern.

Bureaucratic experiences return us in part to an earlier time. Now, formal patterns of supervision rather than informal observing and gossiping guide the individual's conduct; colleagues rather than kinfolk surround his daily life. But, as we see it, this newly stable society is capable of controlling and caring for the lives of its members to a degree that makes unnecessary many of the powerful and internalized standards of the older middle classes. We think of the new middle classes as having standards—standards perhaps not much more or much less fixed than those of entrepreneurial middles. But, in contrast to those of the older type of middle-class person, these standards are buttressed more by social pressures from without and less by such pressures internalized in the individual.

Riesman gives much attention to describing inner-direction and the rise of other-direction in its place. However, he pays less attention to accounting for either. His major formal explanation says that inner-direction appears in a society in which birth rates are rising and death rates declining, while other-direction develops in a society in which both birth and death rates are falling. Unfortunately, he has little to say about the reasons why there should be such a connection between these population changes and the way in which the conduct of participants in such societies is guided and controlled. His explanation of changes in American character and child care in terms of prosperity and abundance and the growth of bureaucracy is similarly informal.

By now the reader knows that we have made major use of bureaucratization and considerable use of the social implications of abundance to explain the new spirit of child rearing in the United States. We did not feel that any plausible connections of a causal sort could be established between that spirit and changes in the birth and death rates. We were struck, however, by the similarities between Riesman's description of the inner-direction of the older middle classes and our own ideas.

Both Riesman's view and ours (though for different reasons) predict a decline of the kind of child-training practices associated with internalization—with self-control and self-denial. The data from our Internalization Indices confirm this prediction. But Riesman's interpretation suggests that something else should be true. Riesman thinks he observes that parents in the new middle classes place more emphasis on the child's learning to accommodate to the shifting desires of his peers and show an accompanying intolerance for the introspective and introverted individual. We tried to capture possible differences in mothers' feelings on this score with the following question (12):

Suppose a fourteen-year-old child were interested in some worthwhile activities that gave him (her) little time to spend with other children. The things the other children are doing are just as worthwhile, but they don't

Entrepreneurial and Bureaucratic Families **111**

interest this particular child. Would you encourage him (her) in going on with his own interests, or would you rather see him (her) change to something he (she) can do with other children.

A comparison of middle-class mothers in entrepreneurial and bureaucratic settings shows no differences in the proportions of respondents advocating that the child follow his own interests or the interests of others.

We recorded not only the answers mothers gave to this question, but the reasons with which they supported those answers. Some said that children must learn interpersonal skills and methods of getting along with other people. Others emphasized that the child could not satisfy his own needs or further his own interests if he lacked friends. However, these reasons are not related to the integration setting of the family.

It is possible that the answers to this particular question fail to show a difference between entrepreneurial and bureaucratic mothers because the question encourages those mothers to reply with stereotyped answers in which many of them do not believe. For one thing, we found it impossible to distinguish between those parents whose intention was to stress the importance of the child's having friends and acquaintances who could be used by the child in the service of his personal interests and those parents who felt that an accommodative style of life, a pattern in which the child would get his goals from the shifting interests of his peers, would be the kind of world for which he should prepare.

In short, such evidence as responses to this question afford does not support the idea of a connection between this interpretation of other-direction and our respondents' integration settings. However, the evidence is neither plentiful nor strong.

Consumption Orientation

We tried to see if we could explain another trend mentioned in Riesman's work (and in that of other commentators on modern life). Riesman gives this expectation the dramatic title of "consumption orientation." We interpret this to mean a willingness to accept gratification in the present instead of looking on life as an investment from which the rewards will be reaped only in the future. This view of life as an investment is what Riesman calls "production orientation." It need not involve sacrifice, but it always involves planning in the present for the production of desired future events.

We asked each of our mothers this question (13):

We are interested in what mothers would do if they really had free leisure time. Suppose your housework were well taken care of most afternoons, you didn't have to work, and you have some extra money. Imagine this started in the summer. What would you do with the free time?

The answers to this question were not critical, in themselves, for our purpose. (Most mothers replied with common, unexceptional activities. As a first choice, about 16 per cent would go shopping, 13 per cent would rest and relax, and about the same number would like to do a little traveling and sight-seeing or go on outings and picnics. Eight per cent thought they would like to sew. About 7 per cent preferred to visit with friends and relatives, and an additional 7 per cent wanted to take part in sports. Approximately 6 per cent would take courses in domestic arts or other subjects. Then followed a wide scattering of answers none of which received as many as 5 per cent of the choices.) All the mothers' choices were interesting in themselves, but the vital information we needed came from asking, for each activity they mentioned (14), "Why would you like to do that, if you had the time?" We hoped to learn whether the mother saw her leisure as providing gratifications she could seize and enjoy in the present or as a kind of investment for the future.

Among the early interviews that we gathered were a pair that give striking illustration of the difference we anticipated. Two mothers said that if they had free time beginning in the summer they would want to lie in the sun and bake. Both, of course, were asked why they would like to use their time that way. One said, "I just like it. It feels so good to lie there and just soak up sunshine—to just feel it going through you." The second expanded, "I have a lot of colds in the winter, and I'd want to get a lot of sun so I wouldn't have so many."

Quite naturally, we expected that entrepreneurial middle-class respondents would be more likely to find their gratifications in the future than would middles with bureaucratic experiences. This proved untrue. No significant differences appear in the tabulations.

Again we must be cautious. No single unvalidated question can be the test of the correctness of a prediction. Further research must be done on this relation of bureaucracy and consumption orientation.

Problem Mothers and Problem Children

The final suggestion which we derived from Riesman's thinking concerns the mothers' ideas of where the responsibility lies when their children misbehave. Perhaps this consideration belongs more

Entrepreneurial and Bureaucratic Families **113**

appropriately with the Internalization Indices. It differs from the others, however, in the theme it appears to emphasize.

The mothers were given this case (15):

You know, there's something which happens in some families. You have friends in for a meal in the evening, and your five- or six-year-old child doesn't behave—he wiggles around and shakes the table and plays with his food. You feel a little embarrassed. How have you or would you handle this kind of situation?

How could you prevent that from happening another time?

The reason for thinking that answers to these questions might be related to an entrepreneurial or bureaucratic middle-class position has to do with internalization. If the child has been trained to control himself (an entrepreneurial emphasis), the appropriate behavior for the parent would seem to be that of getting the child to invoke those internalized controls—to act as if the child were responsible for his acts since he is capable of controlling them. Table 4–5 shows that

Table 4–5

MOTHER OR CHILD RESPONSIBILITY FOR MISBEHAVIOR

Social Position	Mother's Responsibility	Child's Responsibility	χ^2	df	p
Entrepreneurial upper middle	1	28			
			5.63	1	< .01*
Bureaucratic upper middle	10	24			
Entrepreneurial lower middle	15	55			
			.12	1	< .80
Bureaucratic lower middle	11	47			
Total Entrepreneurial middle	16	83			
			1.36	1	< .30
Total Bureaucratic middle	21	71			

* The p value reported here is taken for one tail of the probability distribution.

this expectation is borne out only for the comparison of entrepreneurial and bureaucratic upper middles. The findings are not so sharp as might be expected, but they give enough support to the hypothesis to warrant its continued exploration.

Other Differences in the Middle Classes

This concludes the presentation of the areas in which we expected to find entrepreneurial-bureaucratic differences in the middle classes. Another question remains. Did we find other differences in the middle classes—differences we did not anticipate?

When we chose some items on which to predict differences, we did so with the thought that of the available items, they were the ones most likely to show these trends. Conversely, we did not expect the number of additional significant differences to exceed the number which would be expected by chance. Of the forty remaining items on which we could make comparisons between entrepreneurial and bureaucratic middles, only two showed any difference at or beyond the .10 level of probability. These are reported in Table 4–6.

Computations based on the data in this table for Item 13a show that entrepreneurial middles are less likely (.10 level) than bureaucratic middles to require the child to put his clothes away before age five. This is not a sharp difference between mothers in the two integration settings.

The results for Item 12b can be understood only after giving a short description of the question involved. We presented each mother with a list of reasons why parents might prefer that their children undertake some activities rather than others. The reasons were:

1. It teaches him to think.
2. It develops him physically.
3. It has to do with planning and organization.
4. It gives him plenty of exercise.

We then asked which of these four considerations the mother thought was most important in judging the value of a child's activities, which was second in importance, and so on. Our interest was in learning whether mothers were more likely to stress a child's learning the conceptual and organizational skills mentioned in the first and third reasons or the physical and motoric skills implied in the second and fourth reasons.

Item 12b refers to the consideration that mothers thought was second in importance among the four. It is interesting that entrepreneurial lower middles are more likely than bureaucratic lower middles, and entrepreneurial middles generally are more likely than bureaucratic

Entrepreneurial and Bureaucratic Families **115**

middles taken as a single group, to choose one of the more conceptual reasons as second in importance. (The respective p values are less than .02 and .05.) This may reflect the greater importance of independent thinking and planning in the life of the older middle classes.

Since this number of unpredicted differences could easily have occurred by chance alone, we shall not discuss them further in this context. (We will postpone further interpretation of the meaning of these two items for later chapters where they again become important.) Thus, in a negative as well as in a positive way, we have been able to support our interpretations.

Table 4–6

UNPREDICTED DIFFERENCES BETWEEN THE ENTREPRENEURIAL
AND BUREAUCRATIC MIDDLE CLASSES

			Social Position			
			Entrepreneurial		Bureaucratic	
Item Number	Item	Response	Upper Middle	Lower Middle	Upper Middle	Lower Middle
13a	Require child to put away own clothes	Before five years	7	19	9	22
		At or after five years	13	13	4	10
12b*	Prefer conceptual activities for child as second choice	Conceptual	3	21	6	7
		Motoric	6	15	11	18

* The meaning of this item is discussed in Chapter Nine.

. . . . . *THE LOWER CLASSES*

Earlier in this chapter, we mentioned how little is known about the conditions and experiences of lower-class families under bureaucratic conditions and concluded that it was unwise to attempt predictions of their differences from entrepreneurial lower-class families. Of course, we were highly interested in such significant differences as might appear unheralded. Only five of a total of seventy-three reached or approached significance. Families classified as lower class (upper lower or lower lower) and bureaucratic were more likely than entrepreneurial lower-class families to wean the child from the bottle later than twelve months, begin his urinary training when he is eleven months or older, do nothing if he touches his sex organs, and find him a joy rather than a burden. Further, if the child is grown and in difficulty away from home, they are more likely to help him by bringing him home or giving him money rather than by offering advice. Table 4–7 gives the probabilities.

Table 4–7

COMPARISON OF BUREAUCRATIC AND ENTREPRENEURIAL LOWER-CLASS FAMILIES*

Item Number	Bureaucratic Lowers Tend More Than Entrepreneurial Lowers to:	p
5c, 6b	Wean a child from the bottle after he is 12 months old	$<.10$
7a	Do nothing if the child touches his sex organs	$<.001$
17	Begin a child's urinary training when he is 11 months old or older	$<.10$
30b	Bring the child home or give him money rather than advice if he has difficulty after he leaves home	$<.05$
Coders' rating†	Find the child a joy rather than a burden	$<.05$

* Upper lower and lower lower families were combined since they did not exhibit any significant differences in responses.

† The coders' judgment based on a reading of the whole interview.

Perhaps the most interesting thing about these differences is that there are so few of them. In fact, there are so few that they could easily have occurred by chance. Unlike the middle classes, the lower classes of different integration do not differ substantially in techniques of child training. We cannot be certain, in view of the scant information about these groups, whether this paucity of differences is due to the fact that bureaucratic influences have not yet had an appreciable impact on blue-collar workers or whether some other reasons should be invoked.

There is, however, a certain consistency in the five differences that do appear. In each case bureaucratic lowers resemble the new middle classes more closely than the old. Theirs seems a less stringent style of rearing children.

With these findings in mind, we are ready to go on to the next chapter. There we shall find comparisons of the methods of training youngsters used by middle- and lower-class mothers within the entrepreneurial setting and within the bureaucratic classification.

Entrepreneurial and Bureaucratic Families **117**

. . . . . SUMMARY

In general, our expectations have been borne out. Our data support the predictions of the greater use of internalization techniques by entrepreneurial middle-class mothers and their emphasis on an active, manipulative approach to life. We also have evidence that the indices which we were reasonably certain would show significant differences are just about the only ones to show such differences for our material. We found that only two out of the twenty-two entrepreneurial-bureaucratic comparisons that might have been made in addition to the ones we chose to explore were significant. This is very close to the number of additional significant differences we would expect to find purely by chance. Finally, we did not find a connection between bureaucracy and data concerning Riesman's concepts of other-direction and consumption orientation. We found only a slight association between bureaucracy and data related to his suggestion that modern mothers hold themselves responsible for their children's misbehavior. It must be remembered, however, that our methods would require further strengthening before such findings could seriously dispute the accuracy of Riesman's expectations.

NOTES

[1] Allison Davis and Robert J. Havighurst, "Social Class and Color Differences in Child-Rearing," *American Sociological Review*, 11 (December, 1946), 698–710.

[2] There is some uncertainty whether these conditions should be stated as involving the child's lack of symbols with which to conceptualize his experiences or as involving his repression of feelings that he has conceptualized. Perhaps both situations are involved. Arguments for the former appear in such sources as: Alfred R. Lindesmith and Anselm L. Strauss, *Social Psychology* (New York: The Dryden Press, 1949); Ernest G. Schactel, "On Memory and Childhood Amnesia," *Psychiatry*, 10 (February, 1947), 1–26; David C. McClelland, *Personality* (New York: William Sloane Associates, 1951), 544–549. Some results of making demands on the child at a very early age are presented in Wesley Allinsmith, "The Learning of Moral Standards," unpublished doctoral dissertation, Department of Psychology, University of Michigan, 1954.

[3] We recognize, of course, that people differ in their responses to experiences of guilt. Some of these differences are discussed in Daniel R. Miller and Guy E. Swanson, *Inner Conflict and Defense*. To be published by Henry Holt and Company in 1958.

[4] A statistically significant finding is one that could not easily have occurred by chance alone. Thus if one tosses a penny 100 times, getting 60 heads and 40 tails, he would feel that this could result from chance. If, however, he got 95 heads and 5 tails, he would begin to think something other than chance was

producing the results. In this book, results are called significant if they are marked enough, when evaluated statistically, to occur by chance alone 5 or fewer times out of 100 repetitions of the study.

Unless otherwise specified, probabilities cited in this book are based on the computation of chi-square. When tables of four cells are involved, Yates' correction for continuity has been applied whenever the number of cases expected in a cell fell below ten. For tables of more than four cells, chi-square was computed by the method described in Alexander M. Mood, *Introduction to the Theory of Statistics* (New York: McGraw-Hill Book Company Inc., 1950), 152–164; and in J. E. Keith Smith, "Multi-variate Attribute Analysis," Engineering Research Institute, University of Michigan, August, 1953. This method contains a correction for tables in which there are small numbers of expected cases in some cells.

[5] Talcott Parsons, "An Analytical Approach to the Theory of Social Stratification," *The American Journal of Sociology*, 45 (May, 1940), 852–853.

[6] Edgar A. Guest, "Opportunity," in *Collected Verse of Edgar A. Guest* (Chicago: The Reilly and Lee Company, 1938), 23.

[7] "A Man," *ibid.*, 90.

[8] This may be one of the conditions that has resulted in unprecedented numbers of women entering and remaining in the labor force in prosperous times. Previously women came into the economy in large numbers only in time of war or depression and they left as soon as the emergency was over.

[9] Items 8 and 8*a*.

[10] David Riesman and others, *The Lonely Crowd: A Study of the Changing American Character* (New Haven: Yale University Press, 1950).

[11] In his concept of "inner-direction," Riesman wants to stress certain aspects of behavior which become clear only when compared with other possibilities. What he has done is to speak of three ways in which the individual's behavior may be controlled. In the first case, "tradition-direction," the individual lives in a stable social world that guides his conduct by embodying a set of relatively unchanging standards which it compels him to meet. The individual is thus controlled primarily by the constant pressures of his social environment. Examples might be found, among other places, in some small, primitive communities. By contrast, the second case, "inner-direction," is one in which conduct is regulated by so training the individual that he internalizes a set of standards. The environment may change, but these internalized standards continue to direct his action. In the third case, that of "other-direction," the environment is too unstable to exert effective and continuing guidance or to teach the individual to internalize standards. Nevertheless, he must live with other people and adjust to their behavior. This adjustment is accomplished through constant attention to what others are doing and by ready adaptation to the cues they provide.

[12] Item 31.

[13] Item 33.

[14] Item 33*b*.

[15] Item 32.

CHAPTER FIVE

. . . . CHILD TRAINING,

SOCIAL CLASSES, AND

INTEGRATION SETTINGS

At least since 1946, there has been evidence that mothers in different social classes do not rear their youngsters in the same way, and that techniques of child care peculiar to particular social classes come into use as soon as a baby is born. We too want to report some predictions and findings on the relations between social class and child rearing. Because we find that a family's integration setting affects the way its children are trained, we shall examine the role of social class *within* the entrepreneurial and the bureaucratic situations. First, however, we present the essential findings from a pioneering study of child rearing and social class. It was part of the background for our own research.

In 1946 Allison Davis and Robert Havighurst published a study destined for wide quotation (1). Its title was "Social Class and Color Differences in Child-Rearing." They described their work in this way:

The study consisted of holding guided interviews with mothers of young children, recording their responses on a schedule, and making a statistical analysis of the data from the schedules. All the mothers were residents of Chicago, and most of them lived on the South Side of Chicago.

There were fifty mothers in each of four groups, white middle class, white lower class, Negro middle class, and Negro lower class (2).

. . . .

The middle class sample is probably more representative of upper middle than of lower middle class people, with a high proportion of fathers in professions and managerial positions in business. The lower class sample is definitely upper lower rather than lower lower class . . . (3).

When Davis and Havighurst compared the methods of child care used by middle- and lower-class mothers in white families, some striking differences appeared. Lower-class mothers were significantly more likely to feed their babies only at the breast, to let the babies nurse whenever they were hungry, to wean them after they were twelve months old, and to give them pacifiers. Lower-class mothers also were different in the way they trained youngsters to use the toilet. They were significantly more likely than middle-class mothers to begin bowel and bladder training after the infant was six months old. More lower-class parents completed training their children in bladder control at eighteen months or earlier.

These were only a few of the differences in child training between mothers in the two social classes. Lower-class mothers generally did not require girls to assume such responsibilities as helping with younger children, cooking, sewing, or doing the dishes at as early an age as did mothers of middle-class status. By contrast, middle-class mothers more frequently expected children to take naps in the daytime, to be in the house at an early hour at night, and to continue their schooling for long periods. Whereas middle-class respondents delayed the age at which children are allowed to attend movies alone, such mothers were more likely than those in the lower class to feel that boys and girls could go downtown by themselves at an early age.

Finally, Davis and Havighurst presented some information about the behavior of the children of these mothers. The middle-class respondents were three times as likely as lower-class mothers to say that their children sucked their thumbs or that their youngsters masturbated.

All of these findings caught the attention of many social scientists because such discoveries had implications for the way social classes might affect the personality development of children. Davis and Havighurst summarized their results in this way:

Middle-class families are more rigorous than lower-class families in their training of children for feeding and cleanliness habits. They generally begin training earlier. Furthermore, middle-class families place more emphasis on the early assumption of responsibility for the self and on individual achievement. Finally, middle-class families are less permissive than lower-class families in their regimen. They require their children to take naps at a later age, to be in the house at night earlier, and, in general, permit less free play of the impulses of their children.

Generalizing from the evidence presented, . . . we would say that middle-class children are subjected earlier and more consistently to the influences which make a child an orderly, conscientious, responsible, and tame person. In the course of this training middle-class children probably suffer more frustration of their impulses (4).

This picture of middle-class life and values given by Davis and Havighurst is not what we expected or found among the bureaucratic mothers discussed in the preceding chapter. It is close to what we expected and found for entrepreneurial middle-class mothers. That observation defines the problem for this chapter. For the reasons discussed below we concluded that Davis' and Havighurst's findings should appear when we compared middle- and lower-class mothers of entrepreneurial integration. On the other hand, we came to believe that the findings should not appear when bureaucratic mothers from these two classes were studied.

. . . . . *CHILD TRAINING, SOCIAL CLASSES, AND ENTREPRENEURIAL INTEGRATION*

In Chapters Two and Four we have described the conditions experienced by the entrepreneurial middle classes that should lead them to emphasize self-control and an active, manipulative orientation toward life. We have presented evidence that these emphases appear in the way entrepreneurial middles train their children. Now we want to indicate why we felt that these two emphases, and one other, were less likely to appear among the entrepreneurial lower classes. The reasoning involved is but an extension of the brief picture given in Chapter Two of life in the lower classes.

We view the lower classes in entrepreneurial settings as a people facing a hazardous world and having relatively little in the way of resources. In our sample they are the blue-collar workers who have come into the city from the farm or a foreign land, who, in some few cases, are self-employed, work in small organizations, or get most of their incomes from profits or fees or commissions rather than wages. We see them as assuming that a man must look out for himself in the city, yet usually lacking the education and contacts to make the world a secure place for themselves and their families. People must adjust to their predicament when they confront difficult problems without reasonable assurance that the outcome will be satisfying. They have few incentives to guide and plan their own conduct with care if their efforts will make no difference to them in the future. There is no reason for them to practice self-denial, or to invest their time and energy and money thoughtfully, if life stacks the odds against receiving any return on that investment. Under these circumstances, they come to feel that it is better to embrace such pleasures as life affords and to enjoy them when they come. Therefore we expected the entrepreneurial lower classes to give less emphasis to training their children in self-control and self-denial than the entrepreneurial middles.

Secondly, we expected that these entrepreneurial lower-class families would find less occasion than middle-class families for training children to take an active and manipulative approach to their environments. If the environment holds many insurmountable barriers, it is important to learn not to try the impossible. In such a world, a child would find only grief if he were highly ambitious, if he were set on shaping the world to his own desires.

Finally, we expected entrepreneurial middle- and lower-class mothers to differ in the weight they gave to training for responsible independence. We thought the mothers in the older middle classes would place a greater emphasis on training the child to be personally accountable for his own acts because these active and manipulative children must early come to be worthy of trust or their early independence and self-control will be a threat to those around them. The youngster must acquire a regard for his responsibilities to others so that he will not require close and constant supervision. This is a price paid for a measure of freedom. And, just as the development of responsible conduct involves early practice in acting responsibly and in fulfilling requirements for service to others, it also should force a delay in the assumption of the full responsibilities of adulthood. This delay permits those around the child sufficient time to insure that his behavior will be appropriate, skillful, but, withal, worthy of trust. An individuated-

Social Classes and Integration Settings **123**

entrepreneurial society that finds it difficult to provide constant supervision of its members must make certain that they are responsible to the degree they are independent.

If one examines Davis' and Havighurst's findings about the way middle- and lower-class mothers handle their infants, he finds that much of the information they have is of the sort already presented as part of our Internalization Indices. We used those indices again—this time to test the prediction that the entrepreneurial middle and lower classes would differ in the extent to which they teach their children self-control. Similarly, we used the now familiar Activity Indices to see if the social classes would, as we expected, differ from one another in their emphasis on a manipulative and active approach to the environment. A new set of indices—we shall call them Indices of Individual Responsibility—were brought together to test the third of our predictions, namely that entrepreneurial middle-class mothers would be more likely to stress the training of children in responsibility than would lower-class mothers from the same integration setting.

Findings

Table AI–3 in Appendix One summarizes the results of applying the Internalization Indices. Here a surprise awaits us. Only three of the seven indices in this group show a significantly sizable difference between middle- and lower-class mothers. We find middle-class mothers less likely to give immediate attention to a baby who cries when nothing serious is wrong with him. We find that these same parents are more likely than lower-class mothers to begin bowel training when the infant is nine months old or even earlier. Then, there is the further trend showing that mothers of middle-class status appear more often among those who use symbolic punishments instead of spanking and slapping.

One additional question was answered much as we expected, but the difference it shows between the classes is not significant. It reveals that middle-class mothers are more likely to set a schedule for a baby's meals, rather than feed an infant at times he "demands."

As for the remaining three indices, those having to do with the age at which the baby is weaned, the time at which urinary training begins, and the use of direct or symbolic rewards, the findings neither support our prediction nor do they show trends in an opposite direction. There simply are no differences in these matters between middle- and lower-class mothers.

Suppose we go a step further. Are mothers obtaining high cumulative scores on these Internalization Indices more likely to be middle class? Table 5–1 shows that the trend is consistently in that direction, but that it is not marked. (As in Chapter Four, we present results separately for each of the two forms of our interview schedule.)

Our expectations meet with even less support from the results found in Table 5–2 and, in Appendix One, in the second part of Table AI–3. Here the materials are the Activity Indices. Significantly large differences do appear in the direction we anticipated. However, there are only two of them out of twelve indices. These show that our middle-class mothers are more frequently among those who say children should be put out as soon as possible to solve their own problems and who justify frequently leaving a youngster with a competent baby sitter because this is good for the mother. No other differences of any moment appear between the classes.

Once again, we may consider what happens when we make up a cumulative score for each respondent. Will mothers with high cumulative scores on these Activity Indices be more likely than others to be classified as middle class? Table 5–2 shows that the answer is negative.

This brings us to the Indices of Individual Responsibility. The first four of these indices as given in Figure 5–1 resemble some of the

Table 5–1

CUMULATIVE SCORES ON INTERNALIZATION ITEMS

Schedule Form	Cumulative Score	Entrepreneurial		Entrepreneurial Upper Middles	Entrepreneurial Lower	
		Middles	Lowers		Middles	Lowers
A	High (2–3)	22	44	5	17	44
	Low (0–1)	6	25	0	6	25
	χ^2	2.01			.79†	
	df	1			1	
	p^*	<.10			<.25†	
B	High (3–4)	28	20	10	18	20
	Low (0–2)	13	18	7	6	18
	χ^2	2.03			3.10†	
	df	1			1	
	p^*	<.10			<.05†	

* p value for one-tailed probability distribution.
† Computed from a comparison of entrepreneurial lower middles with entrepreneurial lowers.

Social Classes and Integration Settings **125**

questions used by Davis and Havighurst and for which they found large differences between the social classes. They asked for the age

Table 5–2

CUMULATIVE SCORES ON ACTIVITY ITEMS

Cumulative Score	Entrepreneurial Middles	Lowers	Entrepreneurial Lower Middles	Lowers
High (6–9)	19	35	16	35
Low (1–5)	11	31	10	31
χ^2		.89		.55
df	1		1	
p		<.50		<.50

at which children were expected to help with various tasks around the house. Only one of our questions, that about the age at which a child would be required to run errands to a nearby store, is of the same order. The other three of our questions inquire when the mother expects the child to perform some tasks that, presumably, she has had to do for him at an earlier time, such as putting away his own clothes, picking up his toys, and dressing himself.

Figure 5–1

INDIVIDUAL RESPONSIBILITY INDICES

Item Number	Item
13	Here are some tasks that some parents require of their children. Which of these did you or would you require of (child's name) and by what age?
13a	Require child to put away his own clothes?
13b	Require child to pick up his own toys?
13c	Require child to run errands to nearby store?
13d	Require child to dress himself (herself) completely?
20a	Can you give me an example of something (name) did when he (she) was ten years old and that you felt was very wrong and that you warned him (her) never to do?
22	Some mothers believe that for a child's own good they should know what he (she) is doing most of the time and should supervise him (her) until a certain age. What age would you say that should be?
28	(Again thinking far into the future) at what age do you think (name) will be old enough to be a good husband (wife)?
29	At what age do you think (name) will be old enough to be a good father (mother)?

The other four of our Indices of Individual Responsibility were chosen from widely scattered points in our interview schedule, but we felt that all of them, though for different reasons, reflected a judgment that the child ought to show responsible independence. Thus we assumed that entrepreneurial middle-class mothers would be more likely than lowers to emphasize earlier the child's learning to care for himself. We believed such training should be reflected in the feeling of middle-class mothers that the child will not need close supervision after a relatively early age. (See Item 22.) Again, we felt that mothers who emphasized responsible independence in children would be especially sensitive to, and disturbed by, any signs that the youngster did not give careful and competent attention to tasks assigned in the home or at school. They would worry if he was careless about his own safety. (See Item 20a.) We judged that they would be less likely to mention other childish misdeeds as being of as great seriousness. Finally, we felt that these same middle-class mothers, rather than those in the lower classes, would more probably feel that responsible independence would require a long period of training before such adult responsibilities as marriage or rearing a family should be undertaken. Items 28 and 29 were included to get information on these matters.

As in the case of the Internalization and Activity Indices, we were concerned that the Indices of Individual Responsibility be reliable—that there be some evidence that they had something in common with each other instead of being just a motley collection of questions which we had mistakenly grouped under the same heading. Appendix Two gives the findings from which we conclude that satisfactory reliability does exist for this group of questions.

Now we come to the crucial question. Were we able to predict the answers which entrepreneurial middles and lowers gave to these questions? The results summarized in Table 5–3 and, in Appendix One, Table AI–3 show that we were not.

Just two of these indices produce notable differences of the kind we expected. Middle-class mothers are more likely than those of lower-class status to stop close supervision of a youngster by the time he is twelve years old or even earlier. They are also more likely to mention being disturbed by the child's failure to be careful for his own safety or his lack of responsible performance on tasks assigned in school or at home.

With only these two questions revealing a significant difference we cannot even be reasonably certain that the trends they show reflect class differences in training for individual responsibility. We have a similar feeling about the single additional question for which a difference of some size, though not significantly large, appears. As expected, there is a tendency for middle-class mothers to feel that their children must be twenty-one years or older before they will be ready for marriage.

No conspicuous differences between the social classes appear on any of the remaining five indices. To complete the negative picture, Table 5–3 lends no significant support to the prediction that women obtaining high cumulative scores on these indices are more likely than others to be middle class. A routine check shows that these cumulative scores do not distinguish entrepreneurial families from bureaucratic families at any social class level.

In summary, within the entrepreneurial setting, we gain some consistent but modest support for the judgment that middle-class mothers are more likely than those of lower-class status to emphasize

Table 5–3

CUMULATIVE SCORES ON RESPONSIBILITY ITEMS

Cumulative Score	Entrepreneurial Middles	Entrepreneurial Lowers	Entrepreneurial Lower Middles	Entrepreneurial Lowers
High (4–6)	15	10	8	10
Low (0–3)	16	19	9	19
χ^2	1.19		.28	
df	1		1	
p^*	$<.15$		$<.35$	

* p value for one-tailed probability distribution.

self-control in the teaching of their children. Such significant class differences as appear among the Activity and Individual Responsibility Indices are in the direction we expected, but there are too few of them to be readily interpretable.

It is not clear why so few of our predictions are confirmed. The ones that do succeed occur most often among the Internalization Indices. It is in that group of indices that we have the largest number of items like those used by Davis and Havighurst.

Perhaps the differences we expected between the entrepreneurial middle and lower classes did exist ten or more years ago, but it may be that the bureaucratic trends in American life have diminished the size of those differences in all but a few areas of child care. Perhaps we were wrong in thinking that those differences ever existed. Perhaps the classes were disparate in emphasis on teaching self-control but alike in their emphasis on the themes present in our Activity and Responsibility Indices. Since we have supportive evidence in the preceding chapter that the Internalization and Activity Indices mirror the themes we expected them to reflect, it is less likely that this failure

Table 5–4

UNPREDICTED DIFFERENCES IN CHILD TRAINING BY SOCIAL CLASS
WITHIN THE ENTREPRENEURIAL SETTING

Item Number	Distribution on the Item	Upper Middle	Lower Middle	Upper Lower	Lower Lower	df^*	$p\dagger$
8a	Parents allowed child in bathroom with one or both of them	5	16	12	12		
	Parents did not allow child in	1	6	12	10	1	<.10
9	Would frequently leave child with competent sitter	9	30	29	31		
	Would not	0	6	10	14	3	<.10
30a	Would give unconditional help to child who deceives parents about his failure in earning a living	11	30	32	44		
	Would give conditional help or no help	18	36	33	27	3	<.10
31	Child should follow peers' interests in order to learn interpersonal skills	15	39	46	43		
	Child should follow peers' interests because he may not be happy in life without friends	9	18	12	14	1	<.10
32	Mother responsible for child's misbehavior	1	15	12	7		
	Child responsible	28	55	56	67	3	<.05
33b	Leisure is invested to produce future gratification	3	14	10	4		
	Leisure affords immediate gratification	19	41	45	52	3	<.10

* If the degrees of freedom (df) are 3, the p value is reliable for the four social classes. If it is one, the p value is reliable for the distribution between all middle classes when compared with all lower classes.

† Since these findings are unpredicted, all p values are based on both tails of the probability distribution.

Social Classes and Integration Settings **129**

of prediction occurs because those indices are not valid. However, the Indices of Individual Responsibility are untried and may be invalid. There is no way to decide among these possibilities with our present data.

Other Differences. Having little success in forecasting where important differences in methods of rearing children would be found between the entrepreneurial middle and lower classes, we were interested to see if such differences would appear where we had not anticipated them. There were thirty-nine questions in our interview schedule on which we had not expected the answers of middle- and lower-class mothers to differ. From among these questions a significant difference appears between the social classes in only one instance. There are five other cases in which a difference approaching significance is found. These six questions are listed in Table 5–4. Since such a small number of sizable differences could easily have occurred by chance, we shall not give them any lengthy discussion.

It is worth mentioning that the large proportion of entrepreneurial middle-class mothers who are willing to leave a child with a "sitter" (Item 9) fits well with an emphasis on training youngsters for responsibility. The meanings of the trends in Items 30a and 32 are susceptible to varying interpretations. More upper middle-class parents leave a grown child on his own to solve his problems and feel he should be held responsible for his misbehavior. Thus we may be getting a reflection of greater respect for the child or of less attachment to him. It is also possible that both interpretations are correct. Finally, we are uncertain of the interpretation that should be placed on the distribution of answers on Item 8a. Though we find no social class differences in feelings about the child's handling of his sex organs, entrepreneurial middle-class parents are more likely than entrepreneurial lower-class parents to allow children to accompany adults into the bathroom.

..... *CHILD TRAINING, SOCIAL CLASSES, AND
BUREAUCRATIC INTEGRATION*

In the section that follows, and for the first time up to this point in our analysis, we had no predictions. This came about because we lacked sufficient information about the power position of the lower classes in the bureaucratic setting to enable us to forecast how such persons would compare with those in the middle classes. The existing literature suggested one possible outcome: we should expect few differences between the lower and middle classes as a result of the lesser attention of bureaucratic middles to striving and internalization and as a result of the improved security said to exist for lowers as a product of unionization and the protection of their jobs in large bureaucratic enterprises.

Table 5–5

COMPARISON OF BUREAUCRATIC LOWER CLASSES WITH THE BUREAUCRATIC AND
ENTREPRENEURIAL MIDDLE CLASSES AND THE ENTREPRENEURIAL LOWER CLASSES

Item Number	Item	df	p^*
	Bureaucratic Lowers Tend More Than Bureaucratic Middles to:		
1	Mention fewer pleasant things about having a new baby.	3	<.02
2a	Prevent child from sucking body.	3	<.10
2b	Use mechanical means to prevent body sucking.	3	<.02
3	Delay helping, or not aid, an infant crying for attention.	3	<.05
6a	Wean from bottle later.	3	<.10
7	Say child did not touch his sex organs.	3	<.05
8a	Refuse to allow child to follow parents to bathroom.	3	<.05
12a	Make a motoric first choice.†	3	<.10
13a	Require child to put away own clothes later.	3	<.02
21	Wait until calm to punish child.	3	<.10
22	Stop close supervision later.	3	<.10
	Bureaucratic Lowers Tend More Than Entrepreneurial Middles to:		
5e, 6c	Use demand instead of scheduled feedings.	1	<.05
7a	Not prevent child from touching sex organs.	1	<.02
8a	Prevent child from following parents into bathroom.	1	<.05
14	Begin bowel training later.	1	<.01
17	Begin urinary training later.	1	<.10
20, 20a	Use direct instead of symbolic punishment.	1	<.02
24	Want information about rearing children.	1	<.01
30	Not feel sorry for child who fails and deceives parents.	1	<.02
30b	Bring the child home or give him money rather than giving advice if he has difficulties after he leaves home.	1	<.02
31	Give inner directed reasons.	1	<.05
33b	Evidence consumption orientation.	1	<.05
	Bureaucratic Lowers Tend More Than Entrepreneurial Lowers to:		
5c, 6b	Wean from bottle later.	1	<.10
7a	Do nothing if child touched sex organs.	1	<.001
17	Begin urinary training later.	1	<.10
30b	Bring the child home or give him money rather than advice if he has difficulties after he leaves home.	1	<.05
Coders' rating‡	Find the child a joy rather than a burden.	1	<.05

* Since no predictions of direction were made, p values are reported for both tails of the probability distribution.
† The meaning of this item is discussed in Chapter Nine.
‡ The coders' judgment based on reading of whole interview.

Social Classes and Integration Settings **131**

In our analysis we compared the bureaucratic lowers with bureaucratic middles and with entrepreneurial middles and lowers. Knowing something about the latter three groups, we used them as "fixed points" against which to understand the properties of the relatively unknown bureaucratic lowers. Table 5–5 begins this survey with a report of all differences found at or beyond the 10 per cent level of probability. A total of seventy-three comparisons was made between each pair of social classes.

It is clear from Table 5–5 that there is not a significant number of significant differences between the entrepreneurial and bureaucratic lower classes. A second result, suggested by the first, is that the responses of entrepreneurial and bureaucratic lowers differ in similar ways from the answers of entrepreneurial middles. Of the sixteen differences between entrepreneurial middles and bureaucratic lowers that reach the .10 level or beyond, only two are cases in which the responses of entrepreneurial lowers do not relate to the answers of entrepreneurial middles in the same direction and at similar or better significance levels. Only two more are differences involving a reversal of direction. Since this many discrepancies could have occurred by chance alone if both entrepreneurial and bureaucratic lowers were samples of the same population, we must conclude that they are not significantly different from one another when compared with entrepreneurial middles.

It also appears that middle- and lower-class mothers in the bureaucratic setting do not differ significantly from one another in their answers to our questions. The differences that exist include three of our eight Internalization Indices. On all three of these, the lowers show less tendency to use internalizing behaviors. Four of our ten Activity Indices appear. On each of them there is more likelihood that the lowers will stress activity. The picture that emerges is one in which bureaucratic lowers generally appear to be like entrepreneurial lowers. (As we said earlier, this may mean that the bureaucratic revolution has not touched the lower classes in significant ways.) It also becomes evident that it is the entrepreneurial middles who are most sharply deviant from all other integration-stratification settings.

Finally, it seems that the position of the lower classes, at least with respect to conditions reflected in our questions on the relations of mother and child, is not different between the entrepreneurial and bureaucratic situations. What is different between these situations is the set of experiences of the middle classes. The increased security of the bureaucratic middles has led to a lesser emphasis on the importance of internalization and activity with the result that their child training looks *similar* to that of the lower classes. This is *not* to suggest that the child care of bureaucratic middles is *the same*. Since the reasons for choosing similar techniques in rearing youngsters are probably different for bureaucratic middles and entrepreneurial and bureaucratic lowers—perhaps in the extent to which a sense of safety and well-being rather than one of hopelessness and futility permeates the relation of parent and child—there surely must be some significant differences between the child-training practices of these social classes. What can be said, however, is that our interview schedule was not constructed to pick up these important shadings of practice and feeling. They must be another problem for further research.

Although the number of significant differences between bureaucratic middles and lowers is not large, some of those differences are suggestive of trends. On items having to do with sucking parts of the body and touching the sex organs, the middles are less likely to impose prohibitions on children. Similarly, the middles are less likely to forbid children to follow them to the bathroom. The middles mention more pleasant things about having a new baby in the house, and they are more likely to give immediate attention to an infant crying for attention. On the other hand, middle-class mothers wean their children earlier than do lowers, stop supervising them closely at an earlier age, and more often punish youngsters when the parent is still angry. They also require children to put their own clothes away at an earlier age.

In future studies it will be interesting to test the possibility that bureaucratic middle-class parents are, as these findings suggest, less concerned than lowers about bodily modesty and about evidences of some tendencies toward dependent behavior in their children. Such studies might also indicate that these middle-class mothers show a greater love for, and indulgence of, their youngsters in many ways, but that they are more concerned than lower-class mothers to train their children for responsible conduct at an early age.

. . . . . *COMPARISON OF THE FINDINGS WITH*
THOSE OF OTHER STUDIES

At the beginning of this chapter, we cited findings from a study by Davis and Havighurst in Chicago. The middle-class mothers whom they interviewed were different from the lower-class mothers in their sample on several methods of child care. Our information from Detroit does not provide nearly as many large differences in methods

Social Classes and Integration Settings **133**

of rearing children between these social classes. At this point we want to examine the convergences and disparities between the findings we have reported in this chapter and those obtained in Chicago. We also shall compare our results with those from the two other studies with which we are acquainted that obtained a considerable number of interviews with parents of diverse social class position and which asked several questions similar to our own. One of these is a study undertaken in the Greater Boston area by a team of scientists (5) from Harvard University. The other is an earlier study of our own (6) conducted in the Detroit area.

Findings from Chicago

For convenience, we have arranged Table 5–6 to show how our own results compare with those of Davis and Havighurst for those questions asked by both projects. It must be remembered, of course, that the exact wording of the questions was not always identical in the two studies, nor did the two studies separate behaviors—such as the age dividing early from late weaning—at the same point. Our own findings are not changed, however, when we divide our results at the same ages as those employed by Davis and Havighurst.

We had expected that our findings from a comparison of entrepreneurial middle- and lower-class mothers would be more like those reported by the Chicago project than would the results obtained when we compared the two social classes within the bureaucratic setting. We reached this conclusion because the middle-class mothers in Chicago reared their children with the emphasis on self-control and responsibility which struck us as entrepreneurial. Table 5–6 shows that, as we expected, results like those of Davis and Havighurst do tend to appear when we compare entrepreneurial middles with lowers of the same integration setting or with bureaucratic lowers. This occurrence makes considerable sense in view of our finding that the entrepreneurial and bureaucratic lower classes do not differ appreciably from one another in methods of child care.

When bureaucratic middles are compared with lowers from either integration setting, only one difference resembling a finding from that of the Chicago study is found. This appears in the form of a modest tendency for bureaucratic middles to wean their children earlier than do bureaucratic lowers.

There are many possible reasons why the DAS results do not resemble those from Chicago more closely. First, there is the passage of time. Davis and Havighurst did their study in 1943. We interviewed

Table 5–6

COMPARISON OF THE DAVIS-HAVIGHURST FINDINGS ON SOCIAL CLASS
AND CHILD REARING WITH THOSE OF THE PRESENT STUDY

	DAS Finding*			
Davis-Havighurst Finding	Entrepreneurial Middles vs Entrepreneurial Lowers	Entrepreneurial Middles vs Bureaucratic Lowers	Bureaucratic Middles vs Bureaucratic Lowers	Bureaucratic Middles vs Entrepreneurial Lowers
1 More lower-class children are fed only at the breast.	0	0	0	0
2 More lower-class children are fed on demand.	+ <.20	+ <.05	0	0
3 Middle-class children are weaned earlier.	0	0	+ <.10	0
4 Bowel training is begun earlier with middle-class children.	+ <.05	+ <.01	0	0
5 Bladder training is begun earlier with middle-class children.	0	+ <.10	0	− <.02
6 More lower-class parents complete bladder training by 18 months.	0	0	0	0
7 Middle class expects higher occupational status for children.	0	0	0	0

* In this table, a plus (+) sign at the intersection of a row and column means that the DAS finding is in the same direction as that of Davis and Havighurst and reaches the .50 level of confidence or beyond. Where differences between the social classes were found at the .20 level of confidence or beyond for both tails of the probability distribution, the actual p values are reported. A minus sign (−) appears in this table whenever the DAS finding is opposite in direction to that of Davis and Havighurst and at the .50 level of confidence or beyond. A zero (0) means that the DAS finding did not reach a confidence level of .50.

our sample of mothers ten years later. Countless changes have occurred in the United States in that time and their influence on the rearing of children cannot be estimated with any accuracy. Some disparities between the studies may occur because one was performed in Chicago, the other in Detroit, or because the Chicago mothers are predominately upper middles and upper lowers while the Detroit mothers include lower middles and lower lowers.

Then, too, the parents studied may not be comparable in other ways. Ours come from a random sample of a metropolitan area. Theirs were

> . . . not secured by a random procedure. Rather [their sample] consisted mainly of people who had children in certain nursery schools, some private, and some war nurseries supported mainly by public funds. The South Chicago group consisted mainly of people who lived in the neighborhood in which one of the interviewers had grown up. The Woodlawn lower-class group was obtained by calling at random in certain areas where housing was obviously poor, and passing from one family to another with whom the person being interviewed was acquainted . . . (7).

No one can say how those procedures may have affected their findings, or what may have been the influence on the Chicago results of the fact that Davis and Havighurst generally discarded returns from families in which the mother was not born in the United States.

But, what of the similarities between the results from Chicago and Detroit? At one point, some interesting speculation is possible. As we have said, we have come closest to obtaining findings like theirs when we compared entrepreneurial middles with entrepreneurial or bureaucratic lowers. Is it possible, then, that Davis and Havighurst chose a disproportionate number of their middle-class mothers from among those we would have classified as entrepreneurial?

There is a suggestion that this explanation may be correct. It comes, not from their published report, but from the data in another publication, that of Martha Ericson (8), who used the same sample of mothers. Ericson tells us that, of the forty-eight middle-class mothers interviewed, twenty-three lived in Chicago's Hyde Park area, seven in that city's Englewood area, ten in the Marshall Field Garden Apartments on the "near north side" of Chicago, and eight in the outlying areas of the city's south side. Of the fifty-two lower-class mothers involved, ten came from Hyde Park, twenty-nine lived in the area of the South Chicago Community Center, and thirteen were chosen from Chicago's Woodlawn area.

The selection of forty out of forty-eight of the middle-class mothers from the Hyde Park, Englewood, and near north side areas is the fact to which we want to call attention. These subparts of Chicago are among those that are, at once, the areas having the highest rates for migration into and within the city for white-collar people and those having the greatest concentration of typically urban living arrangements as reflected in the high percentages of persons living in apartments (9).

It is a long and tenuous jump from these migration findings to the similarities and differences in our two studies. However, it seems worth advancing the hypothesis that the middle-class migrants in these areas had an entrepreneurial integration in our society and were, in fact, the ones whose children were found by Davis and Havighurst in the nursery schools from which they selected families for study.

Why should such a hypothesis be entertained? We might reason somewhat as follows. Migration usually represents social as well as geographic mobility. White-collar migrants are likely to include a disproportionate number of people who are trying to improve their jobs or neighborhoods by moving to a new location. Such persons may be more likely than are non-migrants to have an individuated and entrepreneurial view of life—hence, to fall more closely into an entrepreneurial rather than a bureaucratic style of living. Along these lines we may observe that these same areas of Chicago are the very ones that have the highest rates of manic-depressive psychosis (10). Such a finding underscores the contention that these are areas in which white-collar people, perhaps because they are mobile and striving for still higher status, are subject to unusual pressures. Just such mobility and striving would put a premium on training children in self-control and self-denial, the themes to which the items in our Internalization Indices seem related.

We must repeat, however, that what we have just presented is conjecture. Only further research can test such speculation (11).

Findings from Greater Boston

The work on social class in Boston was developed by a scientific team at Harvard University (12). It can be compared at a number of points with our own studies. Of additional and special interest is the fact that its findings are at variance with those from Chicago.

Who were these mothers from Boston? Some estimate can be made from the way in which they were selected in 1951–1952.

. . . The families were selected from two areas in the Greater Boston metropolitan area: One section was largely suburban-residential, the other was a working-class residential area adjoining a large industrial plant. As the first step in selecting a sample, public schools were chosen in neighborhoods which appeared to offer a wide range of social class groups. The

Social Classes and Integration Settings **137**

kindergarten children (aged five to six) in these schools and their parents were taken as the original population for study. Families were then excluded from the target group if either of the child's parents was foreign born, if the child was not living with both natural parents, or if the child was a twin or suffered from some physical handicap . . . (13).

From this description we learn that the method of obtaining mothers to be interviewed differed from that used in Chicago or in the DAS in several important respects. Of special interest in view of the findings from Boston, are the definition given of lower-class families and the characteristics of the "suburban-residential" area from which, presumably, so many of the middle-class mothers came.

Of the families studied, 198 were called "upper-middle" and 174 were classified as "upper-lower." The occupations categorized as upper middle closely resemble those to which we gave the same label, and those apparently called upper middle by Davis and Havighurst. However, the Boston upper lowers seem quite different from those assigned to such a status in the Chicago and Detroit studies. The upper lower mothers from Greater Boston include a group of lower middle families! In fact, we are told (14) that "about one-fourth of the group" consists of lower middle families including such occupations as:

. . . dance-band musician, low-income salesman, construction foreman, self-employed painter and decorator, manager of a small restaurant who helps with the cooking, etc. . . .

The name of the "suburban-residential" area from which many of the Boston middle-class mothers came was kindly supplied to us by the directors of the Harvard project. We find that this suburb is indeed quite different from the kind of area in which most of the middle-class mothers studied in Chicago and Detroit were located. Among the larger Boston suburbs, the 1950 U. S. Census shows this area consistently at or near the top on indices of wealth and comfort. Its citizens have the highest average income, the greatest number of years of schooling, the largest homes, and the smallest ratio of persons-to-rooms in those homes of any sizable community around the city of Boston itself. Their wealth apparently is not so great as that of such Detroit suburbs as Grosse Pointe or Bloomfield Hills, but it distinctly surpasses that of most portions of the Detroit metropolitan area. The population of this community, like the upper middle-class mothers in the Harvard sample, contains a disproportionate number of professional families and of those who own or manage businesses.

These features of the Harvard sample—a substantial proportion of lower middles classified as upper lowers and a selection of upper middles from a particular kind of community—are of special interest because they suggest why some of the Boston findings were obtained. They also permit speculation to explain why, as we shall presently show, their results resemble one part of our findings from Detroit. First, however, let us consider the major Boston findings relating to topics on which there are comparative data from Chicago and Detroit.

1. The classes do not differ significantly in their infant feeding practices: they are similar in age and severity of weaning, and in the proportion of mothers who breast-feed. The upper-middle class schedule infant feedings slightly more rigidly, but not significantly so.

2. The upper lower mothers are more severe in their toilet training. The two classes are similar in the age at which they toilet train their children, but the upper lower mothers employ more punishment and scolding in connection with toilet accidents.

3. Upper lower mothers are much more severe in sex training. They begin modesty training at an earlier age, and insist upon higher standards of modesty. The upper middle mothers are likely to ignore masturbation and certain forms of sex play among children, or will seek to distract the child without making an issue; the upper lower mothers tend to react with considerable emotion, and to punish the child for such behavior.

. . . .

5. Upper lower parents employ physical punishment, deprivation of privileges, and ridicule as techniques of controlling their children more commonly than do upper middle parents.

. . . .

6. The tendency for the upper middle mothers to be more permissive and less severe in their child training than the upper lower mothers holds up when the mothers' education, age, or ethnic origin are held constant (15).

Now, let us compare these findings with those from Detroit. Table 5–7 gives a summary. The results from the Boston-Detroit comparison are equivocal, but the two studies are most alike when the Boston data are matched with those involving the comparison of Detroit's bureaucratic middles with its entrepreneurial lowers. In that comparison, both studies show an absence of class differences on items concerning methods of feeding infants and of toilet training. Both find middle-class mothers more tolerant of the child who handles his sex organs.

We would like to suggest that future studies of social class and child training explore such possibilities as the following to account for the points of agreement and disagreement among the investigations in Boston, Chicago, and Detroit. First, it may be that, by choosing upper middle-class families living in an especially well-to-do suburb,

Social Classes and Integration Settings **139**

Table 5–7

COMPARISON OF THE HARVARD GROUP'S FINDINGS ON SOCIAL CLASS
AND CHILD REARING WITH THOSE OF THE PRESENT STUDY

Harvard Group's Finding	DAS Finding*			
	Entrepreneurial Middles vs Entrepreneurial Lowers	Entrepreneurial Middles vs Bureaucratic Lowers	Bureaucratic Middles vs Bureaucratic Lowers	Bureaucratic Middles vs Entrepreneurial Lowers
1 No class differences in age of weaning.	+	+	− <.10	+
2 No class differences in use of breast feeding.	+	+	+	+
3 No class differences in use of scheduled feeding.	− <.10	− <.05	+	+
4 No class differences in age of beginning toilet training.†	− <.05	− <.01	+	+
5 Upper lower mothers use more punishments and scoldings for toilet accidents.	0	0	0	0
6 Upper middle mothers ignore masturbation or seek to distract child.	0	− <.02	0	+ <.01
7 Upper lower mothers use physical punishment more often.	+ <.01	+ <.02	0	0

* In this table, a plus (+) sign at the intersection of a row and column means that the DAS finding is in the same direction as that of the Harvard group and reaches the .50 level of confidence or beyond. Where differences between social classes were found at the .20 level of confidence or beyond for both tails of the probability distribution, the actual p values are reported. A minus sign (−) appears in this table whenever the DAS finding is opposite in direction to that of the Harvard group and at the .50 level of confidence or beyond. A zero (0) means that the DAS finding did not reach a confidence level of .50.

† We are informed by the Harvard group that "toilet training" in their study refers to bowel rather than urinary training.

the Harvard scientists selected mothers who come disproportionately from a bureaucratic setting. Or, whether the mothers in the Harvard sample are entrepreneurial or bureaucratic, they may include a disproportionate number of upper middles who have clearly "arrived" in the upper reaches of the prestige hierarchy in American life.

There is a second possible explanation of the equivocal pattern of the Boston-Detroit comparison. A fourth of the Boston upper lowers would conventionally be labeled "lower middles." If these were also from the older lower middle class instead of from a bureaucratic integration, they would, of course, appear as more severe in their child training practices than upper middle-class mothers in general and bureaucratic upper middles in particular. This same combining of lower middles with upper lowers in the Boston study may explain why the "lowers" appear more severe than the "middles" in contradiction to the findings from Chicago.

With respect to this second possibility, we must report, however, that the Harvard project finds that:

. . . the relationships of class to child-rearing are in general linear, and that on scales [of child-training] which show the upper-lower group to be more severe, the very lowest groups [within that upper-lower category] . . . are the most severe of all. This suggests that if our sample of "lower" families had been confined to the lowest end of the [socio-economic] scale, the differences between this group and the upper-middle group in child-rearing would have been even greater, in the direction of greater severity in the lower class (16).

This may make the second possible explanation we advance less likely than the first. These are highly intricate matters. The only thing that is certain is that the present findings on the subject are not adequate to resolve the discrepancies that have appeared.

Other Findings from Detroit

The third study with which we want to compare our present findings is one in which we, ourselves, were involved (17). It concerned the ways in which adolescent boys learn to handle inner conflicts. For that study we interviewed the mothers of 232 boys. The boys themselves were subjects in experiments we directed.

Of the boys studied, 120 were seen in 1952 and 112 in 1953. Among the questions asked the mothers of the boys studied in 1953 were several like those we used in the DAS. It is with the results of these questions that we would like to compare the two studies.

All the children in our 1953 study of adolescents were alike in being:

1. Male.

2. In the seventh and eighth grades of the public schools of the City of Detroit.

3. Classified as having an intelligence score of C or above on the schools' placement test, or an I.Q. score of 75 or above on any of the several tests administered by the school system.

4. Not more than one year of age away from the median age for their grade in school.

5. Born north of the Mason-Dixon line.

6. The children of parents who were born in the United States.

7. At the time of study, in residence with both of their biological parents.

8. White.

9. From families having some variety of Christian religious preference.

10. Children of parents whose families originally came to the United States from northern and western Europe.

11. Children of parents whose perception of their social class position agreed with our judgment of their class from their occupation and education.

12. Children who were not manifestly suffering from mental disorders.

The schools from which these boys came were chosen by going over the United States Census reports and selecting those areas in which occupations typical of upper middle, lower middle, upper lower, and lower lower persons were concentrated. This means that boys selected for the 1953 study were likely to live in neighborhoods where there are a large number of families having a social class position similar to their own. The mother of each of these 112 boys was interviewed in the course of our study.

We did not have available all the material used in the DAS to classify mothers as entrepreneurial or bureaucratic in social integration, but we have tried to approximate the groupings used in the present study. Specifically, we were able to compare families in which the husband was self-employed or in which one or both parents were born on the farm with the remainder of our subjects. Using these criteria as a definition of the difference between entrepreneurial and bureaucratic mothers and employing a method of classifying families by social class similar to the one reported for the DAS research, we compared the answers of the mothers of those adolescents with the responses of our DAS mothers. Table 5–8 gives the results on items for which either of these studies obtained significant trends in a particular direction.

We see that the studies agree on five of these eight comparisons. This actually understates the extent of their agreement. For each of these eight items appearing in both studies, comparisons were made between the integration settings for middle- and lower-class responses and between the social classes within each integration setting. Most of that total of thirty-two comparisons made for the data from each study showed no significant differences. Thus, the two studies actually are compared at thirty-two points, and only the three comparisons not preceded by a plus sign (+) in Table 5–8 show a dis-

Table 5–8

COMPARISON OF DAS RESULTS WITH THOSE FROM EARLIER
MILLER-SWANSON STUDY

DAS Item Number	DAS Finding Trend*	$df\dagger$	$p\ddagger$	Earlier Study's Finding $df\dagger$	$p\ddagger\S$
5e, 6c	EMC mothers more likely than BMC mothers to feed baby on schedule.	1	<.05	1	− <.20
	EMC mothers more likely than ELC mothers to feed baby on a schedule.	1	<.20	1	+ <.10
14	EMC mothers begin bowel training earlier than BMC mothers.	1	<.20	1	+ <.05
	EMC mothers begin bowel training earlier than ELC mothers.	1	<.05	3	+ <.01
20	EMC mothers more likely than BMC mothers to use symbolic punishments.	1	<.01	1	0 <.95
	EMC mothers more likely than ELC mothers to use symbolic punishments.	3	<.10	3	+ <.02
21	EMC mothers more likely than BLC mothers to approve punishing when angry.	3	<.10	3	+ <.10
23	EMC parents as likely as ELC parents to disagree over methods of child control.	1	1.00	3	0 <.02

* EMC = Entrepreneurial middle class. BMC = Bureaucratic middle class. ELC = Entrepreneurial lower class. BLC = Bureaucratic lower class.

† If three degrees of freedom are involved in a computation, the p value given is reliable over all four social classes; if one degree of freedom is involved, the p value is reliable for a comparison of all middles with all lowers.

‡ All p values are computed for both tails of the probability distribution.

§ In this table, a plus (+) sign at the intersection of a row and column means that the finding from our earlier study is in the same direction as that of the DAS and reaches the .50 level of confidence or beyond. The actual p values obtained in both studies are reported. A minus sign (−) appears in this table whenever the finding from our earlier study is opposite in direction to that of the DAS and at the .50 level of confidence or beyond. A zero (0) means that the finding from our earlier study or that from the DAS, but not both, showed a difference that failed to reach the .50 level of confidence.

Social Classes and Integration Settings **143**

agreement in their results. This suggests that the DAS findings on several questions can be generalized to the very restricted sample chosen for our earlier studies.

. . . . . SUMMARY

The problem of this chapter is the existence of differences in the way children are trained in middle- and lower-class families. Such differences were reported in a study undertaken in Chicago in 1943. We anticipated that the Chicago finding—that lower-class mothers were more likely than mothers of middle-class status to be "permissive" in rearing children—would recur in our Detroit data when entrepreneurial middles are compared with entrepreneurial lowers. We expected, further, that the Chicago findings would not appear when bureaucratic middles were compared with bureaucratic lowers. These expectations receive some support in our results.

However, we did not find evidence consistent with two of our expectations. We anticipated that Detroit area mothers in the older middle classes would be more likely than lower-class mothers to train their children in an active and manipulative view of the world and to stress responsibility and independence. No such differences appeared between these classes.

A comparison of middle- and lower-class mothers classified as bureaucratic showed that there were an insignificant number of differences between them in the way they trained their youngsters. Similarly, entrepreneurial and bureaucratic lower-class mothers did not differ in methods of child rearing to any notable extent.

On comparing these results with studies made in Chicago and Boston, we found that conclusions obtained from Detroit area mothers showed only a modest correspondence with those found elsewhere. We have offered some possible reasons for the similarities and differences among the studies in these three cities.

Finally, however, we did discover that several DAS results have a strong resemblance to those from another study undertaken in Detroit. We conclude from this that at least some of the findings of the present study present a consistent picture of the social class and integration-setting differences to be found by interviewers in the Detroit metropolitan area at this point in its history.

NOTES

[1] Allison Davis and Robert J. Havighurst, "Social Class and Color Differences in Child-Rearing," *American Sociological Review*, 11 (December, 1946), 698–710.

[2] *Ibid.*, 700.

[3] *Ibid.*, 704.

[4] *Ibid.*, 707.

[5] Eleanor E. Maccoby, Patricia K. Gibbs, and the Staff of the Laboratory of Human Development, "Methods of Child-Rearing in Two Social Classes," in William E. Martin and Celia B. Stendler (eds.), *Readings in Child Development* (New York: Harcourt, Brace and Co., 1954), 380–396.

[6] Daniel R. Miller and Guy E. Swanson, *Inner Conflict and Defense.* To be published by Henry Holt and Co. in 1958.

[7] Davis and Havighurst, *op. cit.*, 704.

[8] Martha C. Ericson, "Social Status and Child-Rearing Practices," in Theodore M. Newcomb and Eugene L. Hartley (eds.), *Readings in Social Psychology* (New York: Henry Holt and Co., 1947), 494–501. We have observed the discrepancy in the total number of middle- and of lower-class subjects mentioned in this report as compared with that of Davis and Havighurst. We are assured by Martha Ericson Dale that the two studies used the same sample.

[9] Ronald Freedman, *Recent Migration to Chicago* (Chicago: The University of Chicago Press, 1950).

[10] *Ibid.*

[11] For a further discussion of possible hypotheses relevant to these points, see: Robert J. Havighurst and Allison Davis, "A Comparison of the Chicago and Harvard Studies of Social Class Differences in Child Rearing," *American Sociological Review*, 20 (August, 1955), 438–442.

[12] Maccoby, Gibbs, and others, *op. cit.*

[13] *Ibid.*, 380–381.

[14] *Ibid.*, 381.

[15] *Ibid.*, 395.

[16] *Ibid.*, 394.

[17] Miller and Swanson, *op. cit.*

EVALUATION
OF THE FINDINGS . . . .

CHAPTER SIX

*O*THER INFLUENCES ON CHILD TRAINING

. . . .

In this chapter and the ones that follow we want to expand and evaluate our findings that a family's integration and social class positions effect the ways in which it trains its children. We want to give as accurate and complete a picture as we can of the significance of those findings.

The first step in that direction is to ask whether we obtain notably greater relations between type of integration or social class and child care when we add other social characteristics of the family to those we have considered. For example, from a knowledge of a mother's

147

integration setting and her social class, we find that we can predict whether or not she will emphasize self-control in training her children. Suppose, in addition, that we distinguished between mothers with at least a high school education and those with fewer years of schooling. Would we find that it is the entrepreneurial middle-class mothers with less than a high school education who tend to emphasize self-control whereas those with a longer period of schooling behave much like bureaucratic middle-class mothers? Would we find, similarly, that other characteristics of these women (such as the extent to which they have risen above, fallen below, or held the same social class position as their parents) require that we modify our ideas of the way they rear children? In this chapter we present several such characteristics of families and see what effects they have on child care. Among the characteristics considered is that of the families' religious preference. For it, we shall have some predictions to make and test.

The general plan, then, will be to continue classifying our respondents as entrepreneurial or bureaucratic and as the members of some social class. To these social characteristics we shall add others, one at a time, and see if these additions make any significant change in the ways in which mothers in a particular social class and integration setting train their children. There are eight additional social characteristics. They are: intergenerational mobility, the size of the community in which the parents were born, the length of the mother's education, the ethnic background of the family, the stratification-consistency of the family's economic position, the stratification-consistency of the family's neighborhood, its race, and the parents' religious preferences. We chose these eight characteristics because existing studies suggested that they might be related to different techniques of child care. Each of these is described and discussed in turn.

It must be stressed that this chapter does *not* hold new conditions, such as the mothers' education, constant, and determine whether integration setting and social class continue to make a difference in child care. That is an important, but different, problem. It is taken up in the next chapter.

. . . . . INTERGENERATIONAL MOBILITY

We have already mentioned the movement from one social class to another that may take place as sons leave home, get a type of job quite different from that of their fathers, and, over a period of years, change their style of life to fit their new economic situations. In terms of stratification, we may say that children thus increase or decrease the amount of power they have as compared with the power position of the family in which they were raised. Increases are called upward mobility. Movements toward less power are called downward mobility. Any change of the amount and stability of power from that of the family in which the person was reared to that of the family he establishes is called intergenerational mobility.

The upward mobility of families and its effects on parents and children was a favored theme of American and English novelists in the nineteenth century. Jane Austen gave a spare, unsympathetic picture of the upwardly mobile in *Pride and Prejudice*. William Dean Howells (1) pictured the tortures of the newly wealthy family, gauche in its manners, snubbed by its neighbors, the husband driven unwillingly to the dance and the club and the tailor's by his ambitious wife and daughters. More recently, there have been several stories like John P. Marquand's *Point of No Return* written on similar issues. In all of these tales, past and present, are drawn the hard life, the self-denial, the careful planning and the tremendous frustrations and costs of upward mobility. Whether the hero begins in the lower or middle classes, whether wealth and power come through enormous effort or through happy circumstance, upward mobility carries a high price tag. It seemed plausible to us that upward mobility might, therefore, be associated with higher scores on our Internalization and Activity Indices—at least when such mobility occurred among entrepreneurial families. In those families, upward mobility might require still greater self-control and an even more manipulative approach toward the world.

Perhaps the great difference between the older and newer American literature that treats this mobility theme is that, in the earlier period, the central figure was likely to be an unlettered man moving, or being driven, away from the fulfillment of the warm obligations of hospitality and kinship and of attention to his family. He left all these for the sake of money. Or he was the man with special technical training, usually in finance or management, who was as coldly impersonal as the abstract concepts he used to master other people. By contrast, although the newer hero of such mobility stories still must pay with great skill and sacrifice for his status, he gains prestige and power, not by striking out on his own against the social barriers, but by being promoted from the lower ranks in a great bureaucratic organization. In this way he can rise without seeming to climb; he can advance without obvious striving. His promotion is sanctioned by the social system. Further, he is rarely promoted for technical skill alone, but for

Other Influences on Child Training **149**

technical competence joined with talents for participating in an upper-class style of life on the job and off and for being able to blend adept human relations in the work situation with its other tools and materials (2). Thus we concluded that upward mobility for bureaucratized families might not be as clearly associated with high scores on our Internalization and Activity Indices.

Downward mobility has also had an extended treatment by professional writers. Tales of the declining power of the "old" families of New England and Pennsylvania are matched with the somber ruins and weeping moss of a whole school of Southern novelists and playwrights. The encrusted pride of the old and the disintegration of the young are familiar plots.

The reports about mobility by historians and social scientists are similar to the novelists' plots. There is a vast, though fragmentary, literature about the results of mobility on character, family, and community (3). Writer and scholar alike suggest important changes in the lives of families involved in mobility. We decided to explore its importance for our data on child care.

In addition to information about the social class of the families studied, we had obtained the occupation of the husbands' fathers. The first thought was to employ that information in rating the childhood social class of the husbands in our sample. However, this plan was discouraged by the realization that we had taken family income into account in social class placements of our respondents and did not have comparable information about the incomes of the husbands' fathers. Another reason for not using such a plan is that the social class position of some occupations had changed in the last forty or fifty years, making hazardous the use of the same divisions we applied to the husbands' occupations (4). Finally, an analysis of intergenerational mobility cannot depend on assumptions about the actual amount of the differences in power from one occupation to another. Such an analysis must proceed through tabulations which take into simultaneous account the type of job from which the family moved and the type into which it went. To do this, using the ten categories in which we coded occupation for husbands and their fathers, would have so reduced our numbers in each husband-father combination that we could never have meaningfully examined the distribution of child-training practices in each.

To get around these difficulties we settled on the simple device of classifying the occupations of each husband and of his father into two groups, "head" or "hand," depending on whether primarily conceptual or manual skills were involved. (This classification omits cases in which the husband's father was a farmer because we lacked adequate information for stratifying the rural population.) The importance we have attached in Chapters Two and Three to movement across this head-hand line was a supporting consideration for its choice. However, we recognized that even such a broad classification of occupations as the one we have employed will misclassify a fair number of persons moving from hand to head types of work who fall into the category of owners of small businesses. Many of these move back to hand occupations when their businesses fail or when they find them unsatisfying as a type of work (5). Some people move in this way several times during their occupational careers.

We used the four categories of social mobility listed in Table 6–1:

Table 6–1

DISTRIBUTION OF RESPONDENTS BY OCCUPATION
OF HUSBAND AND HUSBAND'S FATHER

Husband	Husband's Father	Number	Per Cent
Head	Head	74	19.7
Head	Hand	76	20.3
Hand	Head	60	16.0
Hand	Hand	165	44.0

Answers to all our questions about child training are analyzed as they are distributed by the mobility categories of Table 6–1, with the families' integration and stratification positions held constant. No important number of significant differences and no consistent trends appear. Whether this is due to the grossness of our index of mobility, to some other flaw in method, or to a real absence of relationship between intergenerational changes in amount of power and child training is unknown. It is notable, however, that the application of an index usually considered important for purposes such as ours did not produce any positive results.

. . . . . *SIZE OF PARENTS' PLACE OF BIRTH*

The fact of the father or mother having been born on a farm has already been used as an important index of the entrepreneurial character of the family's experiences when it moves to the Detroit area. In addition, we had information about the size of the birthplaces of those parents who were not born on farms. We decided to explore

Other Influences on Child Training **151**

the possibility that families from smaller communities might, like farmers, have an entrepreneurial outlook. This new approach required an index of community size.

Since there sometimes was a difference in the size of the town or city in which the mother was born as compared with that for the father, we chose the latter's birthplace as our index. This procedure divided the families within each social class and in both entrepreneurial and bureaucratic settings into those in which the father's birthplace was: (1) the Detroit area; (2) places with populations from 2500 to 49,999 people; and (3) places with populations from 50,000 to more than a million persons. We did not find a significant number of large differences between the child-training practices of mothers whose husbands were born in larger places and the techniques of those whose husbands were born in smaller communities.

. . . . . MOTHER'S EDUCATION

From our own observation we considered it possible that educational differences might create differences in methods of rearing children. Existing publications give the impression that a modern college education teaches women to be more permissive than they would otherwise be in handling their children. We divided our sample of mothers into those with eight years or less of schooling, those with nine to twelve years, and those with thirteen or more years of formal education. We also held social class constant within the entrepreneurial and bureaucratic settings. As with mobility, we found no more significant differences than could have occurred by chance alone. Further, these few important differences exhibited no pattern or consistency. There were, however, indications of a trend toward *less permissive* child training with increasing amounts of education at all class levels.

. . . . . ETHNIC BACKGROUND OF THE FAMILY

Every respondent was asked the question: "What was the original nationality of your husband's family on his father's side?" Although we had no specific hypotheses relating particular ethnic origins to child training, there were many suggestions in the descriptive cultural accounts that such connections would be found (6). Sufficient numbers of respondents whose husbands came from English, German, Irish, Polish, and Italian backgrounds were available to allow us to analyze separately the practices of each of these nationality groups. The rest of our sample was divided into a group that came from other Northern and Western European countries and another coming from the remaining Southern and Eastern European countries. Controlling for stratification and integration setting as described above, no significant differences or trends appeared. We must caution, however, that the numbers of people in our various groups are very small and this fact may deplete the evidence for such trends as exist.

..... *CONSISTENCY BETWEEN THE SOCIAL CLASS POSITIONS OF OUR RESPONDENTS AND THOSE OF THE AREA IN WHICH THEY LIVE*

In another study (7) we have found indications that lower-class children who live in predominately middle-class neighborhoods behave in some respects like middle-class children. It was possible, as this evidence suggests, that the effects of the family's integration and stratification situation would be counteracted in significant ways by discrepant influences in its neighborhood. Since Detroit is predominately a blue-collar community, we expected that there would be an especially large number of middle-class people rearing their children in neighborhoods populated primarily by lower-class families. Whether such middle-class parents would be able to act according to standards set by their entrepreneurial, bureaucratic, and social class positions, or whether they would be influenced by their neighbors' standards was uncertain. A necessary preliminary to exploring these possibilities was the classification of Detroit neighborhoods by the social class of their inhabitants.

The U. S. Bureau of the Census divides the Detroit area, as that of other metropolitan communities, into small areas known as census tracts. Much of the census material for the general population is published with tabulations by census tracts. These tracts are intended to reflect the natural neighborhoods of the metropolis and its surroundings. They usually contain a local shopping center and a relatively homogeneous population. They vary greatly in size (8). Those in the densely populated heart of the central city are often only a few blocks in area. On the outskirts, large sections of thinly populated land make up single census tracts. Census information for these tracts (9) provided the basis for judging the consistency of neighborhoods with respect to social class.

Other Influences on Child Training **153**

For each census tract from which a respondent in our sample came, we computed the percentage of employed males in the labor force who were in "head" occupations as against "hand" occupations (10). Very few tracts, and most of them outside the city of Detroit itself, have a statistical preponderance of head workers. This meant that we had to choose as "head" tracts, or as probable middle-class areas, those with more head workers than were present in some others. The problem was to decide on a point at which to separate these two types of area. Since 37 per cent of all our sample of husbands had head occupations, we decided to use that figure as the basis for determining head tracts. If tracts were distributed as our sample is, 37 per cent of the tracts would be likely to be middle class in character. Arranging our tracts in descending magnitude of the proportion of head to hand workers, we set off as head tracts those in the upper 37 per cent of the ranking. The distributions of Table 6–2 resulted.

Table 6–2

DISTRIBUTION OF HUSBANDS' OCCUPATIONS BY THE
OCCUPATIONS OF EMPLOYED MALES IN THE
LABOR FORCE IN THE SAME CENSUS TRACT

Husband's Occupation	Occupations in Census Tract Classify That Tract as:	
	Head	Hand
Head	97	79
Hand	94	207

Tabulating as we have before in all the analyses reported in this chapter, we found no important differences when we examined methods of training children by these neighborhood categories.

. . . . . *CONSISTENCY OF THE FAMILY'S*
ECONOMIC POSITION

Another attempt to make use of an additional aspect of the family's stratification position in our observations involved our looking at the consistency of each household's economic position. Others have noted the importance of discrepancies, such as those between occupation and income, in political behavior (11). Middle-class people with incomes as low or lower than those of many blue-collar workers proved unusually authoritarian, thereby bearing out the frequent observation that such middles are subjected to especially intense thwartings and frustrations. It was possible that such discrepancies between occupation and income would prove important for our findings, too. We separated our respondents into four groups: middle-class persons with family incomes above the median family income for all lower-class people, and those with family incomes at or below the lower-class median; lower-class persons with family incomes below the median for all middle-class people, and those with family incomes at or above the middle-class median. Using this more elaborate scheme, we added these refinements to our previous breaks by social class and integration setting and obtained the distribution of all our child-training data. This time, as before, we were plagued with the small numbers remaining in some parts of our tables. The results showed no interpretable number of significant differences and no particularly suggestive or meaningful trends.

. . . . . *WHITE AND NEGRO PARENTS*

Up to this point, all the findings reported in this book have applied to white families. Our sample of Detroit-area mothers also included a small number of Negro women—about 11 per cent of the total. This chapter seems an appropriate place at which to compare the child-rearing techniques of Negroes and whites.

We conducted interviews in 59 Negro families as compared with 479 in white homes. Although the Negro families are divided, as are the whites, into about equal numbers in the entrepreneurial and bureaucratic settings, the vast majority of them are found in the lower classes. Table 6–3 shows these distributions.

As the table shows, the number of Negro cases in any cell is small and the numbers in the middle classes are tiny indeed. This fact meant that only among the lower classes could we make even suggestive comparisons between Negroes and whites.

Despite this difficulty, we determined to see, in a purely exploratory way, what differences would appear. There were many things to suggest that some should exist (12).

Negroes in the United States represent both a special set of ethnic backgrounds and a stratification position. Coming from many places on the African continent, they brought with them a set of cultural traditions different from those of any white group. It was unlikely, however, that those ways of life would have persisted in any significant degree in the people we interviewed. The immigration of Negroes

Other Influences on Child Training **155**

Table 6–3

Social Position	Whites	Negroes*
Entrepreneurial		
Upper middle	29	1
Lower middle	71	2
Upper lower	69	6
Lower lower	74	18
Total	243	27
Bureaucratic		
Upper middle	34	1
Lower middle	58	3
Upper lower	75	4
Lower lower	69	13
Total	236	21

* Nine cases had insufficient evidence to allow placement as entrepreneurial or bureaucratic. Two more cases did not have data needed for placement by social class.

into this country was almost at an end after 1808, when the Congress prohibited the further importing of slaves. As a monumental report on the conditions of the Negro points out, he is an old American (13); his attitudes toward domestic and foreign politics and toward other ethnic groups in the United States are like those of lower-class whites whose families came in the earlier waves of immigration. He was systematically Christianized. His native traditions were modified and absorbed by force and by natural processes of acculturation through more than a century and a half of living with people of European descent.

At the same time, the Negro was at the bottom of the American stratification order. When the Emancipation Proclamation was issued in 1863, the overwhelming majority of Negroes had less wealth and property, and certainly less prestige, than did almost any whites. Even in much of the North, where interracial hostilities were at a minimum, Negroes were socially isolated from the white population. They were allowed to work in only the most menial and lowest paying jobs. The few of their number who managed to get an education beyond the minimum required by law and became skilled in white-collar, including professional, lines of work, normally found employment only within Negro enterprises.

Warner (14) has described the main outlines of the Negroes' condition by saying that the United States had, simultaneously, a class system and a caste system. The classes existed within the castes and all whites were superior to all Negroes regardless of the social class positions of the individuals concerned. Passage from one caste to another was strongly prohibited by white opinion and made additionally difficult by the difference in skin color that often opened to detection even slow and surreptitious shifts.

Over time, this condition has changed. The castes remain in force, but, especially since the First and Second World Wars, their meaning has changed. The "separate but equal" doctrine reflects these trends in which, in many respects, middle-class Negroes have become the equals if not the superiors of lower-class whites in the scale of power. Increasingly, the races come to the ballot box, the court of law, the public facilities for education, health, and recreation on an equal footing.

Even with this tendency, however, it is reasonable to expect that, for another generation or two, Negroes, regardless of social class, will show the same tendencies in child rearing as do lower- rather than middle-class whites, and that the correspondence will be especially close between their style of life and that of white lower lowers. Eventually, Negro middles may come to use the training practices of white middle-class mothers. The expectations that have already been presented for such whites may now be extended to the Negro community (5).

Table 6–4 lists all the differences between the white and Negro

Table 6–4

SIGNIFICANT DIFFERENCES BETWEEN WHITE AND NEGRO
LOWER-CLASS MOTHERS

Schedule Item	Integration	Negroes Are More Likely Than Whites to:	p
13c	Entrepreneurial and Bureaucratic	Require child to run errands to nearby store before age seven.	$<.10$
17	Bureaucratic	Begin urinary training before eleven months.	$<.05$
19	Entrepreneurial and Bureaucratic	Use direct rather than symbolic rewards.	$<.10$

Other Influences on Child Training **157**

lower classes that reach the 10 per cent level of significance or beyond. These caste differences are so few in number that we cannot make a case for any significant differences between lower-class whites and Negroes with respect to the aspects of training children which we observed. Further, this finding is in keeping with the conclusions of Davis and Havighurst (6) when they compared middle- and lower-class Negro families with white families of similar social class in Chicago. They say:

> The striking thing about this study is that Negro and white middle-class families are so much alike, and that white and Negro lower-class families are so much alike. The likenesses hold for such characteristics as number of children, ages of parents when married, as well as child-rearing practices and expectations of children (17).

It is interesting that two of the three notable trends we have reported are also found in the Chicago data. Davis and Havighurst report that one of the few areas of child care in which lower-class whites and Negroes differ is that of toilet training. Negro mothers begin bowel and bladder training earlier than do white mothers. A second area in which Davis and Havighurst report racial differences is that of age of assuming responsibility. Negro boys and girls cross the street earlier. Negro boys go downtown alone earlier than whites, and Negro girls are expected to dress themselves, go to the store, and begin to cook earlier. We find that Negro children are more likely than those in white families to be required to run errands to nearby stores at an early age. In Detroit we do *not* find the following differences reported from Chicago: more Negro children being fed only at the breast, being fed at the child's demand, and being weaned at twelve months or earlier. However, all such comparisons between the Chicago study and our own must be treated with caution in view of the differences between our two samples (see the discussion in Chapter Five) and the small number of Negro cases interviewed by each project.

. . . . . *THE FAMILY'S RELIGIOUS PREFERENCE*

Returning again to our information from white families, we take up the last of the characteristics that we added to integration and stratification and then related to the training of children. Here, unlike the other parts of this chapter, we felt existing knowledge made some predictions possible. Specifically, we predicted that, when their families' integration and stratification positions were held constant, Protestant and Roman Catholic mothers would:

1. Differ in the way in which they discipline children and in the emphasis they place on the child's becoming responsible for his own behavior.

2. Differ in these matters so that Protestants, rather than Roman Catholics, would give greater emphasis to teaching self-control and personal accountability to children.

3. Not differ significantly in emphasis on teaching self-control and personal accountability to children when such emphasis appears in the parents' methods of child care before the youngster is two years of age.

4. Not differ significantly on any notable number of aspects of child training contained in our interviews other than those listed in the second of these predictions.

It will require some explanation to make clear what we meant by each of these predictions and why we thought they should hold true. We shall begin with an account of why we expected differences in religious preference to show any relation to the way children are trained once we held constant the integration and stratification positions of the families we studied.

Protestantism and Roman Catholicism are unlike some religions in giving elaborate development to the ethical implications of the theological beliefs they support. No serious Protestant or Roman Catholic can be unaware of the position of his faith. God is interested in his moral conduct; and his church has tried to define God's will concerning the way men should behave in many situations.

However, Protestantism and Roman Catholicism are not identical in their conceptions of the relations between God and man or of the ideal moral relations among men. Assuming that any beliefs men hold, including these religious and moral conceptions, are products of the experiences people have and the problems they face, we infer that, to the extent Protestants and Roman Catholics differ in their ideas about morality, to that extent they must have different experiences and problems. What we propose is that the disparities between the moral views of these two religious groups will be reflected in child training and that a family's preference for one of these religious faiths rather than the other may be taken as an index of the nature of the moral problems it confronts.

It has been common among modern historians and social scientists to say that there is a high degree of relationship between the experiences people have in economic life and the moral problems which they face. If, for example, the nature of economic experiences is such that people come to occupy a wide range of different and highly specialized occupations, or that people must change their residence frequently as they move from job to job, then it is more difficult for them to come to feel moral ties to one another—to feel responsible for each other's welfare and to consider the interests of the community and their obligations to it as they make decisions (18). There is considerable evidence for the idea of a close relation between a man's economic and moral experiences. For that reason, many scholars assume that, once the economic positions in a population are held constant, there remain no appreciable differences in moral experiences and ideologies between people of similar economic status.

To make our first prediction plausible, we must assume not only that differences in religious ideology reflect differences in moral and religious problems, but that those problems are not perfectly related to the economic positions defined by entrepreneurial and bureaucratic integration and by social class. Although some of these economic positions should be more congenial to Protestants and others of these positions more congenial to Roman Catholics, we expect, for a variety of reasons, to find substantial numbers of both religious persuasions at each social class level in each integration setting. This distribution of respondents is necessary for a statistical analysis.

We have gone further in our first prediction than simply saying that a difference in techniques of child training would appear between Protestants and Roman Catholics when we control social class and integration setting. We have forecast that this difference would appear in those methods of child care that are related to the way in which children are disciplined and those that are related to the emphasis placed on the child's becoming accountable for his own behavior. This forecast needs to be explained and sharpened.

Our essential point is that, given the questions we asked of mothers, we anticipated that Protestant-Roman Catholic differences would be found only for the interview items related to the training of the child for moral behavior. Still more specifically, we anticipated that differences in child training between the two religious groups would appear with respect to those techniques of moral training which reflect the essential differences in the moral ideologies of Protestants and Roman Catholics. We felt that methods of child care most closely related to these ideological differences would appear with reference to methods of discipline and to an emphasis on holding the child accountable for his own conduct—especially where that conduct has obvious moral connotations. What, then, do we mean by moral behavior as against non-moral behavior? What did we assume to be the essential differences in the moral ideologies of the two faiths? What is meant by "methods of child care especially related to discipline and to holding children accountable for their conduct in moral situations?" These questions are answered in the next paragraphs. When that is done, we shall have given the rationales which underlay the second, third, and fourth of our predictions as well as the first, and we can summarize why each of these four were expected to hold for our findings.

First, we must examine the distinction being made between moral and non-moral behaviors. Moral behaviors spring up when people find each other mutually gratifying and enhancing, and, simultaneously, non-threatening. These moral relations may appear in the interactions people have with each other in a society, a family, a gang, or any other group. The virtues—moral norms—are simply the rules of behavior that people discover they have to follow if this highly rewarding situation is to be preserved. The exact behaviors that might have to be performed to pursue these relations vary from one social situation to another. Within a society these behaviors may take such forms as submitting an honest income tax report or making financial contributions to social welfare agencies. In the family, moral behavior may mean lending money or extending hospitality to relatives. It may mean none of these things. A "virtue" such as honesty can involve just having the right intentions or telling the literal truth in all its details (19). Everywhere, to the degree that relations among men are mutually enhancing and non-threatening, to that degree those relations are preserved only when certain rules of conduct are present— rules exemplified by the common virtues, such as honesty, loyalty, co-operativeness, helpfulness, responsibility, and justice. Those rules are moral, and behavior consonant with them is moral behavior. We shall want to use this conception to identify certain child-training practices as being more or less relevant to moral behavior.

Before doing that, however, we need to be clear about the principal differences, as we see them, in the moral ideologies of Protestants and Roman Catholics. These essential differences gain their sharpest reflection in the formal theologies of these faiths.

It is on the details of salvation from sin—from disobedience to God's will—that the principal differences among Christian groups are found. The traditional names for these details are summarized in the ideas of grace, justification, and sanctification. The first of these, grace, is of central importance for our predictions.

Other Influences on Child Training **161**

Grace is defined as the love and favor God extends to man. This beneficence is given as a result of the nature of God, not because of any particular merit on man's part. It is always present, always available (20). Not by any power of his own, but by letting this love of God become active in his life can a man begin the journey to salvation.

The Roman Catholic view shares the general Christian belief that unaided human nature cannot forsake sin, merit salvation, or apprehend God. Supernatural grace alone can raise the human soul to a new order of being that is capable of knowing, possessing, and enjoying God. But, at this point, a critical feature appears. This sanctifying grace comes from the inexhaustible treasury of Christ's merit. That treasury is at the disposal of the Roman Catholic Church. It is made available to men through the sacraments—the God-ordained and, through the priest, the God-performed acts—which prolong and universalize Christ's earthly activities as the Redeemer of mankind. This grace annuls and wipes out the effects and power of man's inherently sinful nature. It gives its bearers a permanent habit of righteousness and carries the promise and potency of perfection. Only a mortal sin, a highly serious offense against God, can destroy it. The sacrament of the Lord's Supper and penances administered by the Roman Catholic Church serve to remove lesser offenses.

There have been times in Roman Catholic history when some of these views were challenged. However, we probably are safe in assuming that they represent the most common notions on the subject of grace among Detroit's Roman Catholics today.

The many branches of Protestantism have at least this in common, that they reject the doctrine that God's grace is available only at the disposal of the Roman Catholic Church or of any other church. Sometimes the matter is put this way: Roman Catholicism holds that in the overt physical acts of the sacraments, as in communion, baptism, or marriage, God's grace, like a substance, is objectively handed by the priest to the communicants. All Protestants see it as coming directly from God. Its presence in the life of the believer is known subjectively, not through the objective receipt of, or by participation in, any act or substance. All Protestants say with Luther that grace is mediated primarily through God's teachings as preserved in the Bible (21).

When one's purpose is to understand the relevance of theological differences for behavior, he usually faces the task of understanding the behaviorial equivalents of the doctrines themselves. He must try to see why such differences in belief as those between Protestants and

Roman Catholics came into existence. He must assume that they are, themselves, pieces of human behavior and that, like all other behavior, they were caused by the natural experiences of man in the world. Fortunately, sociologists and social historians (22) have developed a considerable understanding of the solution to this problem. Since their works are readily available and contain extensive documentation, we can confine ourselves to reporting and extending their principal conclusions. Like the efforts of these earlier social scientists, our formulations often are clearly speculative. They are not undisciplined by existing knowledge of religion and behavior, but they do go beyond that knowledge to provide a bridge to our information about child rearing. If these formulations err, their faults will be corrected by use in research.

If we follow the approach of the social historians, we interpret the concept of the grace of God as having the behavorial meaning of forgiveness and support, and the concept of God as referring to a purposing community or society. With these ideas the doctrinal differences important for our study can be interpreted. The Roman Catholic doctrine of grace as a substance and the church as the necessary dispenser of that substance must rest on certain experiences. That doctrine stresses the necessity that moral relations in the community or society must be strong and well integrated. The community's governing structure must be widely and wholeheartedly accepted, for it acts as the community's representative in releasing members from guilt and in supporting them in new resolutions to keep the social laws. In such a community, the enforcement of loyalty and morality can come from the application of exterior controls. These must, of course, be exercised with the ceremony proper to the actions of the all-powerful group dealing with its suppliant members. We interpret the doctrine of the nature of grace-as-a-substance as a tenet referring to the immediate reality and effectiveness of the community's action in reconstituting deviants as acceptable participants in its life, in sustaining the conforming in their conformity, and in bringing new members into the orbit of its power.

From its beginnings in the 1500's to the present, Protestantism seems to have spread along with the commercial and industrial revolutions and with political upheavals. It accompanied these shifts, but differed from them. It was a statement of a moral order and a theology in keeping with the new experiences in moral relations that developed in the changing societies of the West. Thus the wider community of the Protestant is changed and changing. He is a man moving from the settled life of the agricultural community into the

Other Influences on Child Training **163**

isolating, separating, individualizing entrepreneurial world. In some lands he is the supporter of the new nationalistic trends that challenge all foreign controls, including those of the Papacy. The preservation of the moral code in his life cannot be assured by the exercise of powerful and ever-present external controls. Governments are falling. Cities rise and with them public opinion and old institutional forms lose much of their control over individual lives. The familiar pattern of the early response to these conditions is to instill into children a set of inner promptings that will keep them faithful to the moral standards through all manner of temptations and obstacles that prevent the accomplishment of this mission. Internal controls must function where external supervision is absent.

The past does not perpetuate itself. If doctrines persist, especially over periods of several hundreds of years, everything that we know about human conduct suggests that they must have roots in conditions which also persist. The conditions that sustain such tenets may not be exactly the same ones from which they sprang. However, to the extent that the doctrines do not change, those conditions must be similar to the original ones in their behavorial consequences.

The point to be made is that Protestantism was in large part a set of ideas generated by the problems of keeping moral relations alive under entrepreneurial, urban conditions, especially among peoples who were only a generation or two or three removed from the rural type of community. Further, although it is doubtful if Protestantism could have survived under conditions in which the original moral contacts were thoroughly eroded, it offered a rationale for life that is quite consistent with the problems of moral relations faced by large parts of the population of the contemporary United States. Similarly, Roman Catholicism continues to find substantial groups of people whose moral relations are appropriately formulated by its doctrines.

These considerations about the fundamental differences in the moral views of Protestants and Roman Catholics lead us to expect that they will differ with respect to some of our Internalization Indices. Roman Catholics should be more likely than Protestants to use "external" disciplines and rewards in controlling their children. Protestants should be more likely to use "internal" symbolic rewards and punishments.

By "external" punishments we have in mind the regulation of behavior from the outside, as in spanking. By contrast, an "internal" punishment, like arousing the child's guilt, stimulates him to control his own behavior. The punishment comes from within the child, not simply from the outside agent. In like manner, we think of giving the child a present as an external reward. Praising the youngster is an internal reward because it is effective only when the child finds a virtuous picture of himself to be rewarding. Thus the reward comes, in part, from within the child. This divergence in method of discipline seems in harmony with the divergence between the faiths in their conceptions of the means by which men are guided toward righteous and moral conduct—the Catholic through the external application of the mystical powers of the religious community, the Protestant through personal self-control and conformity and contrition before God.

Because of this same difference in moral ideology, we expected that Protestant mothers would be more likely than Roman Catholics to act quickly and sternly when a child disobeyed—to punish him at once instead of waiting until they were calm. We also anticipated that the Protestant mothers would more probably feel able, having taught a rather rigorous self-control to their youngsters, to set these youngsters free from close supervision at an earlier age than would Roman Catholic parents. The latter, following the motif of external control, would continue close supervision of their children for longer periods.

But there were some items from our Internalization Indices on which we did not expect the appearance of appreciable differences between these religious faiths. In fact, in our third prediction, we explicitly forecast that no significant differences would appear on certain items. The interview questions we have in mind are those involving methods of child training that we expected the vast majority of our mothers to use only during their youngsters' infancy, roughly in the period before the children are two years old. Thus, we did not expect to find differences between the religious groups with respect to the giving of immediate attention to a baby who cries when "nothing is wrong," the feeding of infants on a schedule or on demand, or the age at which babies are weaned or given bowel or urinary training.

But, why should we not expect differences between these religious groups in those early training practices—practices like early weaning or toilet training—that make the child give up his present desires for some future gain or for the preservation of his present gratifications? Do these not demand the kind of self-control stated earlier as the mark of the Protestant moral problem?

That the child may learn self-control and the denial of the immediate satisfaction of his desires as a consequence of such training we do not contest. However, the specifically *moral* problem as the

Other Influences on Child Training **165**

Protestant faces it is the development of a general pattern of self-control *as a means of supporting mutually enhancing and non-threatening relations*. Such a moral context for training in self-control is not necessarily present when a mother insists that the child perform on the toilet before he understands the mother's reasons. In fact, it almost certainly cannot be present in any sense that the child can understand. He does not yet know what it means to do something because others will be injured or inconvenienced if he fails to act. This is a critical point. For Protestants and for Roman Catholics, interpersonal events have moral aspects only if the consequences for *others*, the continuation of the *mutually* enhancing features of their relations, in addition to the consequences for one's self, are self-consciously taken into account. The child does not enter into a moral relation with the mother when the results of his acts are of concern only to himself. Moral qualities enter their contacts when he makes decisions with the knowledge of their impact on her feelings and future as well as on his own. And the mother usually will not apply moral criteria to his acts until she can assume that he does in fact have such knowledge.

With these points in mind, we did assume that some items from our Individual Responsibility Indices should evidence differences between Protestant and Roman Catholic mothers because, on the one hand, these questions deal with the age at which the child should be held accountable for his own conduct, and, on the other, because that age is late enough so that one may assume that the child can be an active participant in a moral relation--in a relation entailing mutual responsibility with someone else. Those items were the ones having to do with the ages at which children were expected to assume such responsibilities as dressing themselves or picking up their own clothes. We anticipated that Protestant mothers, with their emphasis on making the child accountable for his own conduct, would press him to assume these responsibilities earlier than would Roman Catholic parents. Figure 6–1 presents these and the other items on which we expected differences in methods of child care to appear between the two religious groups.

A special note may be added about Items 13, 19, and 20. Each of these was used earlier as part of the Responsibility or the Internalization Indices. Now we use them as indices of another type. How do we justify this different interpretation of their meaning? The answer is implied in our previous discussion. When we first used these items, our purpose was to show that answers to them would be consistent with, and reflective of, the differences in problem and experience found in certain social positions in the economic system.

Figure 6–1

ITEMS CHOSEN TO REFLECT PROTESTANT AND ROMAN CATHOLIC DIFFERENCES
IN CHILD TRAINING: INDICES OF MORAL RELATIONS

Item Number	Item
13	Here are some tasks that some parents require of their children. Which of these did you or would you require of (child's name) and by what age?
13a	Require child to put away his own clothes?
13b	Require child to pick up own toys?
13c	Require child to run errands to nearby store?
13d	Require child to dress himself (herself) completely?
19	Think about a time when (name) will be (was) ten years old. He (she) has just done something that you feel is very good, or he (she) has been particularly good. What would you do at those times?
20	Now, please think about that same time when (name) will be (was) ten years old. He (she) has just done something that you feel is very wrong, something that you have warned him (her) against ever doing. What would you do at such times?
21	Suppose a four-year-old child does something that makes his mother angry and excited. Should the mother punish the child right away while she is angry, or should the mother wait until she's more calm before she decides what to do?
22	Some mothers believe that for a child's own good they should know what he (she) is doing most of the time and should supervise him (her) until a certain age. What age would you say that should be?

At this point, however, we plan to try to hold constant the influence of the economic positions of these families and examine the meaning of the items in Figure 6–1 when it is removed. Now they are fit candidates to reflect problems and experiences other than those we originally associated with them.

Why have we restricted our thinking about the relation of religious preference and child training to Protestants and Roman Catholics? Why has not the same approach been taken to predict differences between Christians and Jews or between different varieties of Protestants? The answer is that the number of families in non-Christian or in particular Protestant denominations was too small, at least when we controlled those families' integration and stratification positions, to permit a meaningful analysis. Only 2 per cent of our mothers gave some branch of Judaism as their religious preference. Less than 1 per

Other Influences on Child Training **167**

cent listed any other non-Christian group. Just over 1 per cent preferred a Christian religious body of a Greek or Russian rite. Almost 39 per cent were Roman Catholics. Less than 5 per cent of the sample claimed no religious preference. The remainder preferred some Protestant denomination. The two largest Protestant groups, Baptists and Methodists, included only 15 and 11 per cent, respectively, of our respondents.

We expected our hypotheses to hold best for comparisons of the more active adherents of the two religious groups (23). If lower activity often meant, as we guessed, less interest because the religious movement provided less appropriate solutions for the problems people faced, then the effects we have discussed were not so likely to appear. It happens that in our sample of mothers a considerable majority of Roman Catholics said they attended a religious service on the average of once a week. Protestant mothers were not such regular attendants. This fact may be the case in good part because of the lesser importance attached by Protestants to the necessity of regular contacts with the church as a means of keeping within the bounds of the moral life. For this reason, and in order to enlarge the numbers of Protestants who might be compared with active Roman Catholics, we defined as Frequent Attenders those Catholics who claimed they went to church an average of once a week and those Protestants who said they attended at least some time during the year. Table 6–5 shows the distribution of church attendance by Protestants and Roman Catholics.

Table 6–5

FREQUENCY OF CHURCH ATTENDANCE CLAIMED BY PROTESTANT
AND ROMAN CATHOLIC MOTHERS

Frequency of Church Attendance Is at Least:

Religious Preference	Once a Week	A Few Times a Year	Never	Total
Protestant	82	111	40	233
Roman Catholic	159	38	6	203

How do our four predictions fare when the findings in our tables are inspected? The results relevant to the third prediction—that there would be no appreciable differences between these religious groups in practices relating to the teaching of self-control and personal accountability before the third year of the child's life—are most quickly stated. The prediction is confirmed. No significant difference appears between Protestants and Roman Catholics with reference to the ages at which they wean or toilet train children, the immediacy of their response to a baby crying only for attention, or the use of demand as against scheduled feeding with infants.

The fourth prediction stated that Protestant and Roman Catholic mothers would not differ significantly on any notable number of items about child training other than those listed in Figure 6–1. This, too, is confirmed.

Protestants and Roman Catholics were compared on a total of 73 observations related to child training. Since we examined the answers by members of the two religious groups to each of these items and searched for possible consistencies in the middle and lower classes in both entrepreneurial and bureaucratic settings, this made a total of 292 comparisons. Subtracting the 16 items for which predicted relations were tested in the entrepreneurial situation and the additional 16 relations tested in the bureaucratic setting, we have a remainder of 260 comparisons for which we predicted no significant or consistent differences between the religious groups under study. Simply by chance, if our observations were independent, we might expect to obtain as many as 26 significant differences at or beyond the 10 per cent level of confidence from such an analysis of the remaining 260 comparisons. We obtained only 16. They are listed in Table 6–6. Eight of these findings were in the entrepreneurial setting; eight in the bureaucratic. With their total easily obtainable by chance, and with no clear pattern evident among them, we shall not attempt to interpret these unpredicted significances. It can be said that their number did not exceed our expectations.

And what of predictions one and two? Is there a difference between the two religious faiths? Are Protestants more likely than Roman Catholics to emphasize the teaching of self-control and personal accountability in training their children? The answer to both of these questions is generally positive within the entrepreneurial middle and lower classes, but ambiguous within the bureaucratic setting (24). (Table 6–7 summarizes these results. A more detailed report appears in Appendix One, Table AI–4.)

Take, for example, the findings from a comparison of entrepreneurial middle-class mothers of these two religious persuasions. A total of eight questions was listed for this comparison. Significantly large differences between Protestants and Roman Catholics appear in the expected direction on two of these questions. Thus we find that

Other Influences on Child Training **169**

Protestant mothers are more likely to require children to put away their clothes and to dress themselves before they are five years old.

Table 6–6

UNPREDICTED DIFFERENCES OBTAINED BY COMPARING THE CHILD-TRAINING
PRACTICES OF THE FREQUENT ATTENDERS AMONG
PROTESTANT AND ROMAN CATHOLIC MOTHERS

Item Number	Protestants Are More Likely to:	Integration Setting	Social Class	p^*
2	Say child never sucked his body.	Bureaucratic	Lower	$<.05$
4	Breast-feed the child.	Entrepreneurial	Middle	$<.10$
5c, 5d, 6b	Wean child later than twelve months.	Bureaucratic	Lower	$<.10$
8a	Allow child to follow parent into the bathroom.	Entrepreneurial	Lower	$<.05$
9a	Leave child at home with competent housekeeper because it is good for the child.	Entrepreneurial	Lower	$<.10$
		Bureaucratic	Lower	$<.10$
10	Say child should not be put on own as soon as possible to solve own problems.	Entrepreneurial	Lower	$<.10$
	Say child should be put on own as soon as possible to solve own problems.	Bureaucratic	Middle	$<.02$
11a	Say adolescent girls should not shovel walks.	Bureaucratic	Lower	$<.10$
24b	Want to know how to control child; not about child dynamics.†	Entrepreneurial	Middle	$<.05$
27	Believe child will have a factory job.	Entrepreneurial	Lower	$<.10$
30a	Give no help or conditional help to a child who fails and deceives the parents about his failure.	Entrepreneurial	Middle	$<.10$
		Bureaucratic	Lower	$<.10$
35	Say both parents should punish children.	Entrepreneurial	Middle	$<.01$
		Bureaucratic	Lower	$<.01$
Coders' rating	Feel children are burdensome.	Bureaucratic	Middle	$<.02$

* There is one degree of freedom in each computation. All p values are computed from both tails of the probability distribution.

† This item is discussed in Chapter Nine.

Table 6–7

POINTS OF DIFFERENCE BETWEEN THE CHILD-TRAINING PRACTICES OF THE
FREQUENT ATTENDERS AMONG PROTESTANT AND ROMAN CATHOLIC MOTHERS

Item Number	Entrepreneurial			Bureaucratic		
	Middle Class p†	Lower Class p†	Total* p†	Middle Class p†	Lower Class p†	Total* p†
13a	+ <.05	<.70	+ <.30	<.90	+ <.50	<.70
13b	<.70	− <.50	<.70	− <.50	<.70	<.70
13c	<.99	+ <.03	+ <.05	+ <.05	− <.05	<.05‡
13d	+ <.01	− <.50	<.05‡	<.98	<.98	<1.00
19	+ <.50	<.70	<.70	+ <.50	+ <.50	+ <.50
20	+ <.30	+ <.01	+ <.03	<.80	+ <.50	<.70
21	+ <.30	+ <.05	+ <.05	− <.20	<.70	<.20‡
22	<.80	<.80	<.80	+ <.05	+ <.50	+ <.10

* The chi-square values on which these probabilities are based sum those obtained for the middle and lower classes. There are two degrees of freedom.

† The notation in this table gives a symbol for the direction of the findings followed by the level of probability. The direction symbols are as follows: a plus (+) means the results show the direction predicted; a minus sign (−) means the results are opposite to the predicted direction; the absence of a symbol indicates that the p value is greater than .50 making hazardous any statement about trends. All p values reaching the .20 level or beyond and having the predicted direction are presented using one tail of the probability distribution. For the computations within the middle or lower class, there is one degree of freedom.

The predicted direction of responses for each item is as follows: Protestants are more likely than Roman Catholics to:

13a Require child to put away clothes before age five.
13b Require child to pick up own toys before age three.
13c Require child to run errands to nearby store before age seven.
13d Require child to dress self before age five.
19 Use symbolic instead of direct rewards.
20 Use symbolic punishment and restrictions instead of corporal punishment.
21 Punish offenses at once instead of waiting until calm.
22 Stop supervising the child closely at end of twelfth year.

‡ Two-tailed p value because directions of trends in middle and lower classes reverse.

Three other questions produce modest differences, but those differences, too, are in the direction predicted. They show the Protestant parents as more likely than Catholic parents to use symbolic rewards

Other Influences on Child Training **171**

and punishments and to punish children immediately. Thus, five of the eight items contain trends of the kind we anticipated.

Similarly, when mothers who differ according to religious belief are examined in the entrepreneurial lower class, the three significantly large differences that appear are all of the sort expected. In this case, Protestants are more likely to require a child to run on errands to a nearby store at an early age, and to use symbolic rewards and punishments. Two additional differences occur, but not in the predicted direction. Both clearly are not of significant size.

To summarize, within the entrepreneurial setting, and with social class position held constant, five significant differences appear between Protestant and Roman Catholic mothers. All are in the expected direction. Their number is substantially greater than the number of significant differences—less than one—that might have occurred simply by chance among sixteen comparisons (25). We take this as support for our expectations about the differences between Protestants and Roman Catholics.

In the bureaucratic setting, however, the differences between the religious faiths are not so clear and consistent. When social class is held constant, there are three significant differences between Protestants and Roman Catholics. However, this time, one of the three is significantly in the opposite direction from our expectations. Thus we find lower-class Protestant mothers *less* likely to send very young children to nearby stores on errands. It is not possible to conclude that any difference exists between Protestant and Roman Catholic mothers from such conflicting results.

As we stated earlier, we had reasons for greater confidence in our prediction of Protestant-Roman Catholic differences for families in an entrepreneurial situation. Perhaps bureaucratic experiences are such that they tend to make certain Protestant views more like those of Roman Catholics, supplanting stress on self-control with reliance on external controls to guide the child. At any rate, the differences between the religious groups are no longer as clear under bureaucratic conditions.

We may, of course, ask another kind of question. We may inquire whether mothers who answer more of these eight questions in the way we originally expected Protestants to answer are, in fact, more likely to be Protestant in religious preference. Table 6–8 shows that the answer is positive and significant for middle-class mothers in either integration setting, but that, if a mother is of lower-class status, no relation exists between the number of "Protestant" answers she gives and the likelihood that she is a Protestant in religious affiliation (6).

Table 6–8

CUMULATIVE SCORES ON INDICES OF MORAL RELATIONS

Cumulative Score	Entrepreneurial Middle Classes		Bureaucratic Middle Classes		Entrepreneurial Lower Classes		Bureaucratic Lower Classes	
	Prot*	RC†	Prot*	RC†	Prot*	RC†	Prot*	RC†
High (6–8)	9	1	8	4	8	1	5	6
(4–5)	3	6	3	6	7	3	9	9
Low (0–3)	3	4	1	6	10	2	4	7
χ^2	7.87		5.76		1.11		.55	
df	2		2		2		2	
$p\ddagger$	<.01		<.05		<.35		<.40	

* Protestant.
† Roman Catholic.
‡ One-tailed p value.

The important finding shown in Table 6–8 is that the cumulative scores for Protestants tend to be higher than those for Roman Catholics when the Protestants are of middle-class status, and similar to those for Roman Catholics when the Protestants are of lower-class status. One plausible explanation of this finding is that there are some characteristics of lower-class life—perhaps its lesser incentives for self-denial and striving—that minimize the distinctive views of Protestants with respect to child care. However, our data are not adequate to test that possibility.

It also is possible that we obtained some of the results we predicted because Roman Catholics come disproportionately from different ethnic backgrounds than do Protestants. We did something to cancel out differences in ethnicity when we controlled for integration and stratification position. The later, and more heavily Catholic, ethnic groups that came to this country are less likely to appear in the middle classes than are Protestants. However, when all is said and done, the actual data gathered did not lend themselves to a satisfactory test in which ethnicity could also be controlled and the effects of religious affiliation examined. The number of cases would immediately become so small that meaningful results could not be had. Although it is not at all conclusive, we find the most likely available test of the possibility that our findings may be products of ethnic rather than religious differences in a fact elaborated earlier in this chapter—the fact that, when the economic position of the family was held constant, ethnic differences showed no tendency to relate to child-training practices.

Other Influences on Child Training **173**

We have already noted that some items in our Indices of Moral Relations also appear in our Responsibility Indices as described in Chapter Five. The four subparts of Item 13 as well as Item 22 appear in both lists. Because of this duplication of the items in these lists, the Responsibility and Moral Relations Indices are highly related. The coefficient of correlation between them is .88 ± .09. Furthermore, cumulative scores on the Responsibility Indices relate to Protestant and Roman Catholic backgrounds in the same manner as do the cumulative scores on the Indices of Moral Relations. This relation is significant within the bureaucratic setting, and in the same direction, but not significant within the entrepreneurial setting.

Both because of similarity in items and in the meaning attached to those items, it is not surprising that these two indices should be highly related. For the same reasons, it is understandable that Protestants get higher cumulative scores on both indices than do Roman Catholics. It appears, however, that by thinking of the Protestant-Roman Catholic difference in broad moral terms, we can correctly predict those items among the Responsibility Indices which relate as predicted to religious preferences. None of the Responsibility Indices which were not used in the Indices of Moral Relations are related to religious background. In addition, the theoretical framework with which we approached the effects religion should have on child training led us to include in our Indices of Moral Relations a number of items not among those in the Responsibility Indices. Thus, despite some duplication of items in the two indices, we feel that the ideas presented in this chapter concerning religion and child care are not subsumed in our discussion of the Responsibility Indices.

. . . . . CONCLUDING NOTE ABOUT OTHER
INFLUENCES ON CHILD TRAINING

Only one of these eight analyses shows any appreciable number of new and important differences beyond those reported in Chapters Four and Five, and only one other, education, shows any appreciable number of consistent trends. When the categories of entrepreneurial and bureaucratic integratio nand the social classes are held constant, none of several conditions commonly thought important for accounting for family life in the United States seems to make any appreciable difference. This conclusion is somewhat attenuated by the small numbers with which we have had to work and—in such cases as those of the social class character of the neighborhood, mother's education, and ethnicity—by the grossness of our devices. The extent to which our integration and stratification techniques are capable of subsuming other indices of position in American society deserves further exploration.

NOTES

[1] In *The Rise of Silas Lapham* (Boston: Ticknor and Co., 1885).

[2] See, for example, Cameron Hawley's novel *Executive Suite* (Boston: Houghton Mifflin Co., 1952).

[3] Good general sources are: Pitirim A. Sorokin, *Social Mobility* (New York: Harper and Bros., 1927); Reinhard Bendix and Seymour M. Lipset, *Class, Status and Power, A Reader in Social Stratification* (Glencoe, Illinois: The Free Press, 1953).

[4] A discussion of these and related problems appears in Natalie Rogoff, "Recent Trends in Urban Occupational Mobility," in Paul K. Hatt and Albert J. Reiss, Jr. (eds.), *Reader in Urban Sociology* (Glencoe, Illinois: The Free Press, 1951), 406–420.

[5] See, for examples: Seymour M. Lipset and Reinhard Bendix, "Social Mobility and Occupational Career Patterns. I. Stability of Jobholding," *The American Journal of Sociology*, 57 (January, 1952), 366–374; "Social Mobility and Occupational Career Patterns. II. Social Mobility," *ibid.* (March, 1952), 494–504.

[6] Many such suggestions are summarized in Daniel R. Miller and Max L. Hutt, "Value Interiorization and Personality Development," *The Journal of Social Issues*, 5, No. 4 (1949), 2–30.

[7] Daniel R. Miller and Guy E. Swanson, *Inner Conflict and Defense*. To be published by Henry Holt and Co. in 1958.

[8] Calvin F. Schmid, "The Theory and Practice of Planning Census Tracts," *Sociology and Social Research*, 22 (January-February, 1938), 228–238.

[9] United States Department of Commerce, Bureau of the Census, "Census Tract Statistics: Detroit, Michigan and Adjacent Area," *United States Census of Population: 1950*, Vol. 3, Chapter 17, Table 2.

[10] "Head" occupations included: professional, technical, and kindred workers; managers, officials, and proprietors; clerical and kindred workers; and sales workers. "Hand" occupations included: craftsmen, foremen, and kindred workers; operatives and kindred workers; private household workers; service workers, except private household; and laborers, except those working in mines.

[11] See, for example: Morris Janowitz and Dwaine Marvick, "Authoritarianism and Political Behavior," *The Public Opinion Quarterly*, 17 (Summer, 1953), 185–201.

[12] See, for example: Allison Davis and Robert J. Havighurst, "Social Class and Color Differences in Child-Rearing," *American Sociological Review*, 11 (December, 1946), 698–710.

[13] Gunmar Myrdal, *An American Dilemma, The Negro Problem and Modern Democracy* (New York: Harper and Bros., 1944).

[14] W. Lloyd Warner, "Introduction: Deep South—A Social Anthropological Study of Caste and Class," in Allison Davis and Burleigh B. and Mary R. Gardner, *Deep South—A Social Anthropological Study of Caste and Class* (Chicago: The University of Chicago Press, 1941), 3–14.

[15] We are aware, of course, that some students have insisted that the Negro family differs from the white family, not only in its lesser degree of power but in line with certain peculiarities of its situation determined by the period of Reconstruction and the later migrations from the South to the North. For example, Frazier [E. Franklin Frazier, *The Negro Family in the United States* (Chicago: The University of Chicago Press, 1939)] emphasizes the importance of the mother in providing stability for the family and training for the children in the frequent absence of fathers who left home in search of jobs and adventure. This migratory pattern is not unique to Negroes, however, being frequent among lower-class whites. In any event, none of the hypotheses we have advanced about child training seem to be modified by such a predominance of maternal contacts with the children, even if such did or do exist in the Negro community.

[16] Davis and Havighurst, *op. cit.*

[17] *Ibid.*, 708.

[18] See: Robert C. Angell, "The Moral Integration of American Cities," *The American Journal of Sociology*, 57 (July, 1951), Part 2, 1–140.

[19] A good comparative discussion of moral practices is found in Ralph Linton's paper "Universal Ethical Principles: An Anthropological View," in Ruth N. Anshen (ed.), *Moral Principles of Action* (New York: Harper and Brothers, Publishers, 1952), 645–660.

[20] For a brief and convenient review of these doctrines, see the following articles in the *Encyclopaedia of Religion and Ethics*, James Hastings (ed.), (Edinburgh: T. and T. Clark, 1920): James G. Simpson, "Justification," Vol. 7, 615–619; Robert H. Coats, "Sanctification," Vol. 11, 181–184; Hugh R. Mackintosh, "Sin," Vol. 11, 538–544.

[21] See: *Ibid.*

[22] We have made particular use of the following: Max Weber, *The Protestant Ethic and the Spirit of Capitalism* (New York: Charles Scribner's Sons, 1930); Ernest Troeltsch, *The Social Teaching of the Christian Churches*, 2 vols. (London: George Allen and Unwin Ltd., 1931); Talcott Parsons, "H. M. Robertson on Max Weber and His School," *Journal of Political Economy*, 43 (October, 1935), 686–696; Richard H. Tawney, *Religion and the Rise of Capitalism* (New York: Harcourt, Brace and Co., Inc., 1926); Helmut R. Niebuhr, *The Social Sources of Denominationalism* (New York: Henry Holt and Co., 1929); Emile Durkheim, *The Elementary Forms of Religious Life* (Glencoe, Illinois: The Free Press, 1947).

[23] A special analysis of our data shows no significant number of significant differences on the questions we include in our Indices of Moral Relations when Protestants and Roman Catholics who attend church infrequently are compared.

[24] At this point, the nature of our data permits us to make a more refined judgment of the way religion might relate to non-religious behavior than was possible for Max Weber in his famous study of the relation of the Protestant ethic to the rise of Western capitalism. (Weber, *op. cit.*) For example, Weber speaks of that ethic as stressing rationality, the virtue of hard work, an active rather than an accommodative approach to the world, regularity in performance of tasks, and the making of a profit as an obeisance to God. That Protestants in the sixteenth and seventeenth centuries, and in the twentieth as well, are more likely to be among those exhibiting such values than are Roman Catholics is something we do not dispute. We do feel, following Tawney (Tawney, *op. cit.*), that these values were not specifically religious, but the products of the same economic and political changes that bred Protestants as a religious group. When, in our tables, we control for the position of the family in the economy, we are, in an

important sense, removing from consideration those values and ideas that were differentially held by Protestants and Roman Catholics as a result of differences in their positions in the economic life of their society. At the same time, we are highlighting a residue which represents the more specifically moral and religious differences between the two faiths. If anything, this procedure is closer than Weber's own to the spirit of his emphasis on the independent reality of religious movements and institutions from the economy and the state.

[25] Assuming, of course, that our measures are independent of one another.

[26] Appendix Two contains a discussion that shows that the eight items of our Indices of Moral Relations constitute a reasonably reliable rating scale.

CHAPTER SEVEN

THE VALIDITY AND SCOPE OF THE INTERPRETATIONS

We began this book with a problem and a proposal. We wanted to identify the source and significance of the emerging methods of child care. We proposed that those methods stem, at least in part, from the change from entrepreneurial to bureaucratic experiences in American society, and that the significance of these new methods of child care lay in their providing youngsters with skills and attitudes appropriate for living in a bureaucratized society. Later, we proposed that differences in techniques of rearing children would be associated with the social class position of American families and with their religious preferences. Some support for each of these proposals appears in our results.

But, can those results be relied upon? Can they be explained away? Are there alternative explanations, just as plausible as those we have given, that will also account for our findings? In short, how valid are our interpretations? In the first part of this chapter, we shall examine a variety of alternative explanations of our findings.

The remainder of the chapter explores the scope of our findings. Specifically, this means that we shall consider the answers to two questions. First, how strong is the relation between the methods of child rearing we have studied and the social positions—social class, integration setting, and religious preference—which we have employed to account for a mother's choice among those techniques of child care? How much of the variation from mother to mother in methods of training children have we explained? If, for example, we know the social class to which a family belongs, with what confidence can we predict the score it will exhibit on our Internalization Indices?

Second, is there any basis for thinking that findings like ours would be found anywhere else in America, or are they peculiar to the Detroit area? Where should it be possible to obtain results like ours?

. . . . . THE VALIDITY OF THE INTERPRETATIONS

By this time we know that a great many features of a family's social situation—features such as intergenerational mobility and ethnic background—are of no help in explaining differences in child care once we take account of the family's integration and social class positions. Suppose, however, that we consider another possibility. Are the entrepreneurial-bureaucratic disparities in methods of training children really produced by something else? Perhaps those disparities result from differences in education, and the bureaucratic mothers have had more years of formal schooling. Perhaps similar considerations, rather than social class differences as such, explain the discrepancies we find between middle- and lower-class mothers in the entrepreneurial setting. Suppose we look at the facts in the matter.

As in the preceding chapter, we want to judge the effects of several social conditions on child care. As in the previous chapter, we looked for the effects of the following social conditions: intergenerational mobility, the size of the community in which the husband and wife were born, the length of the wife's education, the ethnic background of the family, the stratification-consistency of the neighborhood in which the family lived, the consistency of the family's economic position, and the parents' religious preference. The small number of Negro respondents prevented any searching analysis of the effects of race on child training.

We held each of these seven social conditions constant in its turn, allowing the families' social class and integration positions to vary. The results are consistent and convincing. We found no evidence that any of these seven conditions, rather than stratification and integration, produced our study's results. It is true that many of the significant differences reported in Chapters Four and Five disappeared as the application of controls reduced the number of cases in the cells of our tables. But this same reduction of cases rarely destroyed the trends we have reported. The overwhelming impression gotten from looking at tables to which these controls were applied is that the relations we found between child care on the one hand and integration and stratification positions on the other continue to hold, although they usually are no longer significant. Limitations of space prevent a detailed presentation of our material on controls, but some technical elaboration is given in Appendix Two.

We took one additional social condition into account at this point. Back in Chapter Three we reported the finding that middle-class bureaucratic husbands were more likely to be in professional and clerical occupations than were entrepreneurial middle-class husbands. Conversely, the entrepreneurial middles were more likely to work as managers, owners, or proprietors of establishments or as salesmen. The application of this occupational difference as a control produces findings like those just described when the seven other social conditions were held constant. This is an especially important result. It suggests that the findings of our study, relating integration and child rearing, do not arise from differences in the specific kind of work the husbands perform. It suggests that the source of our findings lies in the complex set of conditions we have called entrepreneurial and bureaucratic—conditions which provide different contexts in which occupations may be pursued. Apparently it is not so much a matter of a man's being a professional worker rather than a manager, or a clerk instead of a salesman, that determines which of the methods of child training included in this study he will adopt. Instead, his choice of techniques of child care seems to be determined by the integration setting in which he performs his tasks.

Some Other Interpretations of the Findings

Having found that the application of several controls to our findings does little or nothing to destroy the direction of association with the families' integration position or social class, we can narrow the range of possible sources of invalidity in our interpretation of those findings. Clearly, our results cannot be attributed, at least in any simple way, to the conditions we have just controlled. But there are other possibilities. Even if experiences like education or intergenerational mobility do not explain the differences in child care that we have uncovered, the conditions to which those differences are related—conditions such as entrepreneurial and bureaucratic integration—are broad and complex. Perhaps it is some few aspects of those complex conditions rather than those conditions in their entirety which produce our findings. The same may be said for the relations of those other involved conditions—social class and religious preference—to child care.

To these intriguing and vexing possibilities only the amassing of more and specially designed studies can provide an answer. Take, for example, the idea of bureaucratic integration. The people we classified under that label are those who worked for someone else in a large organization and who, along with being native Americans, were born in towns and cities. They also were people whose income was principally in the form of a wage or salary. The explanation we have given for the methods of child care used in such families rests on the judgment that all of these several conditions have certain common consequences. Yet, that may not be true. Possibly only one or a few of these ingredients are crucial. Once isolated, they might relate to techniques of child care in a more substantial way than does our first crude identification of the bureaucratized families. The findings in this book are strong enough to justify a more refined and penetrating look into the several ingredients that go into our definitions of the integration settings, social class, and religious preferences. Our interpretations of those findings, based as they are on the best synthesis we could make of available information, will undoubtedly prove inaccurate in part. However, they point the way to a whole series of problems for research that would not have opened up if these first approximations to an explanation were not attempted.

There is another question that can be answered in only this vein. Do the people whom we call bureaucratic or middle class or Roman Catholic or anything else select their style of living and of rearing children as a result of certain social experiences? Or, do they already have that style of living and child care and, having it, drift into social situations most congenial to their interests. Once again, the information from our study can provide no definitive answer. However, it seems highly improbable that the bulk of the people who occupy a particular social position do so because they freely choose that position from among all others. Although our study provides no evidence on the matter, the great mass of knowledge about how most people come to have a particular occupation or a given religious persuasion suggests that their choices are strictly limited by the initial economic position of the families from which they come and by the kinds of occupational opportunities available when they begin their adult careers. When a major historical shift is in process from a rural to an urban place of residence, and from small stores and shops to concerns of greater complexity, most workers have no choice but to participate in that shift or go without employment. For this reason, we feel that the methods of child care now emerging are probably the products of these new conditions.

Another important possibility needs consideration when we remember that our entrepreneurial respondents were placed in that category by one of five criteria. Some of them are called entrepreneurs because they were born on the farm or in a foreign country, some because they are self-employed, still others because they work in small organizations or obtain most of their income from risk-taking activities. In Chapter Three we presented a rationale for calling persons with one or more of these characteristics "entrepreneurial." We also took note of the speculative character of some of this rationale. At this point we can offer tabulations which bear on the rationale's validity.

Do persons born abroad or on the farm really give more entrepreneurial responses than bureaucratized subjects? Or, are the differences we find between bureaucrats and entrepreneurs produced solely by comparing bureaucrats with persons having a more obviously entrepreneurial situation, namely, those who are self-employed, who work in small organizations, or who get most if their incomes from profits, fees, or commissions? Table 7–1 provides some of the answer. It gives the percentage of subjects making an "entrepreneurial" response by place of birth and type of occupation. The questionnaire items tabulated in the left-hand column are those for which we found significant differences between the integration settings.

The number of respondents becomes very small for persons with entrepreneurial occupations who were born outside the United States

Table 7–1

PERCENTAGE DIFFERENCE OF "ENTREPRENEURIAL" RESPONSES BETWEEN
BUREAUCRATIC SUBJECTS AND EACH TYPE OF ENTREPRENEURIAL
SUBJECT—MIDDLE-CLASS SUBJECTS ONLY

Item No.	Native-Born and Urban		Foreign-Born		Native-Born and Farm-Born	
	B^*	E^*	B^*	E^*	B^*	E^*

Internalization Indices

Cumulative Schedule A	32	88†	44	67	50	100
Cumulative Schedule B	34	77†	60	60	63	100
Item 3	44	94†	75	75	67	75
Items 5e, 6c	38	56	50	75	56	75
Item 14	60	67	71	75	70	75
Item 17	23	53†	21	50	43	50
Item 20	72	88	93	100	100	67

Activity Indices

Cumulative	41	58	58	50	43	67
Item 2b	‡	‡	‡	‡	‡	‡
Item 7	47	71	67	75	78	67
Item 9a	53	67	75	50	50	100
Item 10	33	56	75†	67	44	25
Items 11a, b, d	54	84†	58	50	67	67

* B = Respondents have a bureaucratic occupation.

E = Respondents have an entrepreneurial occupation, that is, are self-employed or work for a small organization or obtain half or more of their incomes from profits, fees, or commissions.

† Significantly different from bureaucratic respondents at $<.05$.

‡ Number of cases too small for tabulation.

or on farms, making the percentages highly unreliable. We may, however, examine certain trends apparent in this table.

First, it is clear that a majority of these types of entrepreneurs are more likely than bureaucrats to give an "entrepreneurial" response to each of the twelve items tabulated. All five types of entrepreneurial

Validity and Scope of the Interpretations **183**

subjects exceed the bureaucrats on seven of the twelve items. Four types of entrepreneurs exceed the bureaucrats on four additional items. Three types of entrepreneurs exceed the bureaucrats on the remaining item.

The great unreliability introduced by the small numbers on which some of these percentages are based makes highly tenuous any statements about interactions, but some are present. For example, we find that, on some items, respondents who are foreign-born or farm-born and who also have an entrepreneurial occupation are more likely than those with similar birthplaces but bureaucratic occupations to exceed the percentages for bureaucrats. This is the case for three of the seven Internalization items and partly true for two more. The results for the Activity Indices are far less consistent.

In summarizing, Table 7–1 suggests that:

1. The five types of entrepreneurial subjects each tend to give more entrepreneurial responses to these items than do the bureaucrats.

2. Larger numbers of respondents would permit us to see if having two entrepreneurial characteristics made respondents more likely to give an entrepreneurial response than having one such characteristic. We lack the respondents to make such an inquiry.

The further question arises as to whether greater exposure of middle-class bureaucrats to recent writing on child care might account for their differences from entrepreneurs. This possibility needs further exploration. Since bureaucrats tend to have more education than entrepreneurs, and since more of them have lived in urban settings, they may give more attention and support to columns offering child guidance. Their very habituation to finding norms and guidance from the larger society may encourage them to accept what the newspapers say on the subject of rearing youngsters. On the other hand, we find, as predicted, that bureaucratic parents are more likely than entrepreneurs to spank their children. This action goes counter to the advice given by popular writers such as Dr. Spock. Further, our data show that, when education or size of community of origin are controlled, the differences between integration settings still appear. In conclusion, we regard the possibility raised in this paragraph as unlikely, but unresolved.

Another argument, however, seems decidedly unlikely. It suggests that the differences, modest as they are, which we find between middle- and lower-class entrepreneurs are a product of the concentration of the farm- and foreign-born among entrepreneurial lowers. It says: Perhaps such people are more traditional and authoritarian. This argument seems improbable on two grounds. First, a great many of our entrepreneurial middles also receive that placement because they were born abroad or on farms. Second, we have shown that entrepreneurial lowers are quite like lower-class bureaucrats in their responses to our questions. None of the bureaucrats were born out of the United States or on farms.

We might also wonder if our results do not appear because some ideas about child care that have long since been pressed upon mothers have finally gained acceptance. For several years a special organization, the Cornelian Corner, has devoted its energies to urging mothers to feed their babies at the breast. Some people in, or influenced by, the psychoanalytic movement have pressed for a mode of infant and child care resembling that of the new bureaucratic trends. From the psychoanalytic group have come suggestions that happier and healthier children will be had if mothers will be genuinely generous and spontaneous in expressing affection; if, at the same time, they do not hesitate to set necessary limits to the child's demands; if they train their children when the youngsters are ready and able to integrate new skills; and if parents continue to love and accept their youngsters even when the children show some socially disapproved behaviors.

Although it is possible that some public education along the foregoing lines has occurred, there remains the interesting problem of why it succeeded better with bureaucratic rather than entrepreneurial mothers and why it took until after the Second World War for these notions to be accepted. Our guess is that these ideas from psychoanalytic and other sources, many of which had been in existence for thirty years or more before gaining wide acceptance, were antithetical to entrepreneurial experiences. They had little chance of being adopted by many mothers until a style of living more receptive to them had replaced that of the older middle classes. Bureaucratic integration encourages such a style of life.

There is evidence which supports our guess that the current trends in child care are not products of a long indoctrination of American parents in psychoanalytic ideas. References to psychoanalysis first appear in the year 1910 in American magazines of interest to the general reading public. We have followed their course from that date through the year 1935 to see whether the psychoanalytic implications for child care are mentioned and, if so, to note the treatment they are given. In this work, we have examined all articles for this period that are indexed under "psychoanalysis" in *The Readers' Guide to Periodical Literature*. There are 146 such articles. We did not analyze five of these because they were concerned with methods of constructing and using mental tests or with hypnosis and had no direct connection with Freud or the psychoanalytic movement proper. A very few references listed by *The Readers' Guide* duplicate others in the same list. The bulk of these are found in such magazines as *Current Opinion* and *Current Literature*, each of which consists of summaries of articles that have appeared in other periodicals. We have not removed these duplicate articles from our analysis because we sought a picture of the view of psychoanalysis and of its ideas about child care that was available to the readers of all magazines of general interest classified by *The Readers' Guide.*

The results are surprising. Contrary to the common impression that the great majority of commentators on psychoanalysis were violently unfavorable to Freud, his disciples, and all their works, a simple tabulation shows that only 27 per cent of these articles were entirely or primarily negative in their judgment. This finding assumes even more importance when we remember that the vast majority of these authors were informed laymen, not professional psychologists or psychiatrists. There were only two or three cases in which a psychoanalyst was the author of one of these articles. In short, we are not recording the opinions of apologists for psychoanalysis.

Fifty-seven per cent of the articles were either wholly or primarily favorable to psychoanalytic ideas. Eleven per cent had about equally favorable and unfavorable things to say on the topic; 3 per cent were straight factual reports of what the psychoanalysts were saying with no evaluations by the writers; and there was one article that was critical of a particular point in Freud's work, but otherwise was noncommittal.

Further, those writers whose work was primarily critical were rarely irrational or overly emotional in their comments. In the overwhelming majority of cases they were judicious. They pointed to real gaps in the evidence cited by psychoanalytic workers or took them to task for overstating their case or for being vague and imprecise.

But, to what extent do these discussions of psychoanalysis apply to the training of children? The first important finding is that only 17 per cent of these articles said anything at all about the meaning of these psychological ideas for rearing youngsters. It must not be supposed that even these articles generally stressed the techniques of caring for infants and children which we have associated with today's newer middle classes. Only 9 per cent of the articles referring to implications for child care came close to mentioning such techniques, and these said that the most important thing a parent can do to rear a healthy, happy child is to give him patient love and support and "freedom to grow." It should not be overlooked that, although these themes were present in 9 per cent of the articles referring to child care, they appeared in less than 2 per cent of all articles dealing with psychoanalysis, and that, as we reported in Chapter One, the same themes were to be found, though not with great frequency, in the general articles on the training of children indexed in *The Readers' Guide* even in the nineteenth century.

What implications did the writers on child care draw from psychoanalytic teaching? One or both of the following themes appeared in half of the articles dealing with those implications. The first is the danger of too much love. Max Eastman (1) was typical in saying that "mama's boys" grow up to have infantile, dependent wishes as adults, being shy, lacking confidence, and being unable to stand on their own. The second theme was the danger from the forcible expression of authority, especially by fathers. This action could frighten the child to such an extent that he becomes nervous, or hostile, or secretive about socially forbidden practices. Not a single article suggested that authoritarian parents may crush a child's ability to be creative! This theme of so much contemporary writing on psychoanalysis and child care was completely missing in these articles published before 1936.

Apart from this pair of implications, there was a wide scattering of others, none being mentioned in more than one or two articles. Thus we are told that psychoanalytic research finds that the first months "at the mother's breast" are the most important for shaping a child's personality, but no details were given as to how parents may behave during those months to assure that the child will be well adjusted. We find one author who lampooned the analysts as advocating the coddling of children who need to be spanked. Another reminded parents that children, according to psychoanalysis, are far more sensitive to sexual experiences and sights than was previously supposed, and concluded that mothers and fathers must redouble their efforts to prevent the child from having any contact with sexual knowledge. As might be expected of his comments on any topic in which H. L. Mencken became interested, that long-time editor of *The American Mercury* had a highly personal approach to the interpretation of psychoanalytic thought. He wrote (2):

. . . We know, by Dr. Freud's appalling evidence, what the suppression of the common wickednesses can do to the individual—how they can shake his reason on its throne, and even give him such things as gastritis, migraine and angina pectoris. Every Sunday-school in the land is full of such wrecks; they recruit the endless brigades of lady policemen and male wowsers. A

Validity and Scope of the Interpretations **187**

vice-crusader is simply an unfortunate who goes about with a brothel in his cellar; a Prohibitionist is one who has buried rum, but would have been safer drinking it. . . . But so far no psychoanalyst has done a tome on the complexes that issue out of moral struggles against common decency. . . .

The moral of his editorial: Don't press children or adults too hard to conform to rigid social standards.

If anything is clear from these articles, it is that the readers of these periodicals of general interest were not being subjected to a long and systematic education in the methods of rearing children which we have associated with the newer middle classes. To the extent that the content of these articles is typical of the ideas to which the American reading public was exposed between 1910 and 1935, they lend no support for the argument that, after an extended period of indoctrination, many parents began to accept psychoanalytic ideas that were, at first, hard to assimilate. Nor is such an argument reinforced by the finding that the average of articles discussing psychoanalytic ideas dropped from eight or nine a year in the period between 1915 and 1928 to an average of three or four a year between 1929 and 1946 and remained at about that level until after the Second World War when the number of articles averaged nine to twelve a year through 1954. This pattern suggests two rather widely separated peaks of interest in the topic, not a slow but continuous growth in concern with psychoanalytic ideas.

Such a conclusion opens up two other possibilities. It may well be that the more recently developed procedures for rearing children emerged quite spontaneously from such new conditions as those we have called bureaucratic—that parents, confronting a changed world, simply adapted their own behavior, including the way they treated children, to its changed requirements. It may be that those requirements, in turn, just happened to be congruent with the methods of child care advocated by the psychoanalysts. Again, it is possible that these parents, groping about for techniques of rearing youngsters which would be compatible with that changed world, recalled fragments of information they had learned about psychoanalytic psychology and embraced the implications of those fragments as an intellectual rationale already available to express their growing desires. Whether either or both of these possibilities play an important role is yet another matter which requires continued investigation. It would be especially important to trace the spread of psychoanalytic ideas into the widely read columns and books on child care.

In closing these reflections on the validity of our interpretations, we must point again to the words of caution introduced in Chapter Two.

We have considered but a few of the multiplicity of social conditions and changes in recent American history. We selected conditions which seemed plausibly related to changes in the training of children. When all is said and done, our efforts at controlling these results or checking against other explanations can eliminate only a few of the many alternative interpretations. Consider, for example, the complex impact of such conditions as the following on data like ours: the rising educational level of the whole population, the long period of prosperity from 1945 to the present, the growing practice of seeking authoritative "scientific" advice about child care, or the increase in a rational, pragmatic approach to many aspects of living. The social conditions we have studied are obviously but a few of many which may be important.

. . . . . *THE SCOPE OF THE INTERPRETATIONS*

The points we have just taken up in this chapter bear on the validity of our findings and interpretations. Now we turn to a different problem. What is the breadth or scope of our results? Specifically, how strong are the relations we uncovered between stratification, integration, and religious preference on the one hand and techniques of child rearing on the other? Second, should we expect that these relations will appear anywhere else in the United States? Are they restricted to the Detroit area? We shall take up each of these questions in its turn.

How Much Have We Explained?

As we expected, the newer methods of training children appear to be related to the rise of the newer middle classes. But how strong is that relationship? Do the old and new middle classes differ sharply in the style of rearing youngsters? How much of the difference in techniques of child care is associated with the integration and stratification position of the family or with those considerations plus the parents' religious preference?

To estimate an answer to these questions, one may examine mothers with high or low scores on our cumulative Indices of Internalization, Activity, Responsibility, and Moral Relations. These mothers, it will be remembered, are not all the women in the sample, but those whose responses to each item of an index were judged to represent a greater or lesser tendency to train children according to the theme

Validity and Scope of the Interpretations **189**

of that group of indices. All of this is explained in detail in Appendix Two. For our immediate purpose, however, it is important that these are the mothers whose responses most clearly and consistently evidence a concern for the themes in the indices. Naturally, we would not expect our explanations to hold as well for mothers who gave little evidence of concern with the techniques of child care for which those explanations were designed to account. The mothers who give the clearest and most consistent evidence of such concern are, therefore, the group for whom we should expect to make the best predictions. The earlier chapters have shown significant relations between the social positions of these mothers and their responses to the indices. But, how large are those relationships?

As the discussion in Appendix Two suggests, we can give only an approximate answer to this question. In that Appendix we cite the reasons for feeling that Table 7–2 gives a conservative estimate of the percentage of the differences in the mothers' scores on each of the indices that is associated with some predicted social positions:

Although it was shown previously that many of these results are

Table 7–2

PERCENTAGE OF DISTRIBUTION OF CUMULATIVE SCORES ON VARIOUS INDICES ASSOCIATED WITH DESIGNATED SOCIAL POSITIONS

Cumulative Scores for Indices of	Social Positions*	Percentage of Association
Internalization (Schedule Form A)	EMC vs. BMC	9
Internalization (Schedule Form B)	EMC vs. BMC	15
Activity	EMC vs. BMC	12
Internalization (Schedule Form A)	EMC vs. ELC	2
Internalization (Schedule Form B)	EMC vs. ELC	3
Activity	EMC vs. ELC	†
Responsibility		2
Moral Relations	PMC vs. RCMC	14

* EMC = Entreperneurial middle class.
　BMC = Bureaucratic middle class.
　ELC = Entrepreneurial lower class.
　PMC = Protestant middle class.
　RCMC = Roman Catholic middle class.
† Less than 1 per cent.

too large to have occurred simply by chance, they still do not indicate any very large associations between these several social positions and cumulative scores. Even the highest associations, those between the older and newer middle classes on the internalization and activity scores and between the Protestant and Catholic middle classes and scores on the Indices of Moral Relations, are small in size. They range from 9 to 15 per cent. Thus, even in the case in which the largest association is found, we must conclude that about 85 per cent of the distribution of differences in cumulative scores—those on the Internalization Indices for Schedule Form B—has no relation to the social positions considered.

We have already taken into consideration several conditions which might have made these relations spuriously high. Is there evidence, however, that they may be lower than the "true" relation of child care and these social positions? We will examine four possible answers to this question.

The first answer is negative. Perhaps our explanations, even though having some merit as evidenced by the significant findings of preceding chapters, still may not begin to get at the major sources of the differences that appear in child care among American mothers. This point is discussed more fully earlier in this chapter.

Second, however, it is possible that our indices of child training or of social position are too crude and too subject to error. They may be low in validity. This possibility has previously been considered for the methods we used to classify mothers in the several social positions. Now it must be acknowledged as of possible importance for the various indices of child care as well. For example, we assembled several items to make up a set of Indices of Internalization. But what if, for a great many mothers, several of those items serve maternal purposes in addition to the one we felt the items stressed, that is, represent ends other than that of teaching the children self-control? Those other ends may be quite unrelated to any of the social positions we studied, whereas self-control might, as we anticipated, be closely related. Nevertheless, with our index items standing for two or more things, some quite unrelated to the social positions under consideration, those positions would have but small relation to the methods of child care.

A third possible answer is that both of our sets of indices—those concerning child care and those for the social positions—may be reasonably valid, but that some of them are of low reliability. This fact would mean that these indices really do reflect the conditions in the world they were intended to catch—that, for example, our Inter-

Validity and Scope of the Interpretations **191**

nalization Indices really do mirror differences in mothers' emphases on teaching the children self-control—but that they do not reflect those conditions in a very stable fashion. Valid indices, but indices of low reliability, would show a low degree of association with one another. In Appendix Two we estimate the reliability of our various indices of child care and of our methods for determining a family's social position as best we can with the information available. From those estimates it is possible to make a gross judgment of how closely the social positions and indices of child care would relate if both types of observation were perfectly reliable. Table 7–3 gives those judgments.

Table 7–3

ESTIMATED PERCENTAGE OF DISTRIBUTION OF CUMULATIVE SCORES
ON VARIOUS INDICES ASSOCIATED WITH DESIGNATED SOCIAL
POSITIONS IF ALL OBSERVATIONS WERE PERFECTLY RELIABLE

Cumulative Scores for Indices of	Social Positions*	Estimated Percentage of Association
Internalization (Schedule Form B)†	EMC vs. BMC	70
Activity	EMC vs. BMC	56
Internalization (Schedule Form B)†	EMC vs. ELC	24
Activity	EMC vs. ELC	10
Responsibility	EMC vs. ELC	20
Moral Relations	PMC vs. RCMC	46

* EMC = Entrepreneurial middle class.
   BMC = Bureaucratic middle class.
   ELC = Entrepreneurial lower class.
   PMC = Protestant middle class.
   RCMC = Roman Catholic middle class.

† For technical reasons described in Appendix Two, estimated percentages could not be computed for the Internalization Indices on Schedule Form A.

A comparison of Tables 7–2 and 7–3 shows that these estimated percentages are far larger than those actually obtained. This finding, in turn, tells us that it may be the low reliability of our observations which is responsible in good part for the small size of the associations reported in Table 7–2. If that is true, it encourages the conclusion that our explanations of differences in child training by differences in the families' social positions may be getting at important sources of those differences and that they are deserving of intensive work to improve their reliability.

A fourth and final possible explanation of the low degree of association between methods of rearing children and the social positions listed in Table 7–2 is one we mentioned earlier. It always is more difficult to get a high degree of association between two variables when the range of difference in either is narrow. As we suggested before, the very nature of our society may be narrowing the range of differences in methods of child care available for study. If we are right in thinking that the lives of most Americans have been touched in some measure by the emerging bureaucratic trends then, to that measure, they probably become like one another. The wider difference in child care that might appear if we compared mothers in 1890 with mothers in the mid-twentieth century is, perhaps, narrowed when we examine the disparities among mothers all of whom come from the latter period in history. Consequently, it becomes more difficult to find high degrees of relation between the social positions of those mothers and their methods of handling children.

The entrepreneurial family is, at the present time, a kind of anachronism, gaining less and less support from the values and institutions of the surrounding society. The bureaucratic family is, as of this writing, an emergent type of family, whose ways of living and of caring for youngsters will come into sharp crystallization only after a number of years have passed and experience is gained. Probably the ideal research design would pit two carefully matched groups of mothers, entrepreneurial and bureaucratic, against each other, with the former being selected from 1890 and the latter from 1980. That study is not in our power. Ours is an approximation to what might be had under ideal, though impossible, conditions. Perhaps such an approximation is fated to produce only limited associations when it tests such predictions as those we have made.

Detroit and the United States

As the last of these evaluations of the worth of our findings, we consider where we may expect our results to hold true. If we drew a similar sample of parents and asked the same questions in New York City, would the same findings appear? What would happen if we repeated the study in El Paso or Cincinnati, in Tallahassee or in the countryside and towns in the middle of Nebraska? What if we drew a sample of all American mothers? Would our results be duplicated?

Anyone reading about our findings certainly must keep in mind the warning implied in these questions—the warning that Detroit is not the United States. It not only is a metropolitan area rather than a

Validity and Scope of the Interpretations **193**

rural setting, but it is distinctive among great cities. It is the center of automobile manufacturing in this country. The methods of production, including the extensive use of assembly-line procedures, found in that industry are concentrated in Detroit as nowhere else. Among citizens of great cities in the United States, Detroiters have a relatively high median income, yet, relatively speaking, are more likely than workers in many other cities to be semiskilled and skilled blue-collar employees. Detroit is a city in which most of the labor force is employed in one of a few very large manufacturing enterprises. It is a city in which many of those enterprises are tied together in large combines for the production of a single product, the automobile. Further, it is a city that has grown rapidly and rather recently. A sizable percentage of its leaders and of its ordinary citizens are not native to the area. All such observations reinforce the cautiousness that should be exercised in extending our findings to other localities.

But, if Detroit is not the United States, there is much of the United States in Detroit—many of the conditions that Americans meet everywhere and much of the way of life which they develop to meet those conditions. For that reason we have considerable confidence that the results obtained in this study are not confined to one small area of the country at one point in its history. The explanations we developed did not take Detroit's peculiarities into account. Although those peculiarities may have enhanced the ability of those explanations to account for the way children are trained, it seems unlikely that the success of many of our predictions depends exclusively on conditions idiosyncratic to the Detroit area. Major social trends in this country have a way of spreading out until they affect the lives of almost all Americans. It would be surprising indeed if the shift from entrepreneurial to bureaucratic ways or the differences between the middle and lower classes or between Protestants and Roman Catholics were confined to southeastern Michigan.

. . . . . *CONCLUSIONS*

From these considerations of the stability of our results when several controls are imposed on them, and of the likely validity, reliability, and generalizability of our results and interpretations, we conclude that they are likely to be found again under similar conditions. We have tried to point to further research which would be crucial if confidence in that likelihood were to be strengthened. Now, having shown our reasons for believing that our findings merit further consid-

eration, we would like to speculate about their wider significance for
life in America's families and for the personalities of Americans.

NOTES

[1] Max Eastman, "Mr.–er–er–Oh! What's His Name? Ever Say That?"
Everybody's Magazine, 33 (July, 1915), 95–103.

[2] Henry L. Mencken, "Editorial," *The American Mercury*, 11 (July, 1927), 288–
290.

Validity and Scope of the Interpretations **195**

CHAPTER EIGHT

. . . . *F*AMILY, PERSONALITY,

AND BUREAUCRACY: A

SPECULATIVE ACCOUNT

The meaning of our findings is not derived solely through such formal tests of their validity and reliability as have appeared in the two preceding chapters. Once a workable degree of reliability and validity is assured, it is reasonable to let the imagination flow—to ask whether and how the emergence of welfare-bureaucracy might transform other aspects of American life even as it seems to change methods of rearing children. What of politics? the arts? recreation? There could scarcely be an end to the possibilities once we began. But, in a book about child care, we shall confine our speculation to two areas of American life that have especially intimate relations with the rearing of children—to some likely effects of bureaucratization on the families and on the personalities of Americans (1).

What we have to say is frankly speculative. We feel it is consistent with what appears in this study and with the trends we sense from a general acquaintance with the periodicals and novels and other contents of the mass media of communication in our time. We shall speak as if the picture we give were well documented. Yet, this must be recognized as a style of speaking which we adopt to achieve an uncluttered presentation. The guesses we offer will have their chief value if they prove suggestive for further investigations. In such a frame of mind, we begin this account with some reflections on the family under entrepreneurial and bureaucratic conditions.

. . . . . *THE FAMILY AND BUREAUCRACY*

. . . the family has been in historical times in transition from an institution with family behavior controlled by the mores, public opinion, and law to a companionship with family behavior arising from the mutual affection and consensus of its members. The companionship form of the family is not to be conceived as having already been realized but as emerging. . . .

. . . The most extreme theoretical formulation of the institutional family would be one in which its unity would be determined entirely by the social pressures impinging on family members. The ideal construction of the family as a companionship would focus upon the unity which develops out of mutual affection and intimate association of husband and wife and parents and children. . . .

Of the historical and existing types of families the large patriarchal type most closely approximates the ideal construction of the institutional family. . . . The modern American family residing in the apartment-house areas of the city approximates most nearly the ideal type of companionship family, in which the members enjoy a high degree of self-expression and at the same time are united by the bonds of affection, congeniality, and common interests (2).

When Burgess and Locke wrote this now widely influential description of the family, World War II was in process. The thinking of sociologists in the United States was still powerfully dominated by the spectacle of the growth of cities and the spread of city ways of life in the wake of industrial capitalism. First through Western Europe and the United States and then in the Orient and every other part of the world reached by a burgeoning commerce and industry, the cities had grown and changed. The industrial and, often, entrepreneurial society had begun to appear, and the traditional pattern of the family had shifted to accommodate to these new forces. Generally, in all these places, the preindustrial family was patriarchal, patrilineal, and patrilocal. That is, the father held the principal authority, children were considered more closely "related" to his family than to the parents and brothers and sisters of their mother, and the family lived in close association with the husband's relatives. Among non-literate societies this pattern was broken most typically when the methods of production were such that wife and, perhaps, children could participate on an almost equal basis with the husband. Such is the case in those simple economies where almost every able-bodied member aids in the gathering of food through collecting nuts and fruit, wild vegetables and cereals, and insects and small animals. Hunting big game, caring for large herds of animals, or conducting agriculture on a large scale require more specialized skills and greater strength. The wife could not participate in full equality in such activities and simultaneously manage the home. The surplus of wealth was not sufficient to hire baby sitters, although, in certain peak periods of activity, the younger children might care for any infants in the family while the mother and older children worked to bring in the harvest or plant the seeds for the next crop (3).

The city life that developed with industrialism was one of those conditions that change the family. In the Western world it typically meant that husband and wife had to leave the large group of relatives in the rural area and take up independent residence in the city. The family was no longer as completely patrilocal or patrilineal as before. It continued to be patriarchal (4). With certain notable exceptions, as in textiles and pottery making, the strength of males and their lesser responsibilities for the care of children made them the principal breadwinners in an age in which much heavy common labor was in demand. Women worked in industry when poverty forced them to and their strength and level of skill would permit (5).

The continuous extension of machine techniques and the growth in size of enterprises whittled away at patriarchal patterns, especially in the middle classes. Women could handle an increasing number of jobs as physical strength was replaced by machine power. Fewer children and the easing of many burdens of housekeeping freed women for employment that substantially increased family incomes. The surplus of wealth produced by industry enabled an increasing number of wives to hire someone to take over at least a part of their household duties while they were away at work. Wages and salaries were lower for women, and their services in greater demand in offices as well as in many blue-collar occupations. The equality of wife with husband grew. It increased in the economy and, ultimately, before the law, at the polls, and in the making of family decisions (6).

We find some striking examples of the outcome of these trends in the relations between men and women in the most urbanized parts of the middle classes at the period of the Civil War in the United States and, especially, after the First World War. Suffragette leaders in the nineteenth century were, of course, not typical of their sex, nor were the professional women or the women who found their way into the bohemias of the great cities in the early 1900's. They do give us extreme versions of trends that were spreading rapidly among the female population. There were the women who thought of the attachment to the household and children as servitude imposed by the lusts and selfishness of men and by the outmoded society which they saw males forcing on women. Some of them refused to take even their husband's names which they thought of as badges of servility. They were violently determined equals. They were in that state of revolt given whimsical and pointed form in James Thurber's classic sketches of "The War Between Men and Women" (7). The flapper style was their sign. The dress was emancipatedly short, its hips and bosom were manly flat. Its waist was at an unmotherly low. The wearer was one of the boys.

It was into this urban, industrialized family that there came romantic love in the modern sense. If husband and wife, parent and child were not bound together as tightly as before with the old ties of kin supports and the heavy dependence of woman on man, a new basis for their relation had to develop. It was, as Burgess and Locke suggest, shared affection. In this remaining bond, the relation had to be more intense and sure than before. Romantic love became the test. It was a passion for another person so great that that one was singled out from all others as the only fully satisfying object in the world; so intense that, at the slightest chance of its failure, appetite fled, words were inadequate, and the world barren until it was resumed. And with romance went the criteria of common interests and compatibility. In the relations of equals, interests had to be common and compatible or the marriage failed.

It is our impression that the companionship family described by Burgess and Locke represents, not the growing wave of the family's future, but one of those sudden surges of history that are swallowed in even mightier currents. We, like Burgess and Locke, see the new

Family, Personality, and Bureaucracy **199**

trends documented best among the middle classes, those parts of the population which we believe were the first to experience these new social conditions. The companionship family is an end product of the entrepreneurial society. The bureaucratic order makes different demands on husbands and wives, and on parents and children.

We should like to draw a new and speculative model of the emerging type of family and to speak of it as the *colleague* family. By this term we want to imply that the tendencies which Burgess and Locke describe have, in part, been consolidated for large parts of the population. Women and men are increasingly equal; they are also separate and different. Specialization, that distinctive characteristic of the bureaucratic way of life, has, we believe, created new conditions for relations in families. In our view, the companionship model began as a demand that women should be able to do all the things open to men. It was still a man's world and women tried to enter it by becoming masculine. But the conditions that brought equality and companionship did not stand alone. The same machine technology that enabled women to enter the economy, made the distinctive character of the male role less necessary. The woman, however, was not transformed overnight. The male partner now had to expect to get to know her interests and to share her work in domestic life and in the arts. Further, the older demands that the male be aggressive and independent and dominating decreased with the growth of the greater security and of routinized channels of occupational advance through the more passive means of education and faithful service. In large areas of life it became acceptable and even required that men, like women, have some of the skills and preoccupations traditionally associated with the other sex.

Even in the late stages of the companionship family it was a parliamentary order. Husband and wife were fairly equal partners whose vote on many subjects was of the same weight. We feel that the distinctive characteristics of the bureaucratic order have led to what might be called a neotraditional family. The specialization on the job has entered the home, and the equal partners have been able to see that differences in talent, interest, and function, as long as they are complementary, do not threaten equality. Instead, they may enrich and promote the common life. For this reason we call this type of family the "colleague" family. As specialists at work may find in each other skills they lack, but skills they equally need, and as they may defer to one another's judgment on the grounds of differing competence without feeling that they have personally lost in prestige, so husband and wife may now relate in this way.

One direction in which this trend toward specialization has led is that of the professionalization of the wife's functions. She can no longer learn them satisfactorily from her mother's tutelage and example. They must be rationalized. Their intuitive processes must give way to formal rules and special technical knowledge. They are subject to improvement as the instruments they use are subjected to critical appraisal and functional selection. The women's magazines provide a kind of in-service training, supplemented with the postgraduate work of the mother's study clubs, the meetings with the specialists at the nursery school, the cooking classes, and the growing number of handbooks for preparing unfamiliar or exotic foods.

The aesthetic style conspicuous in latter-day entrepreneurial homes was starkly functional. Its lines were straight, the angles sharp. The model was the machine, designed as a tool and having its beauty in the perfect expression it gave to the purposes for which it was designed. It was a design of economy. The styles since the Second World War have made room for the unexpected corner, the design included for its own sake, the curved and even undulating line. Clothing, painting, and all the arts, domestic and fine, show signs of a general humanizing trend that expresses convenience while leaving room for changing interests and for experiences that may provoke new tastes.

We believe there has been a general strengthening of some of the traditional family patterns along revised lines. We should guess that the requirements for personal stability made by large specialized organizations, together with the economic security they provide, will begin to slow and then lower the rate of divorce and separation in the population and will raise again the criteria of competence and the gifts of homemaking to renewed importance in the choice of a marriage partner. We also find evidences in the novel, the newspaper, the motion picture, television, and the popular magazine that the formal social controls of the large scale organizations are being extended to shape the family and to provide a new sense of obligation.

It is not likely that the children are as subordinated in the household as they were in times past, or that they are the equal decision makers of some companionship families. They are more in the nature of junior partners who are wanted and needed and whose opinions are sought and given careful consideration, but who must have proper seniority before being admitted to full participation in deciding the family's course.

There is also a renewed interest in limiting the child's freedom. As Wolfenstein says, even the U. S. Children's Bureau pamphlet, *Infant Care*, has changed, after a decade of emphasizing the desirability of freedom for the expression of childish impulses, now saying that children need to have some limits set. Many advisers of parents have gone even further in recent years to say that children *want* such limits, that, without them, the world is too unstructured and uncertain for the child's comfort. Some advisers add that, since the child's untutored desires are without limit, he can find happiness only if he is given limited, hence feasible, goals.

The child who is to be trained for the intricate human relations of the bureaucracy is not ready for adulthood, even after receiving an intensive basic course in responsibility training. He must learn the nuances of human relations and must be able to clarify them in his own thinking so that he can study his own relations to others and gain better control over himself and his associates. This training, together with the child's growing independence in our society, requires that parents spend more time with children. The family is again the school for the job, only now it is the school for the job's human relations, not its technical skills.

In the companionship family of the individuated-entrepreneurial society the child was expected to meet other children as friends. That word has long been in the language, but the word's traditional meaning does not capture the singular content it came to have under entrepreneurial conditions. In those circumstances, a man was often cut off from kin and community. He needed warmth and support and some secure human relations. These needs were likely to be met in his contacts with one or two close friends (8). With them, in part by contrast with the rest of his social life, there was a complete interchange of thought and feeling. The friend did what kin and neighbors might have done at an earlier time. The loyalty of friend to friend was sometimes as great at that between brothers. The intense pattern we have found in romantic love is here, the same mutual choice based on unique complementarity of need, but it does not, of course, contain quite the same weight of responsibility and permanence as the marriage relation. One of the special joys of such a role as that of friendship was that it could, at least in law, be broken without complications other than the emotional shock.

To a great extent the relations of parents and children in the family were modeled along the lines of the role of friends. A father was supposed to be a "pal" or a "buddy" or a "friend" to his children. But, like parental patterns, the nature of friendship is changing. The child increasingly meets his peers as colleagues whose favor he must court and whose respect he must win. He cannot acceptably choose one or two with whom to strike up companionship. He must learn to fit in smoothly with all of them. Since, with many, he does not feel a truly close comradeship, he must learn to produce a relationship that uses the symbols of genuine friendship as its currency without the actual commitment of the real thing. He must learn to be a "nice guy"—affable, unthreatening, responsible, competent, adaptive. It is this kind of skill in which the parents must train him. Without the help of kin and community and without the assistance of a set of rigorous controls built into the child in his early days—controls that would soon be outmoded in a changing world—the parents must spend more time at this task if the children are to be "a credit" to them.

Much of the recent discussion by demographers of the size of families has proceeded on the assumption that parents would limit their children to the smallest possible number if only the means were available. The spread of knowledge about cheap, effective, and available contraceptives to much of the population has made this reputed desire a possible choice for most families, yet the birth rate has increased. Not only are more couples having children but more of them are having second and third children. These are not the large families of eight or ten that were relatively common in the 1800's. Nor are they the childless or one child marriages that were common in the early twentieth century. A new kind of expectation about desir-able family size has appeared.

The beliefs of some students of population that most parents desire to keep the number of children to the minimum seems rooted in observations of the middle classes in the entrepreneurial society. Among entrepreneurial middles, each additional child was a strain on the slender resources on which the family's possible social ascent was based. For the parents interested in the children's future, larger family size meant that fathers and mothers could offer less help toward an education and a "start in life" to each boy and girl.

We may expect that the greater security of the bureaucratic middle classes, especially lower middle families, together with the lesser opportunities for social advance through individual enterprise, takes away some of the forces against having more children and permits a rise in the birth rate. But this situation would be true only if there were some powerful positive forces to promote such a rise. It is our impression that parents in the bureaucratized family, like those in the older agricultural family, find children a fulfillment, without many of the difficulties that went with the raising of a family under entre-preneurial conditions. For the wife they are a necessary canvas on which professionalized skills of homemaking can be expressed. For both husband and wife they are an outlet for creative management of social relations, for the parents' learning new things about themselves, and for demonstrating their conventionality and adaptability and "maturity" in the bureaucratic world. If the family is secure in the new sense that the children can find employment near the home of the parents and, with swift transportation and communication, can be part of the parental families for a long time to come, then there is also a renewed sense of self-continuity and self-realization through children that comes to the couple with a family.

Further, the parents in this new order, unlike those of the entrepreneurial society, have a kind of wisdom that their children will continue to need and that cannot be obtained except by long experience in the stable and complex relations of large organizations. The parents may not have their children's new technical skills. This was a gap that made for isolation if not alienation between generations in the entrepreneurial society. The bureaucratic parents do have relevant, hard-bought skills in making the critical judgments of social situations that their children will need. We may expect, then, a reappearance of the parent as the counselor and aid of the children after they become adults and parents in their own right. In this way it is likely that bureaucratic conditions enhance the function of children as a means of self-continuity and companionship for their parents. This, in turn, makes having children more desirable.

Our own data did not enable us to examine the possibility that the birth patterns of bureaucratic families would show a greater tendency to have children or to have more children than would those of entrepreneurial families. This was the case because we did not have information for families having no children. We sampled only those households in which one or more children eighteen years or younger were living. What we have done is to examine the birth patterns obtained by the Detroit Area Study in a different year, 1954. In that year, unlike the one in which we collected our information, the sample consisted of a random sample of adults in dwelling units in the area (9). Table 8–1 gives the results. An inspection of this table does not show any differences in the likelihood of having children among older (forty years of age and beyond) entrepreneurial and bureaucratic wives. Among younger wives, however, a slight but consistent trend appears. We find that bureaucratic wives are more likely than entrepreneurial wives to have some children instead of being childless. This finding appears in all of our comparisons except that between wealthier upper middle-class families in the two integration settings. In one other case, that between entrepreneurial and bureaucratic wives in the less wealthy families that have a lower

Table 8–1

NUMBER OF CHILDREN EVER HAD BY WHITE WIVES LIVING IN THE DETROIT AREA IN 1954: BY SOCIAL POSITION

Number of Children Ever Had	Wives Aged 39 Years or Less								Wives Aged 40 Years or More							
	Family Income: less than $6000				Family Income: $6000 or more				Family Income: less than $6000				Family Income: $6000 or more			
	UM*	LM†	UL‡	LL§	UM*	LM†	UL‡	LL§	UM*	LM†	UL‡	LL§	UM*	LM†	UL‡	LL§
Entrepreneurial Wives																
3 or more	1	3	1	4	6	0	5	0	0	5	8	8	4	4	10	6
2	0	2	4	2	6	3	4	1	0	2	7	7	6	4	6	5
1	0	2	0	3	1	3	0	3	0	0	3	5	2	2	1	1
0	1	0	2	2	1	3	2	4	2	1	6	5	2	1	2	4
Total	2	7	7	11	14	9	11	8	2	8	24	25	14	11	19	16
Bureaucratic Wives																
3 or more	2	7	9	13	9	12	7	4	0	5	2	6	1	8	13	1
2	1	7	11	12	5	5	13	2	0	3	6	2	8	4	6	4
1	2	3	11	3	6	7	9	10	0	0	1	0	3	3	5	1
0	1	1	1	4	4	7	6	4	0	3	1	4	2	5	2	1
Total	6	18	32	32	24	31	35	20	0	11	10	12	14	20	26	7

* UM = upper middle class.   ‡ UL = upper lower class.
† LM = lower middle class.   § LL = lower lower class.

205

middle-class status, no comparison is possible since entrepreneurial lower middles include no childless families and since the total number of such families is smaller than that for bureaucratic lower middles. The probability of obtaining six out of seven comparisons in the predicted direction by chance alone is slightly greater than five in a hundred. Table 8–1 shows no convincing entrepreneurial-bureaucratic differences in childlessness for older wives nor in the number of children had by wives in any income or social class group. We can also report that the birth patterns in this table are not affected by the distribution of Protestants and Roman Catholics in the population or by the number of years for which these couples were married. Thus, even though we do not have strong support for our expectations, these results do suggest that our ideas may have enough merit to be pursued further.

Now we turn to a theme which has been of constant concern in this book. It is that of the effects of bureaucracy on the personalities of Americans.

. . . . . *PERSONALITY, NEUROSES, AND*
         BUREAUCRACY

Again and again we have spoken of certain themes in child training —self-control and an active orientation toward the world—that distinguish the child care of entrepreneurial and bureaucratic mothers. We assume, of course, that these themes also come to distinguish the personalities—the organization of expectations, predispositions, and overt behavior—of these women and of their children.

The nature and consequences of these personality trends appear with unusual clarity when we consider some of their less attractive aspects. We have already spoken of the advantages of the entrepreneurial emphases on self-control and self-denial. These enable the individual to guide his conduct according to rational considerations and to take into account the demands of a difficult and competitive world. But these emphases are likely to have other consequences as well. The man who constantly denies himself for the sake of future gain finds less pleasure in his life. He is likely to know spasmodic waves of depression. His control and his striving become excessive. Even when he can afford to relax—after he has achieved a desired status or is on a holiday—the habits of his upbringing go on. He has to keep busy, compulsively busy, beyond the point at which creation and planning bring rewards. Even if he wants to stop, he cannot.

Sunday, without the ordered and familiar channels of work, can become a bore or a nightmare.

Further, the entrepreneurial middle is fated to meet severe frustration. His high and unyielding internalized standards commit him to behave in ways that cannot always be realized. He feels pressed to strive, yet he sometimes grows tired. The result is guilt and uneasiness, not relaxation. Again, reality will not always grant success to his efforts. Businessmen find themselves in contracting markets and they fail. Students discover that they simply lack the abilities required to get high grades in school. Pressed to achieve but confronted with failure, the individual is in desperate conflict. Unhappily for him, since his stanlards are internalized, they cannot be reasoned away or easily evaded. The person blames himself, becomes depressed, has low self-respect, and may, in addition, have low status in the eyes of his fellows. He judges himself as well as his performance against his internalized standards and the verdict is "Guilty."

Easy relations with other people are also hindered by the kind of control and manipulative activity fostered by an entrepreneurial society. Unduly strong self-control may be associated with unadaptable and disadvantageous stubbornness. Manipulative activity may strike potential friends as crass exploitation or aggressiveness. The individual's habit of paying candid attention to reality and trying to adapt himself to it and it to his wishes may generate a pleasant candor. But that same frankness may be seen by others as bluntness and lack of sensitivity. And the competitive atmosphere that generates rules of fair play may also produce a latent suspicion that people are trying to triumph at his expense.

Another curious consequence of the self-control and isolation of an entrepreneurial society is that, even while it promotes self-control, it makes uncontrollable a substantial part of the emotional life of the individual. A price of self-control and self-denial is the suppression of many impulsive desires. But these do not always stay suppressed. A man becomes ill or tired or has other periods in which continued self-denial becomes difficult. Then these suppressed wishes may appear overtly. Since he has never learned how to express them in acceptable and innocuous ways, they burst forth in wanton fashion. The long suppressed anxieties and hostilities go out of control. Here we have that marked contrast between his usually dispassionate and calculating conduct and a strange lack of control at other times.

Then, too, entrepreneurial conditions foster a kind of egocentricity in outlook. It could hardly be otherwise when a man learns over so long a time that he must be independent, that he must care for himself since no one else will. His responsibilities for most other people are similarly limited. His neighbors are also his competitors. He quite naturally comes to think of his own welfare first; to consider his own needs even at the expense of others.

Although we do not think of bureaucratic life as a paradise, it probably does ameliorate some of these pressures and difficulties found by the older middle classes. This is a point at which our analysis differs somewhat from existing portraits of Bureaucratic Man.

Merton (10), for example, characterizes the well-adapted bureaucratic personality as cautious, precise in performance, impersonal in dealing with other people, unaggressive, rational, and secure. This person is cautious because he must work within the limitations and demands of an explicit set of rules of procedure if he is to succeed. He is precise in performance, because such precision rather than entrepreneurial flair is the basis of his promotion and tenure. He must be unaggressive and impersonal because hostility and dealing with people as unique, special, individual cases disturbs the intricate and preplanned organization of a large enterprise. He is rational because he must constantly attend to the reality presented by his work if he is to perform it with precision and caution. He is secure because his job does reward him with seniority and tenure and a pension, and because others take the entrepreneurial risks.

We do not feel that this is an inaccurate description of bureaucracy's effects on personality in America. We feel it is incomplete. As we urged in Chapter Two, large, complex organizations in the United States today must encourage not only such personal characteristics in their employees as those listed above, but must also cope with the necessity of creating a moral community—a community of responsibility and loyalty—among those employees. We shall not repeat what we already have said about the reasons for this additional and important task of the large enterprise. What we do want to underscore is that a distinctive aspect of life in American bureaucracies is found not simply in security of tenure gained by the rather deadening conformity to routines, but in the security of belonging to a moral community in which the member has a personal stake and in which satisfactions come from participation in a common task as well as from the expert exercise of his technical skills. As we have suggested in Chapter Two, this American situation also is one in which impersonality is mitigated by formal and planned efforts to gain employee allegiance to the organization. These efforts include de-emphasizing the status structure and the development of a style of supervision which takes into account the individual needs of subordinates. Although the resultant feelings of employees that they are participants in the enterprise, not simply faceless numbers, may rest on a spurious sense of self-importance, it is our impression that these feelings are real and significant.

Further, we feel that Merton's description of the bureaucratized personality is more representative of French, German, and other civil service personnel than it is of the bulk of Americans employed by large concerns. We also feel that the emphasis by Riesman (11), Whyte (12) and others on the highly competitive nature of bureaucratic life is not incorrect, but that it is atypical of the general American scene. Riesman speaks eloquently of the striving among bureaucratic employees for advancement to jobs with more responsibility, income, and prestige. Whyte says that even the wives of corporation personnel must become active participants in their husbands' striving. We suspect that these observations apply to the comparatively small number of persons who are executives in large organizations rather than to the bulk of the labor force. It seems, in fact, an ironic development that whereas the security and leisure of most Americans appear destined to grow with bureaucracy, the pressures on the men at the very top of these giant organizations increase rather than decline. Entrepreneurial skills and responsibilities must still be exercised by middle and top management, and the scope of the enterprises concerned has steadily increased.

Speaking, then, as we have throughout this book, of the consequences of a particular kind of bureaucracy—welfare bureaucracy—for most of the labor force, we anticipate a lessening of psychic pressures and strains. We expect that one symptom of this will appear in the kind and frequency of pathological behavior in the United States.

When people are under great stress, and especially when they find no ready escape from intolerable and unmanageable social pressures, they must distort their perceptions of reality to live at all. We may expect such distortions to decline as American life provides increased security.

The older middle classes, oriented toward meeting difficulties by exercising self-control, were likely to repress impulsive behaviors even more harshly when they were faced with difficulties. If they failed, their pattern of response was to blame themselves, with the result that they experienced great depressions and severe guilt. Alternatively, or additionally, they developed obsessional neuroses or became paranoid.

Self-attack is not the only reaction to conflicts which involve the pressure of conscience. The person may repress his impulse. He may

Family, Personality, and Bureaucracy **209**

project it or the internalized standards. If he projects the impulse, he thinks others want to perform the tabooed act. If he projects the internalized standard, he feels that others are condemning him for wishing to enact the forbidden behavior. Finally, as another alternative to self-attack, the person may substitute for the prohibited desire some remotely related but socially acceptable ideas or thoughts which he repeats over and over again. In short, he may become obsessive.

The entrepreneurial lower classes, with less to gain from self-control, were likely to meet an unfriendly world by denying that it was as it seemed. They would retreat to a pleasant though unrealistic fantasy, for, as the popular song had it, "you can't stop me from dreaming," even if reality is harsh. In extreme cases they developed a conversion hysteria or became schizophrenic.

We anticipate that both social classes will find less need for distorting their impulses and their environment than was true under entrepreneurial conditions. In this connection, it may be significant that American psychotherapists report that so-called "character" disorders are relatively more common than they once were (13). The man with a character disorder is not necessarily repressing the true nature of his desires or his environment. He often can report his symptoms, but he either views them as assets or finds that they provide so great a source of pleasure that he cannot give them up. The man's symptoms get him into difficulties in social relations, but his ideas and behavior are often "realistic" in the sense of corresponding to the realities of the environment he has experienced. If mental disorders involving distortions of perception—disorders such as manic depression and schizophrenia—are declining as we expect, then it would be understandable that psychotherapists would find a larger portion of their patients exhibiting other kinds of problems.

It may also be that psychopathologies involving the orifices of the body will decline. The entrepreneurial middles emphasize the early and stringent socialization of behavior connected with those orifices. We find them more likely than the bureaucrats to force the infant to eat at scheduled times instead of allowing him to feed when he is hungry. Entrepreneurial middles also are more likely to prevent the child from sucking his thumb and from touching his sex organs. They make more stringent demands for early control of defecation.

It is possible that future social historians will find that these entrepreneurial practices provided one major source of evidence from which the traditional Freudian emphasis on the importance of the orifices in pathology had its source. That Freudian emphasis suggests, for example, that excessively early or strict demands on the child in connection with the mouth, anus, and other bodily openings may lead the youngster to overvalue such parts of his body. It suggests that excessive demands of this kind may lead the child to develop what his society considers perverted uses of these orifices. Take this instance. Freudian theory proposes that the child who rebels against toilet training and retains his feces against his mother's wishes, may become constipated or stubborn in later life when he is angry. To the extent that these psychoanalytic predictions are supported by future research, we may expect the decline in traumatic socialization of the orifices to be reflected in a decrease in the frequency with which the bodily openings are involved in psychopathological symptoms.

On the other hand, it is possible that there will be an increase in certain pathological symptoms as bureaucratic methods of child care gain wider acceptance. If, for example, we are right in thinking that the sharp entrepreneurial distinctions between the sexes are blurring in bureaucratized families, it may be that children experience increasing confusion about how to behave in ways appropriate for their sex. The period of transition from the erosion of the old entrepreneurial conceptions of suitable behavior for boys as contrasted with girls might be especially trying. We have encountered a number of anecdotal reports that problems of sexual identity are appearing with increasing frequency in psychiatric patients.

We also must not overlook the possibility that the shift from entrepreneurial to bureaucratic standards will produce an increase in the number of people who have difficulty in controlling themselves. When internalized standards are no longer present and the external controls of the bureaucratized society have not yet come into full operation, the individual may be more likely to do things at the spur of uninhibited impulse. Inevitably, he will come to regret many consequences of such uncontrolled and irrational impulsiveness.

To avoid misunderstanding, we must caution against interpreting the things we have been saying as indicating that Americans are becoming a population of placid and affable and contented conformists. It is our understanding that what we have described are significant new conditions in the American economy. We have tried to suggest some consequences these conditions may have for families and personalities. But we have not given a complete picture of life in the United States. Americans continue to differ in interests and goals by region and occupation and by many other experiences. It is scarcely to be expected that bureaucratic tendencies will erase the conflict and competition among these divergent interests, though they may well lessen some of the older differences among Americans. Perhaps our case is made clear by reminding ourselves that even so drastic a practice in child care as the eighteenth and early nineteenth century custom of "breaking" the wills of children, although it may have produced people who found it difficult to violate the moral standards they were taught, did not generate a docile people. Instead, it seems to have been quite compatible with a population in which conflict and active struggles for political power were much in evidence.

In the same spirit, we wish to urge that serious consideration be given to the possibility advanced here that bureaucratization has begun to provide a new level of security and comfort for Americans and a new sense of participation in a responsible moral community. As a consequence, we are less disposed than some commentators to see the growth of "do-it-yourself" projects and of adult education and the apparent increase of interest in morality and religion as symptoms of a population withdrawing from a complicated and confusing world. Instead, we suggest that these may well signify the seizing of newly available opportunities for self-expression in the fine and practical arts, for the development of sophistication about leisure, and for a confronting of the problems of the relations of man to his fellows and to history.

NOTES

[1] Consideration is given in Appendix Four to the possibility that there is a connection between interest in religion and bureaucratization.

[2] Ernest W. Burgess and Harvey J. Locke, *The Family from Institution to Companionship* (New York: American Book Company, 1945), 26–27.

[3] Leonard T. Hobhouse, G. C. Wheeler, and Morris Ginsberg, *The Material Culture and Social Institutions of the Simpler Peoples, An Essay in Correlation* (London: Chapman and Hall, Ltd., 1915), contains descriptions of various family patterns and their relation to economic and other conditions. For somewhat different interpretations consult Julian H. Steward, "The Economic and Social Basis of Primitive Bands," in Robert H. Lowie (ed.), *Essays in Anthropology* (Berkeley, California: University of California Press, 1936), 331–350.

[4] A classic example of this pattern is described in Conrad M. Arensberg, *The Irish Countryman* (London: The Macmillan Co., Ltd., 1937).

[5] It is doubtful that the use of women for physically lighter work is a simple function of their lesser muscular strength. Certainly women in the Soviet Union seem to be employed for the heaviest kinds of manual labor.

[6] As Albert Reiss points out, the worlds of parents and children were further separated by the compulsory attendance laws that put children in the schools instead of the parental world of work, and by the child labor laws that gave youngsters a special status through enforcing idleness.

[7] *The New Yorker Twenty-fifth Anniversary Album: 1925–1950* (New York: Harper and Bros., 1951), unpaginated.

[8] An important discussion of the forms and conditions of friendship appears in

Jyotirmoyee Sarma, "The Social Categories of Friendship," unpublished doctoral dissertation, Department of Sociology, The University of Chicago, 1946.

[9] The very methods used in the present study to place respondents in a particular social class were also employed in the DAS for 1954. However, the 1954 study did not gather all the data for placing respondents in the entrepreneurial or bureaucratic settings that we had obtained in the previous year. Specifically, the 1954 study did not have information on the number of supervisory levels in the work situation or on the portion of its income that the family earned in the form of profits, fees, and commissions. With these restrictions, the definitions of entrepreneurial and bureaucratic found in 1954 were identical with the ones we used in the present study.

[10] Robert K. Merton, "Bureaucratic Structure and Personality," in Robert K. Merton and others (eds.), *Reader in Bureaucracy* (Glencoe, Illinois: The Free Press, 1952), 361–371.

[11] David Riesman and others, *The Lonely Crowd: A Study of the Changing American Character* (New Haven: Yale University Press, 1950).

[12] William H. Whyte, Jr., "The Wives of Management," *Fortune*, 44 (October, 1951), 86–88, 204, 206–208, 210, 213; "The Corporation and the Wife," *ibid.*, 44 (November, 1951), 109–111, 150, 152, 155–156, 158.

[13] An important work on the nature of character disorders is Wilhelm Reich's book *Character Analysis* (New York: Orgone Institute Press, 1949).

Family, Personality, and Bureaucracy **213**

BENCHMARKS FOR THE STUDY OF CHANGES IN CHILD TRAINING . . . .

CHAPTER NINE

*A*N OVERVIEW

OF CHILD TRAINING

IN THE DETROIT AREA

. . . .

With this chapter we come to an ending and a beginning. Here we give the last of our findings about child care. But here we also take a first step to permit a more adequate study of changes in methods of training children.

From time to time we have wished that information comparable to that which we now possess were available for urban America of fifty or a hundred years ago. With such information we could make clear and firm judgments on many questions about which we now can only speculate. And—what is equally important—we would not be forced to use the existing older middle classes as representative of an older style of life. We know they are already touched in important ways by the new styles of living and hence are "impure" examples of their kind. For many purposes, a superior way to study change is to take periodic samples from the stream of history.

What we can do is to make a first investment in providing the materials for later and longitudinal research on changes in child care. We can present the findings from our study in such a way that they may provide benchmarks against which future investigators can match their own results. For this future purpose, we shall no longer separate mothers by race, social class, or any other basis, but shall report how all our Detroit mothers, taken together, answered our questions. We will present a composite snapshot of Detroit's families in the early spring of 1953. Where existing information permits, we shall try to illumine the picture of Detroit mothers by comparing it with information collected from the study of child training in other societies.

We have arranged our findings about the methods of rearing children to correspond roughly to the sequence with which mothers introduce each of these methods. For this reason we begin with expectations about having a new baby. Then we review the ways in which eating, sucking, and defecating are socialized. Following this, we report findings on methods of discipline and on demands that the child act responsibly. The guidance of sex-related behavior is then discussed. Finally, we present our material on the mothers' expectations about the adult roles their children will play. The number of cases for which responses are reported is 582 when the questionnaire item was administered to all mothers. It is 291 when the item was administered to only a random half of the mothers. The interview form in Appendix Three may be consulted to determine whether an item was used with all, or only half, of the mothers.

. . . . . *THE NEW BABY*

In the judgment of our coders, based on the mothers' answers to Items 1, 1*a*, and 1*b*, the infancy of 66 per cent of Detroit's children represented very pleasant experiences to their mothers. Another 18.6 per cent of the mothers were rated as finding a new baby mildly pleasant. Almost 14 per cent were rated as finding him unpleasant (1). Although we have no data from outside the United States with which to compare these ratings, we find it a striking possibility that more than one out of every ten mothers finds the arrival of a new baby more depriving than rewarding.

The attitudes of mothers affect babies through their appearance in specific maternal behaviors. We turn, therefore, to our findings concerning such matters as the feeding of infants, the control of their defecation, the provision of discipline, and training the growing child to be independent.

. . . . . FEEDING

The body regimens of infancy have had much attention in our earlier chapters. There are times when writers in the popular women's magazines speak as if the whole of the child's personality were set by the age of weaning or whether he was breast-fed. Our immediate concern is not with such problems, but with what mothers do.

About 41 per cent of the children in our study were fed solely on the bottle, only 10 per cent were fed solely at the breast (2). A common pattern was that of the 40.1 per cent of the cases in which the mother began by suckling the child at the breast and later switched to bottle feeding. In 7.4 per cent of the cases the child was bottle- and breast-fed from the beginning (3).

Another popular theme in the writings about child rearing is the importance of demand or scheduled feeding. We find that almost 57 per cent of the children studied were on demand feeding and about 41 per cent on scheduled feeding. We were unable to get information about these matters in 2.3 per cent of the cases (4).

Of those children who were fed only by bottle, and for whom weaning was completed, 63 per cent were weaned completely by the end of the twelfth month, 90 per cent by the end of the eighteenth month, 99 per cent by the end of the twenty-fourth month, and 1 per cent at later times (5). The proportions for those who were breast-fed at some time are almost identical.

These findings on age of weaning are one of the few pieces of information for which we can make some fairly accurate comparisons with the practices of a large number of other societies. There are, of course, countless fragments of information on other topics covered in our study, but the methods of gathering and recording the data are not usually comparable with the ones we have used. Weaning information, because it is expressed in terms of a specific number of years, is far more standardized from study to study. It also is a point which American and European anthropologists are likely to investigate among non-literate peoples since it often differs from our own practices.

Recently, Whiting and Child, an anthropologist and a psychologist, have published the results of cross-cultural investigation of child training and personality. It includes a summary of these weaning data for the largest number of societies ever examined for this purpose (6). They began their research by going through all the information in the Human Relations Area Files under the headings of Infancy and of Child Care (7). These files represent a massive attempt to record all reputably known facts about all societies—more especially about all non-literate or primitive societies. The files are incomplete even with respect to existing knowledge, but they give the most comprehensive coverage now available for anyone who wants to make a large number of comparisons of life in a variety of societies. From these files the investigators uncovered considerable information about child-training practices in sixty-five societies. They also added data from ten other societies not yet incorporated into the files. All seventy-five societies are primitive.

From information thus gathered, Whiting and Child conclude that demand feeding is the pattern practiced by most people in all the societies they sampled. As indicated above, this is also true for our Detroit Area mothers. We have the impression, however, that the precentage of Detroit mothers who feed babies on a schedule is higher than that to be found in any of the groups studied by Whiting and Child (8).

Their second conclusion is that the typical society (among the fifty-two cases in their sample for which relevant information was available) is one in which weaning begins at thirty months (9). We have two figures from Detroit. For infants who have had some breast feeding, the median age at which weaning is begun is nine months. For babies fed only on the bottle, the median age is eleven months. Whiting and Child report that the societies they studied range in this respect from those, like our own, which begin weaning before the end of the first year of life to those which wait until the fifth or sixth year. Less than 2 per cent of the mothers in our sample continued breast or bottle feeding beyond the child's second year. It is clear that mothers in the Detroit area wean their children far earlier than is typical in this group of primitive peoples. Unfortunately, we have no comparable material for other literate or urban and industrial societies against which to match our own.

For some time there has been a belief (10) that the newborn baby takes great pleasure in sucking parts of his body. Much conflicting evidence has since been gathered (11) on the problem of whether this pleasure is independent of the joys of eating, as such, in puppies and rats and kittens and in human infants. It still is uncertain whether or not the very act of sucking is pleasurable to the human child as an inherent consequence of his biology.

It will be recalled that we asked if the children in our study ever sucked their thumbs, arms, hands, or "something like that" (12). About 34 per cent of the mothers said the child had. About 64 per cent said, "No" (13). We have already given our reasons for feeling that many of the negative answers to this question represent a distortion of the true facts. Because the truth of these negative answers is in doubt, we are more interested in the detailed answers of the parents who said "Yes." About half of them felt it necessary to do something to stop the child's body sucking. Two-thirds of these used mechanical or chemical preventives like finger covers or jaw braces or evil-tasting liquids. The others tried to divert the child or give him acceptable substitutes (14).

. . . . . *DEFECATION*

Of course there is some overlap in the periods of time involved in weaning and in the beginning of bowel and bladder disciplines, but, for convenience, we have separated our treatment of them. We found that 6.7 per cent of our mothers had not yet started bowel training (15). Of the remainder, 57.6 per cent began between six and nine months, 84 per cent began by the end of the twelfth month, 97.7 per cent by the end of the eighteenth month, and only an additional 2.3 per cent during or after the nineteenth month. Complete bowel control, both day and night, was established by the end of twelve months in 26 per cent of the cases, between the thirteenth and eighteenth months in 36 per cent of the cases, between the nineteenth and twenty-fourth months for 22 per cent, and after the twenty-fourth month for the remaining 16 per cent (16).

The pattern for beginning urinary training is similar. The relevant periods and proportions appear below (17):

Months	Percentage
0–12	66.6
13–18	23.5
19 and above	9.9

Child Training in the Detroit Area **219**

The only appreciable difference is that urinary training seems to begin somewhat later than bowel training in the general population. The following are the data for the age at which, when the question applied, urinary control was completely attained (18):

Months	Percentage
0–12	24.0
13–18	22.0
19–24	25.0
25 and above	29.0

Age at which toilet training was begun, like age of weaning, is specific enough to enable some comparisons with the practices of other societies. In Whiting and Child's sample of primitive groups, information on this point was in the files for twenty-five societies (19). Their cross-cultural tables are not quite comparable to ours since they do not distinguish between the start of bowel and urinary training. However, the results are still of interest since, for toilet training generally, Whiting and Child find the typical primitive society beginning this regimen at eighteen to thirty months. Our mothers start much earlier. They typically begin bowel training at eight to nine months and urinary training at eleven to twelve months. Whiting and Child report a range of times for beginning to teach defecation control running from one to five years. Only 2.1 per cent of our mothers began bowel training after a year and a half, and only 8.3 per cent of them started urinary training later than that age. Again it is evident that mothers in the Detroit area make demands for the socialization of body functions at an earlier date than do most primitives.

In the case of bowel training we also have some information about the way the parents handled the child who "didn't want to get on the toilet, or [who] was uncooperative and wanted to get off the toilet" (20). To begin with, 20.8 per cent of the mothers said they had had no such difficulties with their youngsters or that these difficulties lasted too short a time to be important. Some 3.9 per cent said they had such difficulties but did nothing about them, 24.4 per cent removed the child when he resisted, 18.7 per cent kept him on and tried to make the experience pleasant with diversions and encouragement, and 19.4 per cent, while keeping him on the toilet, accompanied this with close supervision, spankings, or other stern measures (21).

The differences in disciplinary technique connected with toilet training are not restricted to this single situation. We presented our respondents with the case of a child of ten years who had done something with which the mother was extremely upset or angered and asked what she would do. The distribution of answers appeared like this (22):

Punishment	Percentage
Stimulates guilt or shame	2.1
Scolds, threatens	25.1
Restricts behavior and withdraws privileges	44.2
Physical punishment	22.3
Would not punish	2.5
Do something; what, not ascertained	1.1

It seems that the general population of mothers is split into a group of only 22.3 per cent which spanks or slaps the child, one of just over 25 per cent which scolds and threatens, and a large proportion (44.2 per cent) which uses restriction of behavior (e.g., keeping in the house) and withdrawal of privileges (e.g., sending to bed early, cutting allowance). The choice often publicized in the newspapers between physical punishment and the absence of any punishment at all is hardly crucial for most of the population.

In previous chapters we have also discussed symbolic and direct rewards. We have seen that the entrepreneurial and bureaucratic populations in Detroit do not differ in their use of these methods. How does the total population stand in this respect? A question, similar in generality to that for punishment and also involving a ten-year-old child, was asked concerning reward (23). We got the following results:

Reward	Percentage
Psychic reward: satisfactions expected to come from within the child for a job well done	5.6
Other verbal praise	62.2
Special privileges or freedoms	5.6
Material reward: money, gifts, etc.	18.7
Demonstrations of love and affection	1.1
Some reward; what, not ascertained	0.7
No reward	3.2

Child Training in the Detroit Area **221**

And, what might be done by the child to deserve such punishments and such rewards? The examples our mothers gave are not hypothetical. The questions required them to think of their own child at age ten and to tell us what might have angered or pleased the parents a great deal. In their answers, then, we have some record of the problems and pleasures which children afford parents (24). The lists are familiar to any parent. The child who is considered too daring or who shows signs of straying from parental supervision and rules—these are the common problems. In looking over the examples of good behavior we find little emphasis on virtue and altruism in a general way and much weight given to the performance of those acts that signify integration into the common life of the family, in the operation of the home, and in formal school preparation for the child's own future activities. These acts also outweigh the child's avocational

Examples of Misbehavior	Percentage	Examples of Approved Behavior	Percentage
A *Personal behavior problems*		A *Personal achievements*	
Failure to do household chores right	1.4	Helps in household chores	28.3
Scholastic failures	1.4	School work	25.4
Bad personal habits and hygiene (e.g., child is dirty)	3.2	Skills in avocations	4.9
		Personal physical habits and hygiene	2.5
Endanger safety of self	10.6		
Stay out too late or go too far from home	14.5		
B *Social behavior problems*		B *Good social behavior*	
Disobeys parents	17.7	Obeys parents	3.2
Misbehaves with other adults	3.9	Shows good manners or skill in relations with	
Bad company, tough gang	0.4	others than parents	4.6
Destroys property	1.1	Kindness, virtue, etc.	0.7
Misbehaves with other children	6.7		
Endangers safety of others	1.1		
Stealing, truancy, etc.	5.3		
Lying, fibbing	1.4		
C *Other answers*		C *Other answers*	
Misbehavior (not further specified)	1.8	Can't think of anything	5.6
Never does wrong things	1.8	Doesn't know what to expect at ten	1.4
		Does good things but what not ascertained	3.9
		Never does anything good	0.4
D *Not ascertained*	25.1	D *Not ascertained*	19.1

skill as a source of pride and pleasure to most mothers. Cleaning his room or tending a younger sibling or getting good grades in the classroom are more important than the performance of a hobby or the beautifully timed and executed play in a game or on an instrument. These last are not the typical sources of the pleasure of most mothers in their children.

We must precede the findings for another of our questions (25) by repeating our earlier warning that it asks what mothers *should* do; not what they actually do.

Suppose a four-year-old child does something that makes his mother angry and excited. Should the mother punish the child right away while she is angry, or should the mother wait until she is more calm before she decides what to do?

Just over 60 per cent say the mother should wait (though 12.4 per cent of these say they often do not do so themselves). About 37 per cent favor immediate punishment (26). It seems improbable, and in other studies (27) we find suggestions that it is not the case, that over 60 per cent of Detroit mothers wait until their anger has passed before disciplining their children. The interesting thing here, then, is the prevalence of this procedure as an ideal pattern among our mothers.

The tenor of what most mothers do indicates their conviction that the child must feel and be responsible for his own acts. It will be remembered that we asked what the mother would do if a child of five or six years embarrassed her by his behavior at the table when guests were present (28). Despite their ideal pattern, about 80 per cent would scold or spank such a child or send him away from the table. Only 16 per cent would try to divert him, explain the problem to him, or ignore the difficulty (29). The mother is likely, then, to feel that the child must learn to be responsible for his conduct at this early age.

We have some other indications of the timing of demands for responsibility. These appear in the series of questions we asked about the age at which a child should be required to put away his own clothes, pick up his own toys, run errands to nearby stores, and dress himself. We chose these activities because all of them might be performed by a young child (30).

We find that the child between ages two and three has had some demands made for picking up his own toys in most families, that he is typically expected to do something about putting away his clothes and toward dressing himself between ages four and five, and that going to nearby stores will most often be required for the first time at about ages six or seven.

Percentages Required to Perform Certain Tasks at Specified Ages

Age in Years	Put away Clothes	Pick up Toys	Run Errands	Dress Self
0,1	2.8	14.2	*	*
2	12.4	30.7	*	1.1
3	15.5	23.3	4.2	10.6
4	19.8	17.7	8.1	31.1
5	20.5	7.1	20.8	27.6
6	10.6	3.2	23.0	13.1
7 or more	15.3	1.1	42.1	13.1
Never	0.0	0.0	0.4	0.0
Not ascertained	3.2	2.8	1.4	3.5

* Less than a tenth of 1 per cent.

We also have information on another aspect of teaching the child to be responsible. How long should the mother continue close supervision of the growing child? How long should she continue to keep track of what he is doing most of the time (31)? There are wide differences of opinion (32). Slightly over 21 per cent of our respondents would stop by the sixth year. Another 18.4 per cent feel that some time between the seventh and the twelfth year is appropriate. The median mother chooses the thirteenth or fourteenth year. A time between fifteen and seventeen years is chosen by 9.8 per cent. To us, it is surprising that 27.9 per cent say that close supervision should go on for seventeen years or more. This is certainly a large group to feel that the child will not be responsible for himself in late adolescence and young adulthood! It would be important to know if these answers represent the magnitude of the dangers and temptations of urban life as perceived by close to 30 per cent of the population or whether they stand for the inability of these mothers to train children to be capable of handling the experiences presented by their society.

Teaching children to be responsible requires knowledge as well as determination. There are many mothers who wish they knew more about the behavior of children or about methods for making youngsters obey—child dynamics or the control of children. We inquired whether there were any times in the last month when the mother wanted such information (33). Forty-one and a half per cent answered, "Never." Almost 15 per cent wanted it once or twice. Forty-one per cent would have liked it three or more times (34). Perhaps the most striking thing about these figures, at least to those accustomed to seeing parents who are highly self-conscious about their handling of children and greatly in doubt about the correctness of their methods, is the large number of mothers who reported no such feelings in the last month. We were less surprised to find that about two-thirds of those who wanted information were interested in learning how to control and direct the child, a third in understanding his expectations and needs. Most parents still find that their problems arise in adapting the child to their standards, not in fitting their behavior to his developing interests and desires.

Finally, we were interested in the number of families in which the parents disagreed about the standards and methods used in "making the child mind" (35). Of those families with a husband in the household, about four mothers reported disagreement to every five who said it did not occur. Although the disagreements cited vary greatly in character, the father was commonly reported as more rigid in the scope and height of the standards he sets and in the severity of the methods he prefers to use for their enforcement. We choose not to make too much of this result, however, since it is highly susceptible to distortion by mothers wanting to make a favorable impression on the interviewer.

. . . . . *SEXUAL EXPLORATION*

Children develop attitudes toward sexual behavior considerably before the thirteenth year, or before puberty. We have compared social classes and the integration settings with respect to methods of child care related to sexual exploration. Now we give the findings for the general population of the Detroit area.

We asked parents how they reacted when the young child explored his genitals or tried to follow his mother or father into the bathroom. Specifically, we asked if, at or before age five, he had touched his sex organs and whether the parents did something when this happened (36). About 58 per cent of the mothers said that their children had not touched their genitals. Some 34 per cent said their children had. The percentage of cases for which the information was not obtained due to interviewer forgetfulness or reticence seems high. It is 7.6 per cent.

Of those parents who said that the child had touched his sex organs, about the same number said they had done something about it as said they did nothing about it. Of the 17 per cent of the population who said it had happened and that they had done something, 5 per cent

Child Training in the Detroit Area **225**

diverted the child's attention, 7 per cent used gentle physical prevention or talked with the child, 2 per cent administered physical punishment, 2 per cent used shame or ridicule, and 1 per cent threatened or scolded.

If these figures may be believed, they show a level of tolerance that would not have been anticipated from many of the descriptions of American parents' attitudes toward sexual exploration. We are, of course, rather suspicious of the large number who say they never saw their child explore his genitals. Reports from clinical and hospital studies and from observations in nursery schools and kindergartens suggest that such exploration is almost, if not completely, universal.

Similarly, we are skeptical about the finding that one-third of the mothers with children old enough to have tried to accompany them to the bathroom say their youngsters never did so. Of those who said it had happened, about two out of five prevented the child's entrance and, of those permitting it, about one out of three admitted the youngster only with parents of the same sex (37).

. . . . . *INDEPENDENCE AND ASSUMING A SEX ROLE*

For this early period of childhood, we have already reported the use of a question about the mother's willingness to leave a three-year-old boy with a competent sitter for two afternoons a week. We considered this question as providing a kind of index to her feelings about the desirability of the child's not becoming too dependent on her and about her desire for independence from the child. Some 22.4 per cent of the mothers did not feel that it would be wise to leave a child with a sitter for so long a time (38). Most of these said that no one but the mother is really suitable to care for a three-year-old child. Only about one out of nine suggested that the child would not like being with strangers. Of the 75.6 per cent of our mothers who felt it would be all right to let such a sitter take care of the youngster, about a third emphasized that it would be good for the mother, providing her with relaxation, refreshment, new interests and perspectives, freedom for other responsibilities, greater appreciation for the child, or an increase in the child's appreciation for his mother. The considerable majority of the others emphasized the necessity that the child learn to be independent of the mother and to adapt to other people.

Another question involving this theme of independence asked if children should be put on their own as early as possible to work out their own problems (39). About 43 per cent of these mothers thought they should. Forty-six and a half per cent disagreed. Over 7 per cent could not make up their minds (40).

The parents of our children show considerable variation from issue to issue in the extent to which both mother and father undertake an activity or to which it is specialized in the hands of one or the other (41). There are, then, many different models of appropriate sex-related adult behavior available in this population.

Specialization of Adult Roles by Sex

Performed by	Paint Rooms in House	Get Up at Night with Children	Decide on Holidays and Celebrations	Punish Children	Choose Costly Purchases	Wash Dishes
Husband	43.5	3.8	8.9	5.3	12.7	1.9
Wife	12.7	60.3	11.3	29.9	10.3	70.1
Both	39.2	33.7	76.1	61.3	74.4	24.6
Neither	2.4	0.2	0.5	0.9	0.0	1.0
Not ascertained	2.2	2.1	3.1	2.6	2.6	2.4
Total	100.0	100.1	99.9	100.0	100.0	100.0

Such activities as punishing the children or choosing where to go and what to do on holidays or deciding about an expensive purchase are usually shared activities. Others, like painting rooms, getting up at night with children, or washing the dishes are primarily the work of one sex or the other. A large proportion of mothers answer "both" to each of these questions.

We also asked questions about tasks that might be done regularly by adolescent boys and girls (42).

Specialization of Adolescent Roles by Sex

Performed by	Shoveling Walks	Washing the Car	Dusting Furniture	Fixing Light Cords	Making Beds
Boy	64.2	64.2	1.3	52.5	0.7
Girl	0.0	0.3	64.5	0.7	52.2
Both	33.1	28.4	32.1	12.7	45.1
Neither	1.0	5.3	0.7	32.4	0.7
Not ascertained	1.7	1.7	1.3	1.7	1.3
Total	100.0	99.9	99.9	100.0	100.0

In these data, more clearly than in those for adults, it appears that the proportion of parents feeling that tasks may be performed equally by both sexes is about the same whether the behavior was traditionally associated, as in dusting furniture, with the female role, or as in the case of shoveling walks, with the male role in American society. It

Child Training in the Detroit Area **227**

is still true, however, that, in every case, a majority of mothers try to preserve the differences between the sexes. The boy or girl whose performance of these five activities does not follow traditional patterns can still expect censure in many homes.

. . . . . MOTHERS' EXPECTATIONS ABOUT THEIR CHILDREN'S ADULT ROLES

Most parents take into account the period when their children will be adults. Fathers and mothers develop expectations about that future period even when their youngsters are small. That future sets the upper bounds of the period of dependency in which the parents have very large and special commitments to the individual child. About 28 per cent of the mothers in the Detroit area think that their children will be able to assume the responsibilities of marriage by the age of twenty (43). But 21.5 per cent pick twenty-one years, the most popular choice, as the critical point, while 48.7 per cent feel that marriage must be postponed to a later date (44).

Another device for recording the upper boundary of the parents' expectation of having some large commitments to the child is the age at which he is thought old enough to be a good parent (45). In answering this question, only 18.4 per cent said twenty years and only 9.5 per cent said twenty-one. The remainder—the majority of parents —were divided equally into the 33.2 per cent favoring ages twenty-two through twenty-four and the same proportion preferring twenty-five years and over (46). Clearly these ages of marriage are far later than those permitted by the common law in many states and, of course, later than is customary in most non-literate societies. This practice of late marriage reflects the long-term tendency for the age of dependency and semidependency to be extended upward as training requirements in the occupational fields are enlarged. It is also interesting that a sizable proportion of the population, 33.2 per cent, thinks that the right age for parenthood is two or more years beyond that of marriage (47). Knowing whether this difference in age of marriage and parenthood represents a period in which the marriage is expected to "settle down" and be ready for children, or whether it is a last gay fling before the parents are "tied down" to a family, would help us understand much about the process by which people move from youth to adulthood in our society and the spirit in which they meet the coming of children. The pleasure of most mothers at the coming of new babies seems to favor the first rather than the second of these explanations.

The choice of an occupation is another part of the child's future to which most parents give a lot of thought. We asked for the mothers' best guess in the matter (48), giving them a choice between what are essentially head and hand occupations. Some 77.3 per cent said their children would have an office job. Almost 5 per cent would not venture a guess (49). Only 13.1 per cent thought the child would have a factory job. In a population of parents in which 65.3 per cent of the fathers have blue-collar jobs and 68.6 per cent of the grandfathers were similarly employed, this is a startling finding. It holds as true for mothers' guesses about boys as about girls. Clearly, there are hopes here which cannot possibly be realized, hopes that reflect the prestige and power of the white-collar position in American life. There must be powerful frustrations for blue-collar workers whose parents fostered in them the hope of having a different occupation.

We also asked the mothers in our sample about their feelings concerning the relative importance of a child's being able to use the kind of conceptual skills—skills of thinking and planning and administering —that usually accompany white-collar work as compared with the more motoric or muscular skills of exercising and of working with the hands commonly involved in blue-collar work. This is an item for which we are especially sorry we do not have comparable answers for fathers, since the emphasis on physical skills, particularly for boys, may be quite different for mothers and fathers. However, the mother's feelings are also important and, for the general population, reflect the importance of those talents that lead to the more powerful and prestigeful positions in American life. About 80 per cent of our respondents preferred to have their children involved in activities which teach them to think, plan, or organize, while 16.7 per cent favored activities which develop the child's physique or give him plenty of exercise (50).

We also have some information about the skills which mothers feel are needed in the world of work (51). With reference to office or clerical work and to work in factories, we asked, "if a person wants to make money on a job . . . , is it more important for him to have the right kind of personality, or to know how to do that kind of work well?" Only 11.1 per cent said personality was most important for monetary success in the factory, while 38.5 per cent chose it for the office situations (52). But in two-thirds of the cases saying "personality" for either setting, the reason given is that a man's personality affects his chance of getting and keeping a job. Our respondents did not see "the right kind of personality" as desirable because it brings one the personal gratifications of popularity. It is the employable personality, not the personality that brings interpersonal satisfactions, which is usually seen as required on the job.

And what of these parents' views of life's gratifications? It should not be thought, as some novelists of this century like to believe, that modern parents are robots, shaped only for the desk or lathe, and little better than their pencils or machines. Their personal interests are not stifled. They do not advocate that children stifle theirs.

We asked each mother in our sample whether she would encourage her child to follow his own interests or those of others, assuming that both were equally worthwhile (53). We also asked her to assume that, if he followed his own desires, he would have little time to spend with other children. Just over 60 per cent of the mothers said they would encourage the child to do what he liked. Only 36.5 per cent said that they would try to get him to go along with others' wishes (54). Most of the mothers in this minority made their choice on the grounds that the child does not know his long-term advantage, that he will want friends and the joy and help they provide, and that he will take pleasure in being able to handle people with ease.

Further, most of these mothers are able to enjoy life's pleasures as they come. Present gratification need not always be postponed in order to prepare for the future. We find that 56.9 per cent of the mothers chose their preferred leisure activities for the inherent gratification those activities offer. Another 10.6 per cent said that the gratifications they got from leisure were both immediate and longer-term benefits. Only 10.3 per cent chose their leisure preferences because they were sound investments for future gains (55).

Finally, a mother's children play a vital part in her future happiness. Unless our mothers were grossly unable to report their real feelings, there is clear evidence that the greater part of them would feel real regret if, after the child was grown, they were unable to see him (56). Seventy-two per cent would be very lonely and upset. About 15 per cent would be unhappy, but feel they would adjust to the situation. Five per cent said the separation would not make much difference (57). The emotional investment of mothers in their children is obvious when pointed out, but it is sometimes forgotten in an emphasis on the dependence of the child on the parent.

..... CONCLUSION

This composite picture of Detroit's families is not easily summarized. With rare exceptions, it reveals a considerable range of methods for rearing youngsters and of attitudes toward them. Of course, that very range of practices provokes the growth of knowledge, for it stands as a reminder that the social world is always richer in its complexity than our schemes and explanations suggest. We have offered these findings with the hope that they will stimulate work which will enlarge the scope of our understanding.

NOTES

[1] The percentage not ascertained is 1.9.

[2] See Items 4, 5, and 6.

[3] The percentage not ascertained is 2.7.

[4] See Items 5e and 6c.

[5] See Item 6b.

[6] John W. M. Whiting and Irvin L. Child, *Child Training and Personality, A Cross-Cultural Study* (New Haven: Yale University Press, 1953).

[7] For a more complete description of the nature, coverage, and uses of these files, see George P. Murdock, "Feasibility and Implementation of Comparative Community Research with Special Reference to the Human Relations Area Files," *American Sociological Review*, 15 (December, 1950), 713–720.

[8] Whiting and Child, *op. cit.*, 69.

[9] *Ibid.*, 70–71.

[10] See, for example: Sigmund Freud, *Three Contributions to the Theory of Sex* (A. A. Brill, trans., New York: Nervous and Mental Disease Publishing Co., 1920).

[11] For a recent study of this topic and a bibliography of pertinent experiments, see: Theodore H. and Lili R. Blau, "The Sucking Reflex: The Effects of Long Feeding vs. Short Feeding on the Behavior of a Human Infant," *The Journal of Abnormal and Social Psychology*, 51 (July, 1955), 123–125.

[12] See Item 2.

[13] The answers of another 1.7 per cent were not ascertained.

[14] Seventeen per cent of the mothers who said "Yes" did not tell the interviewer what methods they used.

[15] See Item 14. Responses from 2.5 per cent of the sample were not ascertained.

[16] See Item 16. Some 3.9 per cent of the sample did not provide a response to this item. Another 9.2 per cent had not yet completed bowel training.

[17] See Item 17. The percentage of responses not ascertained is 5.6. Almost 12 per cent of the mothers had not yet completed urinary training.

[18] See Item 18. Urinary control was neither begun nor completed by 25.4 per cent of the respondents. Responses were not obtained from 3.9 per cent of them.

[19] Whiting and Child, *op. cit.*, 74.

[20] See Item 15.

[21] The item was not applicable for 6.7 per cent of the mothers since they had not begun toilet training the child. In another 5.3 per cent of the cases, the response of the mother was not ascertained.

[22] About 1 per cent of the cases were those in which a response to this question was not ascertained.

[23] See Item 19. In some 2.9 per cent of the cases no response was ascertained for this item.

[24] See Items 19a and 20a.

[25] See Item 21.

[26] In 2.1 per cent of the cases a response was not ascertained. An additional 0.7 per cent of the mothers say they never punish the child and never become angry.

[27] See Daniel R. Miller and Guy E. Swanson, *Inner Conflict and Defense.* To be published by Henry Holt and Co. in 1958.

[28] See Item 32.

[29] In 3.6 per cent of the cases, the mother's response was not ascertained.

[30] See Items 13, 13a, 13b, 13c, and 13d.

[31] See Item 22.

[32] The mother's response was not ascertained for 6.0 per cent of the cases.

[33] See Items 24, 24a, and 24b.

[34] Another 5.5 per cent said, "Sometimes," while 2.7 per cent said, "Never," but indicated that they regularly read books and articles on child care. The responses of another 2.7 per cent were not ascertained.

[35] See Item 23.

[36] See Items 7 and 7a.

[37] See Items 8 and 8a.

[38] See Items 9 and 9a. In 2.0 per cent of the cases, the mother's response was not ascertained.

[39] See Item 10.

[40] In 3.3 per cent of the cases, a response was not ascertained.

[41] See Items 35, 35a, 35b, 35c, 35d, 35e, and 35f.

[42] See Items 11, 11a, 11b, 11c, 11d, and 11e.

[43] See Item 28. It is of interest that the median age at which American men get married was 22.6 years in 1951. The median age, at marriage, of American females was 20.4 years. These figures are taken from: United States Bureau of the Census, *Current Population Reports, Population Characteristics,* Series P-20, No. 38, April 29, 1952, 3.

[44] The mother's response was not ascertained in 1.5 per cent of the cases.

[45] See Item 29.

[46] The mother's response was not ascertained in 5.6 per cent of the cases.

[47] An additional 4.2 per cent placed the age of parenthood *before* the age of marriage while, in 6.7 per cent of the cases, no response was ascertained.

[48] See Item 27.

[49] In 4.8 per cent of the cases, the mother's response was not ascertained.

[50] See Items 12, 12a, and 12b. Responses for 4.0 per cent of the cases were not ascertained.

[51] See Items 25, 25a, 25b, 26, 26a, and 26b.

[52] In the office situation, 4.7 per cent gave indecisive answers as did 3.3 per cent in the factory situation. The respective percentages of cases for which a response was not ascertained are 0.9 and 1.2.

[53] See Item 31.

[54] Responses for 2.4 per cent of the cases were not ascertained.

[55] See Items 33 and 33a. Another 8.4 per cent said they wanted to do the things they chose for leisure pursuits because they did not get to do them now; 3.1 per cent gave miscellaneous reasons. Responses were not ascertained for 10.6 per cent of the cases.

[56] See Item 34.

[57] Responses were not ascertained for 3.3 per cent of the cases.

CONCLUSION: AGAIN A NEW GENERATION . . . .

We have spoken of society and of children. We close with reflections about some problems of parents.

What answer can be given the parent who asks, "But what does it all mean for me? What is the best way to raise a child?" In 1930 the editors of a distinguished symposium on "The Intimate Problems of Modern Parents and Children" could reply (1):

> For the first time in the history of human society, the child is being honored as a personality, having a mind and body and intimate life of its own that adults must learn to respect. It is difficult to exaggerate the revolutionary character of this discovery of the child's personality. All our faith in a new society—more humanistic than any of old, more creative and joyous and inspiring—is linked to this newfound realization of *the radiant potentialities of the child's mind (and body!)* when bullying and repression and dishonest adult ethics shall have vanished from the school and the home—and society at large.

The entrepreneurial society in America was long tempered with hope. There were frontiers to exploit. There were ploughboys who really did become President. Friends and neighbors did find their fortunes in the expanding economy and political freedom of a new social world. This hope was a trouble and a spreading infection to established orders. Lyman Beecher (2), then in full confidence of his eighteenth century New England Calvinism was alarmed to find, on returning to his pastorate from a short trip:

> Nearly a dozen persons, children and youth, had in my absence begun to hope [that they could influence God and assure themselves a future in Heaven]. I felt alarmed. . . . A few, no doubt, through excessive ignorance, mistook their first impressions for religion, and began to rejoice in safety, and not in God. . . .

Men were free from many traditions, free from much effective supervision of their lives. An early response to this freedom was loneliness. But, from opportunities to "live one's own life" came new delights and a spirit of individual pride and worth and enjoyment. The progressive education movement celebrated this free and lifting progress of the individual by calling for methods of teaching that would encourage each child to grow and create. This emphasis on the free individual was the spirit of the psychological advice of the early 1900's. The individual, supreme in his uniqueness, was the thing to comprehend. The child was like the doctor's patient, an individual to be diagnosed separately and dealt with by methods best suited to his particular temper and interests. "The clinic and the class room are becoming indistinguishable" (3). By 1941, a prominent psychoanalyst, Erich Fromm, was writing of man as terrified by an unbounded future and interpreting the sullen Fascist movements of the 1920's and 1930's as massive attempts to "escape from freedom" (4).

A comprehensive history of child care is yet to be written (5), but it certainly will show that the "best" way to raise a child is infinitely complicated by the rate of change in modern society. In a very real sense, each generation of Americans has come to a new world and has lived to see much of it outmoded. Child training is always a problem in such a society because it always occurs under changing conditions. Like its environment it is in flux. There has always been a new generation—new in its problems and skills, and tastes and theoretical vogues. It is unlikely that this changing will end in our time. The state of cold war that transforms many traditions to those more compatible with a nation ever under arms, ever watchful, ever concerned about its strength and resilience and solidarity, cannot fail to shape the training of children. Whether we make history or adapt to it, we are always in and of it, and an understanding of behavior cannot escape the conditions of time and place in which it appears.

The psychological therapist, because he comes to know a wide range of ways in which children can be treated, is better able than many laymen to see any one of these methods of child training as viable. He can consider which techniques of child care will be most suitable for producing a child who can fit into the particular social world in which that youngster must live and yet not be overwhelmed by it. Such a therapist, knowing that the way he trains his own children is *only one* among many methods, is partly freed from insisting on the less essential details of rules and discipline if the child resists. Similarly, if we know that bureaucratization, not some immutable natural law, is what creates our concern that children be able easily to make numerous friendships, we will be more tolerant of a child's desire to spend some of his time alone.

All these statements illustrate a general point. If men, knowledgeable about the problems and opportunities within which they live, can see that the way of life they develop is a means to solving *particular* problems, not *all* problems, they may find themselves freed from excessive restraints and pressures. Then they may be able to grant their children a similar freedom. If, through an appreciation of social history, men can transcend their time, there is a greater possibility that they can use their experiences for their own advantage instead of being completely shaped by them. Perhaps, then, from the vantage of the fuller scope of men's experience they can exploit their inheritance as history's heirs. And this possible development is a very special responsibility for the future research programs of the sciences of human behavior.

NOTES

[1] Victor F. Calverton and Samuel D. Schmalhausen (eds.), *The New Generation: The Intimate Problems of Modern Parents and Children* (New York: The Macaulay Co., 1930), 11–12.

[2] Quoted in Constance M. Rourke, *Trumpets of Jubilee* (New York: Harcourt, Brace & Co., 1927), 22.

[3] Calverton and Schmalhausen, *op. cit.*, 13.

[4] Erich Fromm, *Escape from Freedom* (New York: Farrar and Rinehart, 1941).

[5] One of the few attempts is the now outdated but still valuable work of George H. Payne, *The Child in Human Progress* (New York: G. P. Putnam's Sons, 1916).

APPENDICES . . . .

D ET AILED TABLES

. . . .

Table AI–1

FINDINGS FROM THE USE OF THE INTERNALIZATION INDICES

Social Position	Items													
	3		5c, 5d, 6b		5e, 6c		14		17		19		20	
	a	b	c	d	e	f	g	h	i	j	k	l	m	n
Entrepreneurial														
Upper middle	9	0	4	1	6	2	13	6	7	11	17	3	17	2
Lower middle	27	9	17	10	16	12	23	8	17	15	22	7	28	2
Upper lower	26	11	24	11	15	20	15	12	12	12	19	8	18	8
Lower lower	27	18	21	19	18	20	12	12	10	11	19	5	19	7
Bureaucratic														
Upper middle	8	10	7	3	4	12	9	5	3	11	12	3	11	3
Lower middle	9	15	12	8	10	11	19	14	8	22	23	9	22	10
Upper lower	23	12	20	7	12	20	17	17	12	19	28	10	30	7
Lower lower	20	7	15	11	11	16	13	21	7	23	28	9	26	13

a. Give delayed attention to crying baby or give no attention.
b. Give immediate attention to crying baby.
c. Wean the baby by the end of twelve months.
d. Wean the baby later than twelve months.
e. Feed the baby on a schedule.
f. Feed the baby on demand.
g. Begin bowel training before the baby is ten months old.
h. Begin bowel training at or after the baby is ten months old.
i. Begin urinary training before the baby is eleven months old.
j. Begin urinary training at or after the baby is eleven months old.
k. Use symbolic rewards.
l. Use direct rewards.
m. Use symbolic punishments.
n. Use direct (physical) punishments.

Table AI–2

FINDINGS FROM THE USE OF THE ACTIVITY INDICES

Social Position	Items 2		2a		2b		7		7a		7	
	a	b	c	d	e	f	g	h	i	j	k	l
Entrepreneurial												
Upper middle	6	3	1	1	0	0	7	1	1	0	0	1
Lower middle	22	14	7	7	4	0	24	10	9	0	2	3
Upper lower	27	12	3	9	0	0	26	10	9	0	2	6
Lower lower	31	15	7	8	4	2	29	11	11	0	1	6
Bureaucratic												
Upper middle	8	10	1	9	0	1	8	7	2	3	0	2
Lower middle	15	10	5	5	1	4	8	15	7	6	1	6
Upper lower	21	14	8	6	6	2	24	9	5	4	0	5
Lower lower	18	11	5	6	5	0	15	13	6	7	0	6

a. Say the child never sucked parts of his body.

b. Say the child sucked parts of his body.

c. Say the parents felt it necessary to do something about the child sucking his body (if he did so).

d. Say the parents did not feel it necessary to do something about the child sucking his body (if he did so).

e. Use harsh means (mechanical and chemical) to stop the child who sucked his body.

f. Did not use harsh means to stop the child who sucked his body.

g. Say the child did not touch his sex organs.

h. Say the child did touch his sex organs.

i. Say the parents felt it necessary to do something when the child touched his sex organs.

j. Say the parents did not feel it necessary to do something when the child touched his sex organs.

k. Use harsh means (spankings, threats) if they did something when the child touched his sex organs.

l. Did not use harsh means if they did something when the child touched his sex organs.

Items											
9a		10		11a, b, d		11c, e		35a		35b, f	
m	n	o	p	q 2-3*	r 0-1*	s 2*	t 0-1*	u 1*	v 0*	w 2*	x 0-1*
9	0	4	3	7	2	3	6	13	15	18	10
18	12	21	12	25	11	20	16	30	43	35	38
15	13	14	23	29	10	22	17	26	40	39	28
19	10	18	24	27	15	20	23	30	41	36	35
5	10	6	11	8	9	5	13	18	16	11	23
12	7	7	16	11	10	12	11	20	35	29	26
16	11	17	13	23	12	12	23	36	39	33	42
14	8	9	16	18	10	14	15	37	34	32	38

m. Feel it is good to leave a child at home frequently with a competent woman while the mother shops or visits because the mother benefits.

n. Feel it is good to leave a child at home frequently with a competent woman while the mother shops or visits because the child benefits.

o. Agree that a child should be on his own as soon as possible to solve his own problems.

p. Do not agree that a child should be on his own as soon as possible to solve his own problems.

q. Feel that only males should perform activities traditionally associated with their sex among adolescents.

r. Feel that others than males may perform activities traditionally associated with males among adolescents.

s. Feel that only females should perform activities traditionally associated with their sex among adolescents.

t. Feel that others than females may perform activities traditionally associated with females among adolescents.

u. Feel that only males should perform activities traditionally associated with their sex among adults.

v. Feel that others than males may perform activities traditionally associated with males among adults.

w. Feel that only females should perform activities traditionally associated with their sex among adults.

x. Feel that others than females may perform activities traditionally associated with females among adults.

* The number of preferences given by respondents for having tasks performed by a person in the conventional sex role.

PREDICTED DIFFERENCES IN CHILD TRAINING BY SOCIAL CLASS
WITHIN THE ENTREPRENEURIAL SETTING

Item Number	Practices	χ^2	df^*	$p\dagger$
	I. Internalization Indices			
3	Give immediate attention to crying baby. Give delayed attention or none.	8.90	3	+ <.03
5c, 6b	Wean the baby after twelve months. Wean the baby at or by twelve months.	.30	1	<.70
5e, 6c	Feed the baby on demand. Feed the baby on a schedule.	2.44	1	+ <.10
14	Begin bowel training after nine months. Begin bowel training at or before nine months.	3.91	1	+ <.03
17	Begin urinary training after ten months. Begin urinary training at or before ten months.	.01	1	<.95
19, 19a	Use direct rewards. Use symbolic rewards.	.36	1	<.70
20, 20a	Use direct punishments. Use symbolic punishments.	7.80	3	+ <.05
	II. Activity Indices			
2	Say child sucked body. Say child did not suck body.	.48	1	0 <.50
2a	Felt it unnecessary to stop child who sucked body. Felt it necessary to stop child who sucked body.	.69	1	+ <.50
2b	Used mild means to stop child who sucked body. Used harsh means to stop child who sucked body.	.23	1	<.70
7	Say child touched his sex organs. Say child did not touch his sex organs.	.28	1	<.70
7a	Felt it unnecessary to stop child who touched sex organs. Felt it necessary to stop child who touched sex organs.	‡	1	1.00

Item Number	Practices	χ^2	df*	p†
	II. Activity Indices—(continued)			
7b	Used mild means to stop child who touched sex organs.			
	Used harsh means to stop child who touched sex organs.	.01	1	<.95
9a	Felt it good to leave child frequently with competent sitter because child benefits.			
	Felt it good to leave child frequently with competent sitter because mother benefits.	9.53	3	+ <.03
10	Child should not be on own as soon as possible to solve own problems.			
	Child should be on own as soon as possible to solve own problems.	5.15	1	+ <.03
11, a, b, c, d, e	Among adolescent males, traditional sex specialization need not continue.			
	Among adolescent males, traditional sex specialization should continue.	.05	1	<.90
	Among adolescent females, traditional sex specialization need not continue.			
	Among adolescent females, traditional sex specialization should continue.	‡	1	<.98
35, a, b, c, d, e, f	Among adult males, traditional sex specialization need not continue.			
	Among adult males, traditional sex specialization should continue.	.07	1	<.80
	Among adult females, traditional sex specialization need not continue.			
	Among adult females, traditional sex specialization should continue.	.86	1	0 <.50

* If the degrees of freedom (df) are three, the probability applies to the differences among the four social classes. If it is one, the p value applies to the difference between all middle classes versus all lower classes. The significance of the differences among the four social classes was computed for each questionnaire item. If and only if, that difference was not significant, the p value was calculated for a comparison of all middle-class respondents as against all lower-class respondents.

† When a distribution is in the predicted direction, p values are based on one tail of the probability distribution.

‡ χ^2 is less than .01.

Table Al-3b

PREDICTED DIFFERENCES IN CHILD TRAINING BY SOCIAL CLASS WITHIN THE ENTREPRENEURIAL SETTING

Item Number	Practices	Upper Middle	Lower Middle	Upper Lower	Lower Lower	x^2	df*	p†
	III. Individual Responsibility Indices							
13a	Require child to put away own clothes after four years old. Require at four years or younger.	13 / 7	13 / 19	10 / 18	16 / 11	6.12	3	0 < .20
13b	Require child to pick up own toys after two years old. Require at two years or younger.	11 / 8	18 / 15	15 / 13	15 / 12	.02	1	< .90
13c	Require child to run errands after six years old. Require at six years or younger.	9 / 10	16 / 17	11 / 18	11 / 15	.71	1	0 < .50
13d	Require child to dress self completely after four years old. Require at four years or younger.	13 / 7	15 / 17	12 / 16	16 / 12	.16	1	< .70
20a	Child's misdeeds threaten harm to him. Misdeeds threaten harm or offense to others.	10 / 7	14 / 12	4 / 13	5 / 11	6.72	3	+ < .05
22	Stop close supervision after twelve years old. Stop at twelve years or younger.	7 / 11	12 / 12	13 / 10	20 / 6	7.41	3	+ < .05
28	Good spouse after twenty-one years old. Good spouse at twenty-one years or younger.	17 / 12	34 / 35	27 / 40	32 / 42	2.42	1	+ < .10
29	Good parent after twenty-three years old. Good parent at twenty-three years or younger.	7 / 12	12 / 19	8 / 19	15 / 13	.16	1	< .70

* If the degrees of freedom (df) are three, the probability applies to the differences among the four social classes. If it is one, the p value applies to the difference between all middle classes versus all lower classes. The significance of the differences among the four social classes was computed for each questionnaire item. If and only if, that difference was not significant, the p value was calculated for a comparison of all middle-class respondents as against all lower-class respondents.

† When a distribution is in the predicted direction, p values are based on one tail of the probability distribution.

Table Al-4

FINDINGS FROM THE USE OF THE INDICES OF MORAL RELATIONS

Social Position	13a		13b		13c		13d		19		20		21		22	
	a	b	c	d	e	f	g	h	i	j	k	l	m	n	o	p
Entrepreneurial middle class																
Protestant	13	3	11	5	9	6	11	4	13	3	16	0	7	9	8	6
Roman Catholic	3	5	4	4	4	4	1	7	12	5	14	3	4	15	11	5
Entrepreneurial lower class																
Protestant	10	7	9	8	14	3	9	8	17	7	19	5	14	11	5	17
Roman Catholic	2	1	3	0	0	3	3	0	6	3	3	7	2	9	3	5
Bureaucratic middle class																
Protestant	12	4	6	11	13	4	10	7	15	2	11	4	4	13	12	2
Roman Catholic	13	5	9	10	8	11	11	8	14	5	12	7	10	9	7	8
Bureaucratic lower class																
Protestant	11	9	12	8	8	12	8	12	16	4	15	2	6	14	11	8
Roman Catholic	11	17	15	13	18	10	11	17	18	9	20	8	11	17	12	16

a. Require child to put away clothes before age five.
b. Require child to put away clothes at or after age five.
c. Require child to pick up own toys before age three.
d. Require child to pick up own toys at or after age three.
e. Require child to run errands to nearby store before age seven.
f. Require child to run errands to nearby store at or after age seven.
g. Require child to dress self before age five.
h. Require child to dress self at or after age five.

i. Use symbolic rewards.
j. Use direct rewards.
k. Use symbolic punishments.
l. Use direct punishments.
m. Punish offenses at once instead of waiting until calm.
n. Wait until calm before punishing offenses.
o. Supervise child closely until the end of the twelfth year.
p. Supervise child closely beyond the end of the twelfth year.

Table AI–5

CUMULATIVE SCORES ON INTERNALIZATION ITEMS

		Entrepreneurial			Bureaucratic		
Schedule Form	Cumulative Score	Upper Middles	Lower Middles	Total Middles	Upper Middles	Lower Middles	Total Middles
A	2–3	5	17	22	6	7	13
A	0–1	0	6	6	4	11	15
B	3–4	10	18	28	5	10	15
B	0–2	7	6	13	8	18	26

Table AI–6

PERCENTAGE OF RESPONDENTS REPORTING SELECTED CHARACTERISTICS
BY SOCIAL CLASS AND INTEGRATION SETTING

	Social Position			
	Middle Class		Lower Class	
Selected Characteristics	Entrepreneurial $N = 99$	Bureaucratic $N = 86$	Entrepreneurial $N = 139$	Bureaucratic $N = 145$
Age of Child				
18 years	1	1	0	0
16–17	9	5	11	6
14–15	9	6	12	7
12–13	5	6	6	6
10–11	8	6	8	11
8–9	12	7	12	10
6–7	11	7	7	9
4–5	13	21	10	15
2–3	11	19	14	14
12–23 months	11	13	11	8
0–11 months	8	8	7	14
Total	98	99	98	100

| | Social Position | | | |
| | Middle Class | | Lower Class | |
Selected Characteristics	Entrepre-neurial N = 99	Bureau-cratic N = 86	Entrepre-neurial N = 139	Bureau-cratic N = 145
Sex of Child				
Male	48	59	44	46
Female	51	41	56	54
Total	99	100	100	100
Ordinal Position of Child about Whom Interview Was Taken				
4th or more	11	5	11	6
3rd	11	12	10	11
2nd	30	24	33	22
1st	18	24	22	26
Only child	24	33	21	29
No answer	5	2	3	5
Total	99	100	100	99
Age of Husband				
50 or over	16	8	13	2
45–49	12	12	12	10
40–44	14	7	16	14
35–39	20	24	14	22
30–34	18	22	22	20
26–29	15	19	20	21
21–25	4	7	4	10
Total	99	99	101	99
Income of Head of Family				
$6000 or more	44	35	14	17
$5000–$5999	17	13	23	21
$4000–$4999	17	30	20	32
$3999 or less	16	14	39	27
No answer	5	7	4	2
Total	99	99	100	99

Selected Characteristics	Social Position			
	Middle Class		Lower Class	
	Entrepre- neurial $N = 99$	Bureau- cratic $N = 86$	Entrepre- neurial $N = 139$	Bureau- cratic $N = 145$

Occupation of Husband's Father				
Professional, technical, and kindred	6	8	2	4
Farmers and farm managers	20	2	40	7
Managers, officials, and proprietors, except farm	23	25	17	12
Clerical, sales, and kindred	5	6	1	5
Craftsmen, foremen, and kindred	5	25	18	28
Operatives and kindred	21	22	16	28
Private household workers, service workers	12	4	3	5
Farm laborers and foreman	3	0	0	1
Laborers, except farm and mining	0	4	1	7
Not in labor force	3	0	0	0
No answer	1	4	1	2
Total	99	100	99	99

Years of School Wife Completed				
13 or more	17	24	1	4
12	49	49	28	38
9–11	27	23	29	41
8 or less	6	4	40	16
No answer	0	0	2	0
Total	99	100	100	99

Family's Residence Status				
Own home	81	76	69	65
Rent home	18	24	31	35
Total	99	100	100	100

Selected Characteristics	Social Position			
	Middle Class		Lower Class	
	Entrepre-neurial N = 99	Bureau-cratic N = 86	Entrepre-neurial N = 139	Bureau-cratic N = 145
Family's Religious Preference				
Protestant	45	51	56	37
Roman Catholic	41	40	35	53
Other	10	4	4	1
No answer	3	6	4	8
Total	99	101	99	99
Original Nationality of Husband's Father's Family				
Northwestern Europe	43	42	43	38
Central Europe	39	40	34	41
Eastern Europe	3	5	3	6
Southern Europe	5	4	5	6
Canada	2	0	1	1
Other	6	6	7	6
No answer	1	4	6	1
Total	99	101	99	99
Age of Wife				
50 or over	7	5	7	1
45–49	10	10	9	4
40–44	20	11	14	8
35–39	13	14	15	21
30–34	23	26	21	19
26–29	15	18	18	26
21–25	11	16	16	20
Total	99	100	100	99

Selected Characteristics	Social Position			
	Middle Class		Lower Class	
	Entrepre-neurial N = 99	Bureau-cratic N = 86	Entrepre-neurial N = 139	Bureau-cratic N = 145
Population of Birthplace for Husbands Born in the United States and Not Born on Farms				
Detroit Area	59	53	49	55
50,000 or more	25	29	34	32
49,999 or less	16	18	17	13
Total	100	100	100	100
	N = 56	N = 83	N = 41	N = 140
Husband's Occupation				
Professional, technical, and kindred	14	34	1	0
Managers, officials, and pro-prietors	47	29	0	1
Clerical, sales, and kindred	27	26	0	1
Craftsmen, foremen, and kindred	1	0	48	49
Operatives and kindred	3	0	47	42
Private household workers, service workers	7	11	2	4
Laborers, except farm and mine	0	0	1	3
Total	99	100	99	100
Years of School Husband Completed				
13 or more	31	58	7	7
12	36	19	23	27
9–11	17	18	31	43
8 or less	15	5	39	23
No answer	0	0	0	0
Total	99	100	100	100

STATISTICAL PROCEDURES

The purpose of this appendix is to report four procedures in some detail: the selection of the sample of mothers interviewed, the construction of cumulative indices of child care, the estimation of the degree of association between various social positions and the techniques mothers use in rearing children, and methods of control used in Chapter Seven. We begin with a description of the sampling procedures (1).

251

In [Chapter Three] a brief description of the sample design has already been presented. The following is a somewhat more detailed statement of the sample design.

The sampling procedure employed for selecting dwelling units is technically called "three-stage area sampling." It is an "area sample" because the procedure involves the identification of dwelling units with area segments (blocks); the selection of the dwelling units is dependent on the selection of these segments. The first stage involves the selection of census tracts (known as primary sampling units) from among all the tracts in the Detroit Metropolitan Area. The second stage involves the selection of sample blocks from among all the blocks within the tracts selected in the first stage (the primary sampling areas). The third stage involves the selection of sample dwelling units among the dwelling units located in the sample blocks. This is a probability sample because the probability of selection of every dwelling unit is known: it is the product of the probabilities of selecting the tract, of selecting the block within the tract, and of selecting the dwelling unit within the block.

The basic sample rate for the study was one in 643. The sample was selected so that every private dwelling unit has approximately one chance in 643 of being selected.

The procedure for selection at each of the three stages is the widely used method known as systematic sampling. In the first stage of selection, all of the tracts in the Detroit Metropolitan Area were placed in a systematic order and a measure of size (based on population estimates) was assigned to each tract. Then a sampling interval (K) is applied after choosing a random starting number from one to K. The random start and every Kth number thereafter determine the selection of a particular primary sampling unit (tract, town, or township). By the same type of procedure, blocks are selected within each selected census tract and likewise dwelling units within the sample blocks. The census tracts in the sample were systematically selected by ordering geographically the "Administrative and Planning Areas" developed by Mr. James Norton for the United Community Services of Metropolitan Detroit (2). This means in fact a stratification of the sample by these "Administrative and Planning Areas." Of the 79 Administrative and Planning Areas, 65 are represented in our sample. Interviews were taken in 80 census tracts and in 282 different blocks.

. . . . . MEASURES OF SAMPLING ERROR

We have already pointed out in the introduction that apart from "reporting" errors, there are sampling errors that result from the fact that interviews were taken with a sample rather than with the entire population. The size of the sampling error can be estimated.

The sampling error measures the limits on either side of the obtained figures within which the true population value has a given probability of falling. It is customary to give as "the sampling error" a figure representing two standard errors; this represents the limits within which the true value will lie 95 out of 100 times.

Thus, the percentage of respondents reporting ownership of television sets in our sample is approximately 80 per cent. This figure is based on a sample of 1157. Entering Table AII–1 (the table of sampling errors) with a sample size of 1150 and a reported percentage around 80, yields a sampling error figure of 3 per cent. Hence, the expectation is that a similar survey of the entire population would give a result between 77 and 83 per cent. Such expectations would be

Table AII–1

SAMPLING ERRORS FOR PERCENTAGES BASED ON
DIFFERENT SIZED GROUPS

Sample Size	Reported Percentage Around			
	5 or 95	10 or 90	20 or 80	50
50			12	14
75		7	10	12
100		6	8	10
150	4	5	7	9
175	4	5	7	8
200	4	5	6	8
250	3	4	6	7
300	3	4	5	7
400	3	4	5	6
500	3	3	4	5
582	2	3	4	5
1150	2	3	3	4
1300	2	3	3	4
2550	2	2	3	4

borne out in the long run 19 times out of 20. Moreover, there are two chances out of three that the true value lies between 78.5 and 81.5 per

Appendix Two **253**

cent. That is, not only is the true value to be within one sampling error of the obtained value, but the chances are two out of three that it is within one-half the sampling error.

The sampling error varies somewhat for the different findings of the survey. Despite these differences, tables representing the approximate magnitudes of the sampling errors of the various estimated percentages will give a general picture of the degree of variability that should be attached to the estimates.

. . . . . *COMPARISON OF OUR SAMPLE RESULTS WITH INFORMATION FROM OTHER SOURCES*

One way of checking the general adequacy of our sample selection and interviewing is to compare our findings with those obtained from other sources where that is possible.

Since our survey was made not too long after the 1950 U. S. Census, it is possible to compare some of our findings with census data. Where comparisons are made with census data for the Detroit Metropolitan Area, it should be noted that the "Detroit Standard Metropolitan Area," as defined by the census, covers a somewhat larger area and population than our Detroit Metropolitan Area.

Table AII–2 shows that the Detroit Area Study data on number of persons per dwelling unit correspond very closely to those of the Census.

Table AII–2

NUMBER OF PERSONS IN DWELLING UNITS FOR THE DETROIT
METROPOLITAN AREA: COMPARISON OF FINDINGS OF U. S.
CENSUS (1950) AND DETROIT AREA STUDY: 1953

	Percentage of Dwelling Units	
Persons in Dwelling Units	1950 U. S. Census	Detroit Area Study: 1953
1 person	6	7
2 persons	28	28
3 persons	24	24
4 persons	20	22
5 persons	12	9
6 persons	6	5
7 or more persons	5	5
Total	100	100

Table AII–3 indicates a close correspondence between our findings and the U. S. Census report on home tenure, that is, the proportion of dwelling units owner-occupied and the proportion of renter-occupied.

Table AII–3

TENURE STATUS FOR OCCUPIED DWELLING UNITS FOR DETROIT AREA:
COMPARISON OF FINDINGS OF U. S. CENSUS (1950)
AND DETROIT AREA STUDY: 1953

	Percentage of Dwelling Units	
Tenure Status	1950 U. S. Census	Detroit Area Study: 1953
Owner occupied	65	65
Renter occupied	35	35
Total	100	100

The United States Census found that 16 per cent of the population of Detroit was non-white in 1950. This compares with a finding of 15 per cent non-white in the Detroit Area Study for 1953.

Table AII–4 shows a close correspondence of occupational distribution for the U. S. Census and the Detroit Area Study.

Table AII–4

MAJOR OCCUPATION GROUP FOR WORKERS* IN THE DETROIT AREA:
COMPARISON OF FINDINGS OF THE U. S. CENSUS (1950)
AND THE DETROIT AREA STUDY: 1953

	Percentage of Population	
Major Occupation Group	1950 U. S. Census	Detroit Area Study: 1953
Professional, technical, and kindred workers	9	9
Managers, officials, and proprietors	9	10
Clerical, sales, and kindred workers	22	18
Craftsmen, foremen, and kindred workers	19	20
Operatives and kindred workers	27	29
Service workers, including private household	9	9
Laborers	5	4
Not reported	1	1
Total	100	100

* The data from the U. S. Census are for employed persons 14 years of age or older. The data from the Detroit Area Study are for persons in the labor force, 21 years of age or older.

Appendix Two **255**

The preceding tables indicate that the sample results of the Detroit Area Study correspond closely with findings from other sources on a variety of characteristics. The comparisons shown are not selected to prove this point. They are similar to those made with other sources.

..... THE FORMATION AND RELIABILITY OF CUMULATIVE INDICES

Throughout this book we make important use of indices of some theme of child training—for example, of self-control. These indices represent the combination of responses made by mothers to several questions.

Several standard methods exist (3) for combining an individual's responses. We chose our method with a view to violating the fewest assumptions underlying such a combination of responses and as one that could be used with all of our indices. The latter point will now be elaborated.

If each of the items combined in an index is independent of the other items in the same index, a number of methods are available for combining those items. Such independence does appear in the case of the items comprising our Activity Index and the Internalization Index based on Schedule Form B. (These and the other indices are discussed below.) However, the items comprising the indices of Responsibility, of Moral Relations, and of the Internalization Index for Schedule Form A are not independent of one another. Table AII–5 presents those inter-item relations that reach the .10 level or beyond for these latter indices.

A second reason for using the method of combining items which appears here was the desire to obtain a result that would catch the interactions among items. Especially when items are related to each other to a slight but consistent degree and in a consistent direction, they may interact to comprise a respectably reliable and discriminating instrument. Such interaction appears to have occurred in all of our indices. The findings for the Internalization and Activity Indices where total index reliability and discrimination power are high, although inter-item relations are not significant, suggest that each of the items within an index reflects a different aspect of a particular behavior pattern instead of each mirroring the pattern in anything like its entirety.

The method we chose for combining responses to the items in an index is quite simple in nature. It may be illustrated with the items for the indication of internalization. We had already dichotomized the answers to each of the questions in our list of Internalization Indices so that, for every question, we could classify responses as leading to self-control or as not likely to produce that result. There are seven items in the Internalization Indices. Four of these, Items 14, 17, 19, and 20, were asked of the half of our sample of mothers who answered the questions on Schedule Form B. The remaining three groups of items (3, 5c and 5d and 6b, and 5e and 6c) were asked of the half of the respondents who were interviewed using Schedule Form A. What we did was to score each mother, in the sample who answered the questions on Schedule Form B, as showing evidence of using internalization training on four, three, two, one, or none of the Internalization Indices asked of them. In this way we obtained a cumulative score for each respondent. The same procedure was repeated for mothers who were asked the questions on Schedule Form A.

Here, and everywhere else that we used cumulative scores, the number of cases in our tables dropped. This happened because mothers who answered one question in a set of items, say the Internalization Indices, may have failed to answer other questions in the same set or

Table AII–5

INTER-ITEM RELATIONS

Index	Items	χ^2	df	p
Moral Relations Index and	13a and 13b	16.12	1	<.001
Responsibility Index	13a and 13c	4.41	1	<.05
	13a and 13d	13.71	1	<.001
	13b and 13d	5.84	1	<.02
	13c and 13d	11.58	1	<.001
	13b and 19	10.32	1	<.01
	13d and 19	6.36	1	<.02
	21 and 22	3.25	1	<.10

because they may have answered some questions in ways that could not be interpreted as leading to more or less self-control or to more or less of whatever it is that the set of items is believed to represent. A table using a cumulative index should be considered as showing the distribution of answers for mothers who responded to *all* of the items in the index in such a fashion that their responses could be considered as representing the theme believed common to those items.

As in the case of the Internalization Indices, the combining of items for other indices was complicated by our use of two schedule forms with random halves of the sample of mothers. Thus ten of the twelve groups of items listed in the Activity Indices (all but Item 35) had been asked of the same mothers—those responding to Schedule Form A. It is on the answers to these ten groups of items that the cumulative Activity scores are based. Of the eight Responsibility Indices, six (all but Items 28 and 29) were asked of mothers answering Schedule Form B. The cumulative Responsibility scores are computed from those six items. Fortunately, all eight of the Indices of Moral Relations were on the same form of the schedule, Form B. As a result, cumulative scores for these items could be computed for the entire set of eight.

How reliable are the cumulative scores for the four sets of indices? How stable are those scores when obtained repeatedly from the same natural phenomena? Even under ideal conditions only a rough answer could be obtained to such a question, and the conditions with which we worked are far from ideal (4). The closest we can come to estimating something of the reliability of these cumulative scores is to use the well-known odd-even procedure, correcting the resulting coefficients by the Spearman-Brown formula to estimate the reliability of the whole set of items used in a given index. Unfortunately, this method, while giving results influenced by the reliability of the items, also gives a result influenced by the extent to which the items in an index reflect the same or different underlying themes. These two influences cannot be separated in the coefficients produced.

Given these limitations, we can report the following odd-even reliability coefficients (corrected by the Spearman-Brown formula):

Internalization Indices (Schedule Form B)	$.296 \pm .075$
Activity Indices	$.387 \pm .072$
Responsibility Indices	$.498 \pm .086$
Indices of Moral Relations	$.641 \pm .136$

No reliability coefficient could be computed for the Internalization Indices for Schedule Form A since there were only three such items— a small and odd number. However, by the method used, all other indices show significant reliability coefficients.

Finally, we may ask whether these several cumulative indices are independent of one another. This can be answered only for indices that are on the same form of the interview schedule. Thus Internalization Indices appear on Schedule Forms A and B, but the cumulative indices for Responsibility and Moral Relations are only on Schedule Form B, while those for Activity are on Form A. The possible intercorrelations are shown below.

Internalization and Activity Indices	$.103 \pm .089$
Internalization and Responsibility Indices	$.106 \pm .167$
Internalization and Morality Indices	$.105 \pm .088$
Responsibility and Morality Indices	$.881 \pm .093$

We have said that certain themes in child care should be more characteristic of the older than of the newer middle classes, of entrepreneurial middles than of entrepreneurial lowers, and of Protestants than of Roman Catholics. Many of our predictions are supported by our findings at respectable levels of confidence. In addition to those findings, we sought to learn the degree of association between these several social positions and the techniques of rearing youngsters that we predicted would be related to them (5).

For this purpose we have examined the correlations of the cumulative indices of Internalization, Activity, Responsibility, and Moral Relations with the relevant social positions. By working with the answers of mothers obtaining scores on these cumulative indices, we are examining those of our respondents who show the greatest evidence of concern with the themes of child care that we feel are reflected in each of the indices. It should follow from our theory that among these mothers, if among any, there would be a substantial association beween methods of child care and their positions in society.

There are no very satisfactory measures of association for data such as ours which do not meet assumptions of continuity and normality of distribution. Many of the problems and possibilities are reviewed in a recent article by Goodman and Kruskal (6). As a conservative method of estimating association in data like ours, we present in Table AII–6, the values obtained by computing Cramér's measure (7) for our results. This statistic provides a measure of association that can meet the familiar assumptions required either for a coefficient of contingency (C) or for Tschuprow's coefficient (T). However, it is superior to C or T since "it lies between 0 and 1 and actually attains both end points appropriately."

In column F of Table AII–6, we report the values of Pearsonian r's computed from the same data. Although our materials meet fewer of the assumptions required for the use of this statistic than for the computation of Cramér's measure, the comparison of the two may help the reader gage the degree of association present between the several social positions and methods of child care.

In column G of Table AII–6 are the Coefficients of Determination (r^2). Even though they must be recognized as the crudest kinds of estimate, they do suggest that, using the social positions, we have managed to account for no more than 15 per cent of the variance in any of our cumulative indices and for considerably less in most cases. Their values are very similar to those for Cramér's coefficient.

Such an estimate points to the large amount of work required before we shall be able to predict any sizable amount of the variations in child care found among our respondents. But, in what direction should that work move? Is the problem one of having invalid indices of social position or child training? Is it a matter of sharpening and modifying our theory? Is it, in considerable degree, a problem of improving the reliability of the indices? Only on this last point do we have data from our present study that enable an estimate, however gross.

Since we do have coefficients of reliability for each of our indices of child rearing and since it probably is reasonable to suppose that the reliability of our observations of the social positions is very high (we shall arbitrarily estimate it at 1.00), it is possible to estimate the maximum correlation that could be obtained between the social positions and the methods of child care given observations with the degree of reliability of those we employed. Those maximum correlations are found in column E of Table AII–6. When the actual Pearsonian correlations found between the social positions and techniques of rearing youngsters are divided by these estimated maximum correlations, the dividend that results is an estimate of the percentage of that maximum potential relation which was actually obtained (8). This is the familiar correction for attenuation of obtained Pearsonian coefficients of correlation. The corrected coefficients appear in column H of Table AII–6.

Given the limitations on computing Pearsonian coefficients for these data and the equally limited validity of our reliability coefficients, the absolute numbers in these corrected coefficients should not be taken too seriously. Perhaps the major point they suggest is that the low reliability of our indices of child care may be a major source of the low correlations we obtain between those indices and the social positions. When that low reliability is taken into account, these corrected coefficients imply that there may be a substantial relation between many of the social positions and the indices of child rearing.

. . . . . *THE APPLICATION OF CONTROLS IN CHAPTER
SEVEN*

Limitations of space make it impossible to present detailed tables which show the results of applying controls even to those items on

Table AII–6

AMOUNT OF VARIANCE FOR WHICH THE CUMULATIVE INDICES ACCOUNT

Cumulative Scores for: (A)	Social Positions* (B)	Reliability of Cumulative Scores† (C)	Cramér's Coefficient (D)	$\sqrt{C} \times \sqrt{1.000}$ (E)	r_{AB} (F)	r_{AB}^2 (G)	$r_{\infty\infty}$ (H)
Internalization (Schedule Form A)	EMC vs. BMC	‡	.11		.374 ± .135	.091	‡
Internalization (Schedule Form B)	EMC vs. BMC	.296 ± .075	.10	.544	.381 ± .110	.145	.700
Activity	EMC vs. BMC	.387 ± .072	.06	.622	.347 ± .129	.120	.558
Internalization (Schedule Form A)	EMC vs. MLC	‡	.02		.145 ± .102	.021	‡
Internalization (Schedule Form B)	EMC vs. MLC	.296 ± .075	.05	.544	.175 ± .113	.031	.237
Activity	EMC vs. MLC	.387 ± .072	.01	.622	.061 ± .103	.004	.099
Responsibility	EMC vs. MLC	.498 ± .086	.02	.706	.138 ± .130	.020	.200
Moral Relations	PMC vs. RCMC	.641 ± .136	.26	.800	.367 ± .1347	.135	.459

* EMC = Entrepreneurial middle class. BMC = Bureaucratic middle class. ELC = Entrepreneurial lower class. PMC = Protestant middle class. RCMC = Roman Catholic middle class.

† Reliability coefficients as predicted by the Spearman-Brown formula.

‡ Split-half reliability could not be computed since there was an odd number (3) of items.

which we obtained significant differences. Our methods can be illustrated, however, and their results clarified.

For an example, we consider Table AII–7 which summarizes the result of controlling the education of middle-class mothers while letting their integration settings vary. The items listed are those for which we report significant differences between entrepreneurs and bureau-

Table AII–7

CONTROL BY YEARS OF SCHOOL MOTHER COMPLETED

Years of School Mother Completed

Item Number	0–8	9–12	13 or More
2b	−	+	−
3	+	+.05	+.10
5e, 6c	+	+	+.05
7	0	+.03	+
9a	+	0	+
10	0	+.01	+
11	+	+	+.005
14	+	+	0
17	+	+	+.03
20	+	+.03	+

crats. A plus (+) sign in a cell means that the reported difference appeared. A zero (0) means that the reported difference did not appear—either because there is no difference between the integration settings or because the difference revealed is opposite in direction to that expected. A minus sign (−) means that, for some reason, no comparison could be made.

Thus, among mothers who completed from nine to twelve years of school, there was one case in ten comparisons which did not exhibit a difference in the expected direction. Application of a statistical sign test shows that we might expect to find nine of ten comparisons in the expected direction as a chance occurrence about once in a hundred trials. (These items meet the requirement of such a test that the items concerned be independent.) The probabilities from the columns for mothers with zero to eight and thirteen or more years of schooling are $<.06$ and $<.02$.

Our table contains two further pieces of information. It shows the probability values of differences which reach or exceed the .10 level and it permits us to judge whether the pattern of signs differs appreciably among the columns.

We find that mothers with nine to twelve years of schooling exhibit four significant differences on these items, mothers with thirteen or more years of education showing the same number. The absence of significant differences by integration setting among mothers with zero to eight years of schooling is due, at least in part, to the small number of cases concerned.

An appropriate measure of the extent to which the columnar patterns of signs differ is the Cochran Q Test. [This is described in Sidney Siegel's *Nonparametric Statistics for the Behavioral Sciences* (New York: McGraw-Hill Book Co., Inc., 1956, pp. 161–166).] A significantly large Q indicates that the patterns do differ appreciably. Such differences could occur if there were interactions between the items and the conditions in some of the columns. The Q value for Table AII–7 is 1.50 and p is a non-significant $<.30$.

From the systematic application of these methods where they were appropriate and from the inspection of the raw-data tables on which they are based, we reached the conclusions reported in Chapter Seven:

1. That the trends we report in earlier chapters continue to appear after controls are applied although:

2. All cells in all columns are no longer significant because of the reduction of numbers.

3. There seem to be no appreciable interactions between the items and the contents of particular columns.

NOTES

[1] This discussion of the design and reliability of the sample consists of selections taken from: Detroit Area Study of the University of Michigan, *A Social Profile of Detroit: 1953* (Ann Arbor, Michigan: University of Michigan Press, 1953), 32–35.

[2] See: Council of Social Agencies of Metropolitan Detroit, *Administrative and Planning Areas in Metropolitan Detroit*, 1951.

[3] These are reviewed in: Lyle V. Jones and Donald W. Fiske, "Models for Testing the Significance of Combined Results," *Psychological Bulletin*, 50 (September, 1953), 375–382.

[4] The problems of reliability are discussed in: Helen Peak, "Problems of Objective Observation," in Leon Festinger and Daniel Katz (eds.), *Research Methods in the Behavioral Sciences* (New York: The Dryden Press, 1953), 243–299.

[5] We want to give most grateful acknowledgment to Dr. Hubert Blalock for his advice on the interpretation of several of the newer measures of association.

[6] Leo A. Goodman and William H. Kruskal, "Measures of Association for Cross Classifications," *Journal of the American Statistical Association*, 49 (December, 1954), 732–764.

[7] *Ibid.*, 740.

[8] For a representative discussion of this method, see: Quinn McNemar, *Psychological Statistics* (New York: John Wiley and Sons, Inc., 2nd edition, 1955), 159–160.

*T*HE INTERVIEW SCHEDULE

Detroit Area Study
January, 1953

. . . . . *FORM A*

We want to ask you some questions about the activities of children. Some of these questions are about the child at a very young age and others about what may happen at an older age.

1. When a new baby comes, a woman has to do many new things. What do you think are the most pleasant and unpleasant things about having a young baby in the house?

1a. What other pleasant things would there be?

1b. What other unpleasant things would there be?

We're interested in talking with mothers about one child. Suppose we think especially about your (number of years) year old. Now, what is his (her) name?

2. Did (child's name) ever suck his (her) thumb, or arm, or hand, or something like that?

(IF YES)

> 2a. Have you thought it necessary to do anything about it?
> (IF YES)　2b. What was that?

3. Mothers have different ways of handling a crying child of five months. Suppose that you were busy preparing the family dinner and the baby was cranky and crying—if you thought nothing was wrong with him (her), and he (she) only wanted attention, what would you do?

4. Now, some questions about feeding. Was (name) breast-fed at any time?

(IF BREAST-FED AT ANY TIME)

> 5. We'd like to know (name's) age at different times when you made changes in feeding.
> 5a. When he (she) stopped breast feeding as the main way of feeding at meal time.
> 5b. When he (she) started feeding from a bottle.
> 5c. When he (she) gave up using the bottle entirely.
> 5d. When he (she) gave up breast feeding entirely.
> 5e. Did you feed him (her) at special times when he (she) was a baby, or when he (she) seemed to want to eat?

(IF BOTTLE-FED)

> 6. We'd like to know (name's) age at different times when you made changes in feeding.
> 6a. When he (she) stopped nursing from a bottle as the main way of feeding at meal time.
> 6b. When he (she) gave up using the bottle entirely.
> 6c. Did you feed him (her) at regular times when he (she) was a baby, or when he (she) seemed to want to eat?

7. Have you or your husband done anything at any time when (name) [was 5 years old or younger and] he (she) touched his (her) sex organs?
(IF NO)　7a. Did he (she) ever do that?

8. Most small children want to follow their parents into the bathroom. (As a small child) did (name) try to follow you or his (her) father when you or he had to use the bathroom?
(IF YES)　8a. How did you handle that?

9. Suppose a mother has a very good woman who will stay with her 3-year-old boy two afternoons a week while she goes shopping and visiting. She decides not to do this because she feels 3-year olds are too young to be away from their mothers so often. How do you feel about this?
9a. Why would that be?

Appendix Three **265**

10. We hear a lot these days about different ways to bring up children. Some people think children should be on their own as early as possible to work out their own problems. Do you agree or disagree?

11. Here are some things that might be done by a boy or girl. Suppose the person were about 13 years old. As I read each of these to you, I would like you to tell me if it should be done as a regular task by a boy, by a girl, or by both.

11a. Shoveling walks.
11b. Washing the car.
11c. Dusting furniture.
11d. Fixing light cords.
11e. Making beds.

Card I

12. Here is a list of reasons why parents prefer that their children do some activities rather than others.
(1) It teaches him to think.
(2) It develops him physically.
(3) It has to do with planning and organization.
(4) It gives him plenty of exercise.
12a. Tell me which you think most important.
12b. Tell me which you think is second most important.

13—23 (Not asked in Form A)

24. Have there been times in the last month when you've *wanted to* find out about what behavior to expect from children at a particular age, or about how to get children to do something?

> 24a. About how many times in the last month did you *want* to do that?
> 24b. What were the things you *wanted* to find out about?

25. (Looking pretty far into the future) suppose your child had an office or clerical job—if a person wants to make money on a job like that, is it more important for him to have the right kind of personality, or to know how to do that kind of work well?
(IF SAYS BOTH) 25a. Which is more important?
25b. Why would that be?

26. Now suppose he's working on an assembly line in a factory—is it more important for him to have the right kind of personality or to know how to do that kind of work well?
(IF SAYS BOTH) 26a. Which is more important?
26b. Why would that be?

27. If (name) has one of these kinds of jobs when he (she) grows up, what is your best guess as to which it is most likely to be—a factory job or an office job?

28. (Again thinking far into the future) at what age do you think (name) will be old enough to be a good husband (wife)?

29. (Not asked in Form A)

30. Suppose, later in life (name) leaves home to earn his (her) own living, and lets you think that he (she) is succeeding very well. But, when you go to visit him (her) you find he (she) has really been having a very hard time. How would you feel?
30a. Would you do anything?
(IF YES) 30b. What?

31. Suppose a 14-year-old child were interested in some worthwhile activities that gave him (her) little time to spend with other children. The things the other children are doing are just as worthwhile, but they don't interest this particular child. Would you encourage him (her) in going on with his own interests, or would you rather see him (her) change to something he (she) can do with other children?
31a. Why would that be?

32. You know, there's something which happens in some families. You have friends in for a meal in the evening, and your five- or six-year-old child doesn't behave—he wiggles around and shakes the table and plays with his food. You feel a little embarrassed. How have you or would you handle this kind of situation?
32a. How could you prevent that from happening another time?

33. We are interested in what mothers would do if they had really free leisure time. Suppose your housework and children were well taken care of most afternoons, you didn't have to work, and you have some extra money. Imagine this started in the summer, what would you do with the free time?
33a. Is there anything else you would do?
(*Separately for first two activities mentioned*) 33b. Why would you like to do that, if you had the time?

34. What difference do you think it would make when you are older and (name) has grown up if you weren't able to see him (her)?
34a. How do you mean?

35. Here are some things that might be done by a husband or wife. As I read each of these to you, I would like you to tell me if, in your home, it is usually done by you, by your husband, or by both of you.
(IF NOT DONE BY EITHER) 35′. If it were done by one of you, which would it be?
35a. Painting rooms in the house.
35b. Getting up at night to take care of the children if they cry.
35c. Deciding where to go for a holiday or celebration.
35d. Punishing the children if necessary.
35e. Picking out more expensive things like furniture or a car.
35f. Washing dishes.

. . . . . *FORM B*

We want to ask you some questions about the activities of children. Some of these questions are about the child at a very young age, and others about what may happen at an older age.

1. When a new baby comes, a woman has to do many new things. What do you think are the most pleasant and unpleasant things about having a young baby in the house?

1a. What other pleasant things would there be?

1b. What other unpleasant things would there be?

We're interested in talking with mothers about one child. Suppose we think especially about your (number of years) year old. Now, what is his (her) name?

2—12 (Not asked in Form B)

13. Here are some tasks that some parents require of their children. Which of these did you or would you require of (child's name) and by what age?

13a. Putting away his (her) own clothes.

13b. Picking up his (her) own toys.

13c. Running errands to a nearby store.

13d. Dressing himself (herself) completely.

14. Now, let's talk about some other problems of early training. How old (in months) was he (she) when you began bowel training?

(Skip to Question 17, if bowel training not yet begun)

---

15. What did you do when (name) didn't want to get on the toilet, or was uncooperative and wanted to get off the toilet?

16. By what age did he (she) have complete bowel control, both day and night?

---

17. How old was your child when you *began* to train him (her) not to wet himself (herself)?

(IF BEGUN) 18. How old was he (she) when he (she) completely stopped wetting himself (herself) during the night?

19. Think about a time when (name) will be (was) 10 years old. He (She) has just done something that you feel is very good, or he (she) has been particularly good. What would you do at those times?

19a. Can you give me an example?

20. Now, please think about that same time when (name) will be (was) 10 years old. He (She) has just done something that you feel is very

wrong, something that you have warned him (her) against ever doing. What would you do at such times?

20a. Can you give me an example?

21. Suppose a 4-year-old child does something that makes his mother angry and excited. Should the mother punish the child right then while she is angry, or should the mother wait until she's more calm before she decides what to do?

22. Some mothers believe that for a child's own good they should know what he (she) is doing most of the time and should supervise him (her) until a certain age. What age would you say that should be?

22a. Why that age?

23. Have you and your husband differed in your ideas about making (name) mind you?

(IF YES) 23a. Can you give some examples of the things on which you differed?

24. Have there been times in the last month when you've wanted to find out about what behavior to expect from children at a particular age, or about how to get children to do something?

(IF YES) | 24a. About how many times in the last month did you *want* to do that?
24b. What were the things you wanted to find out about?

25. (Looking pretty far into the future) suppose your child had an office or clerical job—if a person wants to make money on a job like that, is it more important for him to have the right kind of personality, or to know how to do that kind of work well?

(IF SAYS BOTH) 25a. Which is more important?

25b. Why would that be?

26. Now suppose he's working on an assembly line in a factory—is it more important for him to have the right kind of personality or to know how to do that kind of work well?

(IF SAYS BOTH) 26a. Which is more important?

26b. Why would that be?

27. If (name) has one of these kinds of jobs when he (she) grows up, what is your best guess as to which it is more likely to be—a factory job or an office job?

28. (Again thinking far into the future) at what age do you think (name) will be old enough to be a good husband (wife)?

29. At what age do you think (name) will be old enough to be a good father (mother)?

30. Suppose, later in life (name) leaves home to earn his (her) own living, and lets you think that he (she) is succeeding very well. But,

Appendix Three **269**

when you go to visit him (her) you find he (she) has really been having a very hard time. How would you feel?

30a. Would you do anything?

(IF YES) 30b. What?

31. Suppose a 14-year-old child were interested in some worthwhile activities that gave him (her) little time to spend with other children. The things the other children are doing are just as worthwhile, but they don't interest this particular child. Would you encourage him (her) in going on with his own interests, or would you rather see him (her) change to something he (she) can do with other children?

31a. Why would that be?

32. You know, there's something which happens in some families. You have friends in for a meal in the evening, and your five- or six-year-old child doesn't behave—he wiggles around and shakes the table and plays with his food. You feel a little embarrassed. How have you or would you handle this kind of situation?

32a. How could you prevent that from happening another time?

33. We are interested in what mothers would do if they had really free leisure time. Suppose your housework and children were well taken care of most afternoons, you didn't have to work, and you have some extra money. Imagine this started in the summer, what would you do with the free time?

33a. Is there anything else you would do?

(*Separately for first two activities mentioned*) 33b. Why would you like to do that, if you had the time?

34. What difference do you think it would make when you are older and (name) has grown up if you weren't able to see him (her)?

34a. How do you mean?

35. Here are some things that might be done by a husband or wife. As I read each of these to you, I would like you to tell me if, in your home, it is usually done by you, by your husband, or by both of you.

(IF NOT DONE BY EITHER) 35′. If it were done by one of you, which would it be?

35a. Painting rooms in the house.

35b. Getting up at night to take care of the children if they cry.

35c. Deciding where to go for a holiday or celebration.

35d. Punishing the children if necessary.

35e. Picking out more expensive things like furniture or a car.

35f. Washing dishes.

Sample No. _____

Adult No. _____

1. Race: (BY OBSERVATION)   White ☐   Negro ☐   Other _____
   (Specify)

2. Sex: (BY OBSERVATION)   Male ☐   Female ☐

3. Age: (From Face sheet) _____

4. Relationship to Head of Household: (From Face sheet) _____

5. About how long have you lived here in the Detroit Area? _____

(IF NOT ENTIRE LIFE)	6. Where did you live most of your life before you came here?
	(STATE AND TOWN) _____
	7. Where were you born? _____
	8. Have you ever lived on a farm? Yes ☐ No ☐
	(IF YES) 8a. Where and when was that?
	(Where?) _____
	(Which years?) _____

9. How long have you lived in this house? _____ years.

10. Do you own this house or are you renting?
    Owns ☐   Rents ☐   Other ☐   (explain) _____

11. How many grades of school did you finish?
    (CIRCLE HIGHEST GRADE COMPLETED.)

    1   2   3   4   5   6   7   8   9   10   11   12   More

    (IF ATTENDED COLLEGE)   11a. How many years of college did you

    attend? _____

12. Do you own a television set?   (BY OBSERVATION, IF POSSIBLE)
    Yes ☐
    No ☐

13. What is your occupation?   (What sort of work do you do?)

_____

    (lathe operator, stock clerk, housewife—if unemployed or retired, also ask
    what he or she does when working.)   If retired, check here ☐
    (IF APPROPRIATE)   13a. What kind of business is that in?

    _____

    (steel mill, grocery store, bank)

Appendix Three **271**

13b. Do you work for yourself or someone else? Self ☐   Someone else ☐

| (IF WORKS FOR SOMEONE ELSE) | 13c. Are you employed now? Yes ☐   No ☐

(IF UNEMPLOYED NOW)
13d. How long have you been unemployed?

_____ |

(IF WORKS FOR SELF)

14. How many people do you normally employ? _____

15. Is anybody who lives here a veteran? Yes ☐   No ☐

| (IF YES) | 15a. Who is that? _____ Adult No. _____

15b. What was the highest rank he held in the service?

_____ |

16. What was your total family income in 1952, considering all sources, such as rents, profits, wages, interest and so on?

Under $1000	$1000–1999	$2000–2999	$3000–3999

$4000–4999	$5000–5999	$6000–6999	$7000–7999

$8000–9999	$10,000 or over

(*DO NOT ASK IN 1 ADULT HOUSEHOLDS*)

17. How much of that was the income of the head of the family? _____

CENSUS DATA FROM MOTHERS

(OMIT NEXT THREE PAGES, Q. 18–35b,
EXCEPT FOR MOTHERS OF CHILDREN 18 OR UNDER)

18. Does more than one-half of the family income come from something other than wages and salary, for example, from fees, commissions or profits?

Yes ☐   No ☐   (IF YES)   18a. Specify source _____

19. How long have you been married? _____years.

20. Have you had any children other than those who live here in the house with you? Yes ☐ No ☐
(IF YES) 20a. How old are they? _____

21. Do you have a religious preference? Yes ☐ No ☐

21a. What religious denomination is that? _____
(Specify)

22. Do you attend religious services? Yes ☐ No ☐

(IF YES) 22a. Would you say you attended: Once every week ☐
About twice a month ☐
About once a month ☐
A few times a year ☐

Now, about your husband (ASK Q. 23–26b EVEN IF HUSBAND IS NOT IN HOUSEHOLD.)

23. What was the highest grade of school completed by your husband?

1   2   3   4   5   6   7   8   9   10   11   12   More

(IF ATTENDED COLLEGE) 23a. How many years of college did he attend? _____

(ASK EVERYONE EXCEPT NEGROES)
24. (The forefathers of all Americans came from outside the United States originally.) What was the original nationality of your husband's family

on his father's side? _____

25. What is your husband's occupation? (What sort of work does your husband do?)

_____

(lathe operator, stock clerk—if unemployed or retired, also ask what he does when working.) Check here if retired ☐
(IF APPROPRIATE) 25a. What kind of business is that in?

_____

(steel mill, grocery store, bank)

25b. Does he work for himself or someone else? Self ☐ Someone else ☐

(IF WORKS FOR SOMEONE ELSE) | 25c. Is he employed now? Yes ☐ No ☐
(IF UNEMPLOYED NOW)
25d. How long has he been unemployed?

_____

(IF WORKS FOR SELF)
25e. How many people does he normally employ? _____

Appendix Three **273**

26. What is (was) your father's occupation? (What sort of work does (did) he do?)

_____

(lathe operator, stock clerk—if unemployed or retired ask what he does (did) when working.)

26a. Does (did) he work for himself or someone else?
Self ☐   Someone else ☐

(IF FOR SELF)
26b. How many people did he usually employ? _____

27. A large city like Detroit is made up of various kinds of groups—Many people say that a big city is made up of class groups. If you had to place yourself in one of these groups, would you say that you are in the —?

Middle Class   ☐
Working Class ☐
Upper Class   ☐
Lower Class   ☐

(IF "MIDDLE" OR "WORKING" CLASS)
27a. Would you say that you are in the upper half or the lower half of this class?

Upper half ☐
Lower half ☐

(ASK QUESTIONS ON THIS PAGE ONLY IF HUSBAND
IS MEMBER OF HOUSEHOLD)

28. About how long has your husband lived here in the Detroit area? _____

(IF NOT ENTIRE LIFE)

29. Where did your husband live most of his life before he came here? _____
(State and town)

30. Where was he born? _____

31. Has he ever lived on a farm? Yes ☐   No ☐
(IF YES) 31a. Where and when was that?

(Where?) _____

(Which years?) _____

32. Now, thinking of his job, does anyone work under him?   Yes ☐   No ☐
    (IF YES)   32a. Does anyone work under those people?   Yes ☐   No ☐

33. Does he work under anyone?   Yes ☐   No ☐
    (IF YES)   33a. Does anyone work over his boss?   Yes ☐   No ☐

34. Does your husband belong to a labor union?   Yes ☐   No ☐
    (IF YES)   34a. How long has he belonged to some union?   _____ years.

35. What about his father's occupation?   (What sort of work does (did) he do?)

    _____

    (lathe operator, stock clerk—if unemployed or retired ask what he does
    (did) when working.)

    35a. Did he work for himself or someone else?   Self ☐   Someone else ☐

    (IF FOR SELF)
    35b. How many people did he usually employ? _____

. . . . *R*ELIGION AND
BUREAUCRACY

By Guy E. Swanson
AND Jean Isaacson

A central thesis of this book's discussion of bureaucracy and child care states that a consequence of welfare bureaucratic life is a renewed sense of participation in an orderly, normative, and moral community. In Chapter Four, for example, this thesis is employed to predict that the bureaucratized middle classes will be more likely than entrepreneurial middles to use corporal punishment in disciplining their children. In Chapter Eight, this thesis is contrasted with the frequent prediction by social scientists that bureaucratization accelerates the decline of normative and moral relations in urban societies.

This appendix presents data relevant to the idea that, in the United States, bureaucratization is associated with a more vital normative community than entrepreneurial conditions permitted. These data represent only a beginning at establishing such a thesis. They are offered both to elaborate and further clarify the nature of welfare bureaucracy as conceived in this book and to indicate additional implications of that conception. Just as there is a more elaborate and technical discussion of the statistical procedures in Appendix Two, so here we give a more technical and elaborate account of a central part of the theory.

The idea has long been current that the urbanization of a society leads to a decline of popular belief and interest in religion. This may be true. The evidence is ambiguous. What we want to propose is that bureaucratic urban conditions as described throughout this book provide a situation that is more likely to foster religious belief than are the conditions provided by an individuated-entrepreneurial urbanism. After outlining this proposal, we shall present a preliminary test of its validity.

As might be expected, research on this topic requires a working definition of religion. We begin at that point.

. . . . . *RELIGION AND VARIETIES*
OF URBAN LIFE

Our work uses a particular conception of the essentials of religion. It assumes that the distinctively religious view holds reality to be the product and expression of purpose. Whatever their differences, all religions, as we consider them, have in common the judgment that the universe is not a mechanism without direction, dead dust hung in space, but that its nature and processes reflect intention. Deity stands for that which has the relevant intentions that create and shape reality.

What conditions would a religious view reflect? We assume that it stands for experiences of transcendent purpose encountered in the course of relations with other people.

For social relations to be experienced as purposeful, the social world must be orderly (1) and of such a nature that something of its direction or course can be known. Further, its direction and order must *transcend* the known intentions of individuals and of special interest groups. They must, in Durkheim's phrase (2), seem exterior to all these and must exercise guidance and constraint over them.

There are theoretical reasons (3) for saying that the physical world is not experienced as operating in terms of purpose unless that imputation follows from first learning of purpose and direction in social relations. Further, as Durkheim (4) suggests, it is likely that only experiences provided by the organization of a unit as large and pervasive as a total society are adequate to provide these "transcendent" social conditions.

This is not a complete statement of the conditions now thought to be required for religious experience, and space does not permit its elaboration. The statement does, however, give the essential ideas about religion used in the work reported here.

Given this conception of religion, it is understandable that the rise of entrepreneurial urban societies described earlier in this book would destroy the conditions that constitute the religious in experience. The individuated-entrepreneurial society is one in which people are separated from one another. Certainly to the extent that this kind of integration developed, all sense of being involved in larger purposes was weakened, and, in its place came more fragmentary, disjointed experiences, lacking the unification of common direction.

However, as has been elaborated in Chapter Two and at many other points in this book, the rise of welfare bureaucracy brings with it many conditions that moderate or nullify the decline of ordered and moral relations produced by an entrepreneurial situation. At a number of places in preceding chapters it is argued that in a prosperous and expanding economy, organized into large units which depend on relatively skilled blue- and white-collar employees, continued organizational operation requires a greater involvement of the labor force in determining and understanding the conditions of its work. Several reasons were given for this conclusion. First, enterprises need to compete successfully with one another to retain their employees, since workers with some specialized skills are in short supply. Second, the problems of supervision multiply as the skills of the labor force increase. This is the case because it becomes less and less possible for supervisors to judge the adequacy of subordinates' performances as those subordinates gain a level of skill, the nature and efficient exercise of which are not fully understood by supervisors. Although this occurs among blue-collar workers, it is especially relevant as a description of the work of white-collar employees whose "product" is not the kind of easily measured unit that lends itself to the test of time-and-motion studies.

Under these conditions, as preceding chapters have summarized, the developing solution to management's problem of retaining and utilizing its labor force is to create a sense of responsibility to the company and the job in its employees. Since this is, essentially, a moral relation it can be established only if management shows a personal concern with its employees' interests above and beyond that connected with the conditions of work tied most closely to the technological operations on the job. Consultation with workers about the methods, goals, and plans of work, clean washrooms, good lighting, attractive color schemes, the de-emphasis of the status system in the organization and the use of collective symbols—our "team," our "industrial family"—are among the devices that serve this end. The consequence is that an increasing proportion of the labor force gets acquainted with many of the plans and purposes of the giant organizations in which it is employed, can sense its own part in a vast collective effort, and feels some share in determining, and in being directed by, that joint program. Similarly, earlier parts of this book have asserted that the success of mass political organizations in turning the efforts of government toward controlling the future and in forcing officials to report on their purposes and to reveal the course of their efforts gives a sense of plan and direction to the individual as part of a massive collective movement through history. Similar experiences of transcendent collective purpose are an outcome of the ever expanding web of contacts and services, both private and governmental, that tie people together in the fabric of the great urban communities. Finally, the population's growing familiarity with the structure of the urban society as a result of continued experience with that structure, provides yet another condition bringing a more ordered and integrated conception of the social world. People come to know the "levers" and channels of urban life and how to manipulate them. What once were nameless and faceless relations among strangers become expected patterns of existence.

What we want to underline is that welfare bureaucracy leads to a return of experiences of transcendent purpose—of religious experiences —and, simultaneously, of morality, as aspects of the social relations of American society.

. . . . . *METHOD*

The population on which these ideas about different types of social integration and religion were tested consisted of 208 students enrolled in three sociology courses at the University of Michigan in the spring of 1955—an introductory course offered only to upperclassmen and graduate students, a course in marriage, and a course in the sociology of religion. These courses were chosen because they admit students who, at the junior year of college or beyond, are well past the commonly observed uncertainties of new students in the university, and so are presumably able to give a more stable and articulate response to questions about many issues. Second, the first two of these courses, which also are the ones from which most of our respondents came, enroll students having a wider range of college "majors" than appear in most other upperclass courses. The various social sciences, humanities, and professional schools are represented. However, we find that few students in these courses are majoring in the physical sciences or in engineering or medicine.

Each student in these courses received a copy of the questionnaire we administered to get information. The respective class instructors then made some standard remarks. They said that the questions were constructed to get at student feelings about religion and ethics and to relate those feelings to some background information. All class members were encouraged to complete the forms and were reminded of the importance for research purposes of obtaining answers from all respondents. The students also were assured that, should any of them have reservations, they were free to refuse participation. The questionnaire ended with spaces for the respondent's name, address, and telephone number. Students were told that they need not fill in this information. It was stressed, however, that the study would profit if it was possible to talk with some respondents after the questionnaires were examined and that the identifying information would make this possible. Ninety-six per cent of the students in these classes returned completed questionnaires. Of these, about 90 per cent reported their names and addresses. Three forms were discarded because the students were not Americans. Six additional questionnaires could not be used because the respondents failed to give enough information to determine their position in an entrepreneurial or bureaucratic setting and their social class. This left 208 usable forms. One hundred and forty of these came from Protestants, 30 from Roman Catholics, and 38 from Jews. All respondents lived in towns or cities. None were farmers' children. Students were categorized as having a structurally entrepreneurial or bureaucratic integration in our society using the criteria given in Chapter Three.

It is always possible, of course, that a family is structurally entrepreneurial in its integration, yet has begun to think about and participate in a bureaucratic style of life. Structurally bureaucratic families may, for some reason, pursue an entrepreneurial style of life. To the foregoing structural integration indices was added a device for classifying the family's behavioral integration. This consisted of asking the respondent for the names of the magazines his mother and father read, and of grouping these magazines into those emphasizing the themes characteristic of the middle-class American version of entrepreneurial organization—themes of ambition and striving, entrepreneurship, individualism, and the realization of gratification in the future—as against those magazines stressing the more bureaucratic themes of adaptability, cooperation and coordination, and the enjoyment and elaboration of an immediately gratifying way of living (5).

The magazines read by the parents of each student were classified as entrepreneurial, bureaucratic, or uncodable. In the latter group were placed all periodicals that did not appear to us as emphasizing either the entrepreneurial or the bureaucratic themes. Then we computed, as a percentage of all magazines read by the parents, the proportion classified as entrepreneurial and the proportion coded as bureaucratic. The parents of each student were given a behavioral integration score by subtracting the percentage of periodicals they read having an entrepreneurial emphasis from the percentage stressing bureaucratic themes. Arranging the parents' scores in ascending order, we formed a group having a relatively bureaucratic behavioral integration from those with scores above the median. The remainder we shall call entrepreneurial in behavioral integration.

The methods for placing respondents' families into appropriate social classes was described in Chapter Three. This method indicated that we had no families which would, to use Warner's terms, be classified as lower lower. There were also only a few upper-class families. We combined these upper-class cases with those categorized as upper middle class.

. . . . . *FINDINGS*

The small number of Roman Catholic and Jewish students made impracticable any meaningful breakdowns of their answers by so large a list of independent categories. That task appeared even less feasible when we discovered that the range of responses of each of these religious groups was drastically restricted. For these reasons, the principal part of our findings comes from examining the Protestants. We also present some limited results for Roman Catholics and Jews.

Findings for Protestants

Findings for Shift Scores (SS). Is there a greater vitality of interest in religion on the part of bureaucratic respondents than among entrepreneurial respondents? To rate vitality of religious belief, we sought evidence that our respondents found religious matters real enough, and important enough, to want to pursue them further. Did they perceive in themselves any signs of growing and deepening belief? Were they sufficiently concerned about religion to feel that their children should be better informed about it than they themselves had been? In short, we sought indications that the respondents had an active interest in religion. In this exploratory study, our questions to detect activity of religious interests were crude and simple. They read:

Has the strength of your belief in a religious philosophy of life: increased, decreased, or remained the same over the last few years?

Would you say that, in the last few years, you have: become more sympathetic, less sympathetic, or remained the same in your feelings toward a religious philosophy of life?

Do you feel that you would like to give your children more, less, or the same amount of religious training as you were given?

Every respondent was given a cumulative score for his answers to these questions, with an arbitrary weight of one being assigned to each response involving an increase, a zero to indications of no change, and a minus one to an answer reflecting a decrease.

Table 1 presents the results for the structural and behavioral integration categories. Since no differences appeared in the answers of persons in the several social classes, all responses are grouped together by integration settings. For the same reason, this practice is continued in all tables in our report.

Table 1

FREQUENCY OF SHIFT SCORES FOR PROTESTANTS

Shift Score	Structural Entrepreneurial		Structural Bureaucratic	
	Behavioral Entrepreneurial	Behavioral Bureaucratic	Behavioral Entrepreneurial	Behavioral Bureaucratic
+3*	12	8	8	7
+2*	6	13	7	3
+1†	18	12	2	5
0†	6	4	3	1
−1†	4	3	1	1
−2†	2	1	2	0
−3†	2	1	0	0
Total	50	42	23	17

* Combined for chi-square analysis.
† Combined for chi-square analysis.

We may now examine Table 1. A chi-square analysis (6) of the differences between respondents in the structurally entrepreneurial and bureaucratic categories shows that the bureaucrats are significantly more likely to have high and positive shift scores ($p = <.03$). This difference remains even when we control for the subjects' behavioral integration ratings ($p = <.05$).

Similar analyses, this time comparing subjects in entrepreneurial and bureaucratic behavioral integrations, produce no significant differences. Further, there is no evidence of a significant interaction between the structural and behavioral integration classifications in producing the pattern of responses we obtain.

From these findings, we conclude that the evidence from the Shift Scores gives support to our prediction that persons classified as structurally bureaucratic would be more likely to show signs of increasing in interest in religion than would those coded as structurally entrepreneurial. No support is offered for our expectation that the same trend would appear when behaviorally entrepreneurial and bureaucratic subjects were compared.

Findings for Evaluated Shift Scores (ESS). One difficulty in interpreting our original Shift Scores (SS) rises from the possibility that the respondents do not change their interest from the same initial degree of religious belief and practice. If, for example, students who were coded structurally or behaviorally entrepreneurial in integration were strong believers in the faiths of their fathers, it might be impossible for them to say that their interest in religion had increased. Perhaps it was already present in the highest possible degree.

This particular possibility proves untrue. We asked the respondents to answer the following item:

The feelings of my parents and myself toward the religious belief and practices that have been traditional in my family are (check):

	Strongly Unfavorable	Moderately Unfavorable	Apathetic	Moderately Favorable	Strongly Favorable
Father	_____	_____	_____	_____	_____
Mother	_____	_____	_____	_____	_____
Self	_____	_____	_____	_____	_____

The first important finding from their responses is that many students who say that they and their parents are strongly favorable receive the maximum possible SS—a plus three. In addition, a student's SS and the response he makes to this item on feelings about the religious beliefs traditional in the family are not related. Thus our SS results are not explained by the respondents' feelings about the religion traditional for their family, nor by the feelings of their parents on that subject. Further, these attitudes of the subjects and their parents toward the family's traditional religion are unrelated to the SS, and their feelings on these same matters are unrelated to their structural or behavioral integration classifications.

Another question remains about the meaning of the SS. Presumably, the student who says his parents are strongly favorable toward their religious beliefs and who perceives an increase in his own belief may be returning to the interests of his family or he may be sensing an increase in interest beyond that of his family. The first case is one of positive regression. The second is one of genuine increase. What happens to the relation of the SS and integration when we take these matters into account?

We constructed some Evaluated Shift Scores (ESS) to provide an answer. The new coding categories were:

Increase: (a) The student sees himself as more interested in the family's religion than the mean amount of interest he reports for his parents and has an SS of plus two or plus three, or—

(b) The student sees himself and his parents as equally interested in the family's religion, and, if the student's interest is "strongly favorable," he has a plus three SS; if his interest is less than "strongly favorable" he has at least a plus two SS.

Stable: (a) The student sees himself and his parents as equally interested in the family's religion and the student has an SS of plus one or zero, or—

(b) The student sees his parents and himself as being strongly favorable toward the family's religion and he has an SS of plus two.

Positive Regression: The student sees himself as less interested than his parents in the family's religion and has a positive SS.

Negative Regression: The student sees himself as more interested than his parents in the family's religion and has a negative SS.

Conflicted: The student's SS derives from evidence both of tendencies to increase and decrease in interest in religion.

Decrease: The student sees himself as less interested or as much interested as his parents in the family's religion and has a negative SS.

There are several results of reclassifying SS by these criteria. Cases in which the parents and children are strongly favorable toward the family's religion and the child has an SS of less than plus three are called stable instead of increasing. Some decreasers become negative regressors. Some former increasers, and some who showed little or no movement, are now called either positive regressors or conflicted. Although these devices are somewhat arbitrary, they should serve to reduce any inflation in the number of genuine increasers. They may well err in overcorrecting on that score. Table 2 presents the distribution of our Protestant cases by these ESS.

Once more we compared the structurally entrepreneurial and bureaucratic subjects. This time we found that, with behavioral integration ratings controlled, the bureaucratic subjects are significantly more likely to be increasers than are entrepreneurial students ($p = <.05$). If the behavioral integration ratings are not controlled, no difference appears between students in the two types of structural integration.

Table 2

FREQUENCY OF EVALUATED SHIFT SCORES FOR PROTESTANTS

	Structural Entrepreneurial		Structural Bureaucratic	
Evaluated Shift Score	Behavioral Entrepreneurial	Behavioral Bureaucratic	Behavioral Entrepreneurial	Behavioral Bureaucratic
Increase	14	13	9	9
Stable	14	13	7	1
Positive regression	10	5	1	5
Negative regression*	1	0	0	0
Conflicted*	3	0	2	1
Decrease*	6	4	2	1
Total	48	35	21	17

* Combined for chi-square analysis.

Similarly, we find that, when structural integration is held constant, our behaviorally bureaucratic subjects are more likely than the others to be classified as increasers ($p = <.05$). If structural integration is not controlled, students in the two types of behavioral integration do not differ in interest in religion.

Finally, the data in Table 2 show that there is a significant degree of interaction between the structural and behavioral integration settings to produce the responses given by our subjects ($p = <.03$). For example, the data show that it is the subjects who are structurally and behaviorally entrepreneurial who are *least* likely to be increasers; that it is those who are structurally and behaviorally bureaucratic who are *most* likely to be increasers. Other interactions appear in this complex table but, in the absence of some prior theory, the small number of cases involved probably does not justify our speculating about their meaning.

From these findings, we again conclude that our hypothesis gains support. With structural integration controlled, behaviorally bureaucratic subjects are significantly more likely than others to be increasers. With behavioral integration controlled, structurally bureaucratic subjects are significantly more likely than others to be increasers. However, although these differences are significant and in the expected direction, they are of a magnitude suggesting that we are able to explain but a small part of the variations in our respondents' answers.

Other Indices of Religious Interest. Having found some support for our hypothesis in the SS and ESS results, and having discovered that our respondents' feelings about the religion traditional in their families was unrelated to their integration setting, we turned to examine three other sources of information in our questionnaires. The first consisted of a question about frequency of attendance at religious services. The second was made up of some open-ended questions about reasons for needing or being interested in religion, and the third consisted of three forced-choice questions requiring a statement of greater interest in the theological as against the ethical content of religion. The answers to these questions relate neither to our two indices of shift in religious interest nor to the integration settings of our subjects.

The lack of relation between evidences of an increase in religious belief and interest on the one hand and frequency of church attendance on the other may indicate that the beliefs and interests reflected in our indices have little bearing on the lives of our respondents. Although this is possible, it is not necessarily the case. Almost all of our Protestant subjects attend some religious service at least once a month. Inasmuch as Protestant ideology permits the individual considerable freedom from participation in institutional religious programs as long as his beliefs are correct, it is quite possible for the relation between strength of belief and frequency of participation to be much less than perfect. Further, it must be remembered that we are dealing with college students, most of whom are living away from home. Separated from their families and other customary social settings, it is likely that many students do not follow the patterns of participation habitual to them in their home communities.

Since, through an open-ended question, we were able to establish that these students could and did distinguish between ethics and theology, considering "a religious philosophy of life" as one springing from theological assumptions, we must assume that, in general, the respondents understood the distinctions in the forced-choice items. Thus we can say that students increasing in religious interest and belief understand this to mean increased interest in theology. However, the lack of a relation between their shift scores and a primary interest in theology as against ethics may mean that some students are interested in theology for its own sake, whereas others are concerned primarily with its ethical implications.

Other Explanations of the Findings. We tried to discover conditions other than the ones we had predicted that might be responsible for our findings. Several variables show no relation to the distribution of results in Tables 1 and 2. These include age on last birthday, sex, the size of the respondents' home towns, the specific basis (e.g., parents born on a farm, breadwinner self-employed, etc.) on which a family was classified as having an entrepreneurial integration, and the amount of education of the parents. Certain other conditions deserve more extended comment.

To test the hypothesis that an increased interest in religion might be due to fears generated by the international situation, or the complexity of domestic political and economic problems we asked a set of three questions:

Rank *all* of these statements according to your feelings about the possibility of a future war. Rank the most likely as (1), and so on:
  (*a*) There is a strong possibility for a peaceful settlement of our international problems.
  (*b*) There is a strong possibility that we will enter into a devastating war.
  (*c*) We are certainly about to enter into a devastating war.

Rank *all* of these in accordance with your ideas about man's capabilities. Rank as above:
  (*a*) With the right leadership there is a possibility that we will pull through these hard times.
  (*b*) We will surely find a solution to today's problems.
  (*c*) No man or group of men can solve the tremendous problems that face man today.

If we enter into another war, what are our chances of winning? Rank *all* of these probabilities as above:
  (*a*) If it happens, we will probably win the next war.
  (*b*) We will probably lose if there is another war.
  (*c*) There is a strong possibility that we will lose the next war.

Each alternative in each of these items was given an arbitrary weight from one to three in the ascending order of the pessimism it expressed, and the weights were totaled to form a cumulative score for each respondent. There is no relation between these scores and the respond-

Appendix Four **287**

ents' shift of interest in religion. This fact corresponds to our judgment that experiences of collective purpose, not of fragmenting panic, underlie religious interests.

Another possible explanation of our findings might lie in the argument that intelligence would be associated with interest in religion. It has sometimes been suggested that a negative relation exists between these things. The theoretical difficulties involved in measures of intelligence are patent, but, as a very crude check, we did obtain the respondents' grade averages in the university. These averages, of course, are as likely to reflect ambition, persistence, application, and verbal skills as they do innate intellectual ability. We do find that subjects classified as structurally entrepreneurial have significantly ($p = <.02$) higher average grades than do those in structurally bureaucratic positions. If these grades reflect ambition and striving, this finding is consistent with our view of entrepreneurial middle-class values. However, there is no relation between these average grades and religious interest.

Again, it has been suggested that extremes of economic security or insecurity affect interest in religion. We asked:

How important have financial worries been in your family since you can remember?
(a) They were a constant source of concern.
(b) They were a frequent source of concern.
(c) They were sometimes sharp, but generally not a major source of concern.
(d) They were never a serious source of concern.

The answers to these questions relate to social class, but they are distributed quite at random with respect to the religious shift scores.

Although these alternative explanations are not supported, some additional properties of our data were revealed when we studied the small group of interviews we were able to obtain from our subjects before they left Ann Arbor for the summer holiday. All the subjects we interviewed were girls.

One point that caught our attention came from the remarks of three girls who had in common an increased interest in religion since joining the Protestant Episcopal Church. Two were formerly Methodists. One was a Congregationalist. Each of these girls who joined the Episcopal Church valued its "churchliness" and spoke of her appreciation for its greater attention to a systematic presentation of beliefs than was given by the denomination from which she had come.

This finding suggested a hypothesis that sheds still further light on the meaning of some of the results from our shift index. The Protestant Episcopal Church, like its Anglican ancestor, represents a faith stressing life in an integrated and relatively stable community. Unlike most of the other Protestant denominations, with the partial exception of Lutheranism, it rose as a consequence of the pressure of competing nationalisms rather than as a result of the individuating tendencies of the early commercial or industrial society (7). It is quite possible that as those individuating tendencies subside and a more integrated society appears, religious forms like those of the Episcopal Church will again become especially appropriate for expressing people's experiences with morality and transcendent purpose.

The Lutheran movement, compounded of rising nationalism and the commercial revolution, is an intermediate case. It too emphasizes the importance, for the believer's salvation, of his integration in a stable moral community.

The hypothesis we have explored states that those who remain stable or increase their interest in religion, or who show tendencies to return to the degree of faith held by their parents, are more likely, if they are structurally or behaviorally entrepreneurial, to come from the individuated Protestant groups (e.g., Methodists, Presbyterians, and Baptists). Evidence of such increase, of stability, or of positive regression toward religious belief should appear more strongly among Episcopalians and Lutherans if the family is classified as structurally or behaviorally bureaucratic. Conversely, entrepreneurial Lutherans and Episcopalians should evidence a decline in their children's interests in religion. Other Protestants should show such a decline under bureaucratic conditions.

To isolate persons with stable and positively regressing beliefs, we must use ESS results. Further, since the number of Episcopalians and Lutherans is very small, we anticipated that our findings would be only suggestive.

The results of this new analysis of the ESS scores did not match our expectations. The trends we expected did not appear. There were no significant differences of any kind apparent in our data.

Then our attention was called to another study which had collected information relevant to our hypothesis. In the course of an investigation involving 236 undergraduates enrolled in some of the more elementary psychology courses at the University of Michigan, Wesley Allinsmith and Thomas Greening asked their subjects.

Regardless of how often *you* attend religious services, and regardless of your attitudes toward *organized religion*, how devout or intensely religious do you consider yourself to be (circle one)?

very devout   devout   not especially devout   not devout at all

They also obtained the information necessary to classify these students as entrepreneurial or bureaucratic in integration and to identify the social class to which their families belonged.

It seemed to us that, although not designed to reveal shifts in religious belief, the answers to their question on devoutness might, like our ESS scores, be expected to relate to the type of integration of the families of the two kinds of Protestants. Table 3 presents the findings.

Table 3

FREQUENCY IN DEVOUTNESS CATEGORIES BY STRUCTURAL INTEGRATION
SETTING AND TYPE OF PROTESTANT BACKGROUND

Devoutness Categories	Episcopalians and Lutherans		Other Protestants	
	Entrepreneurial	Bureaucratic	Entrepreneurial	Bureaucratic
Very devout or devout	4	3	24	13
Not especially devout or not devout	3	1	10	17

The numbers of cases are small, but it shows, as we anticipated, that white students both of whose parents are Episcopalians or Lutherans are more likely to say they are "devout" or "very devout" if the family is classified as bureaucratic than if it is coded as entrepreneurial. Conversely, white students, both of whose parents prefer an individuating Protestant denomination, are more likely to evidence greater devoutness when their families are called entrepreneurial than when we classified them as bureaucratic. A comparison of the two Protestant groups, controlled for integration setting, shows that these trends in the expected direction are significant and at about the .03 level of confidence.

Now we faced a puzzle. Why should the hypothesis be consistent with the Allinsmith-Greening data and not with our ESS tabulation?

We began the search for an answer to this question by considering the likely differences between the two bodies of data. We noted these points:

(1) The devoutness question obtains answers which refer to the individual's feelings about religion in general. So do our three questions concerning shifts in sympathy for, and belief in, a religious philosophy of life. However, the ESS code then corrects the answers to our three questions in terms of the attitudes of the subjects and their parents toward the religious beliefs traditional in their families.

This correction thus ties the ESS code, in part, to feelings about a particular religious denomination.

(2) The hypothesis under consideration predicts a relation between integration setting and *positive attachment* to *a particular variety* of religious belief. Hence we included positive regressors and those who remain stable along with the increasers in judging positive attachment. By contrast, the hypothesis previously tested by the use of ESS predicts a relation between integration setting and *salience* of interest in religion *in general*. We identified increasers as those for whom religious interests were most salient.

(3) Persons given any particular ESS classification, say "increase," may differ considerably in the absolute intensity of their feelings toward religion. Thus increasers may have been very devout and may since have become even more strongly confirmed in their faith, or they may not have been devout at all but are now becoming more sympathetic toward religion. This is as we intended. However, the devoutness question classifies subjects according to the intensity of their feelings, and that alone.

These three points led to the idea that perhaps the individual must believe rather strongly in the doctrines of a particular denomination before they can be expected to affect his conduct. Perhaps it was by tapping degree of belief that the devoutness question allowed the results, which we had anticipated, to appear. Perhaps, by being rather independent of degree of belief, our ESS code failed to produce the expected findings. We decided to take degree of belief into account as best we could and reexamine our data.

Our next step was to locate those among our subjects who might be expected to be like the students in the several devoutness categories. We concluded that the following equivalences were at least roughly accurate:

Devoutness Classification	ESS Code
(1) Very devout or devout	Subjects saying that they were moderately or strongly favorable toward the religious belief and practices traditional in their families, who also were coded as increasers, as stable, or as positive regressors on the ESS Code.
(2) Not especially devout or not devout	Subjects saying that they were unfavorable or apathetic toward the religious belief and practices traditional in their families, or who were coded as decreasers, conflicted or as negative regressors on the ESS Code.

Table 4 gives the results obtained by this regrouping of the ESS data.

Table 4

FREQUENCY OF EVALUATED SHIFT SCORES (CORRECTED FOR STRENGTH OF RELIGIOUS BELIEF) BY STRUCTURAL INTEGRATION SETTING AND TYPE OF PROTESTANT BACKGROUND

Corrected Evaluated Shift Scores	Episcopalians and Lutherans		Other Protestants	
	Entrepre-neurial	Bureau-cratic	Entrepre-neurial	Bureau-cratic
High devout	14	10	43	15
Low devout	10	2	12	6
Total	24	12	55	21

The pattern in Table 4 is not so striking as the one obtained from the Allinsmith-Greening data, but it is in the expected direction. When degree of belief is taken into account, and structural integration controlled, Episcopalians and Lutherans are more likely to be coded as increasers, stable, or positive regressors when they are classified as bureaucratic. Conversely, other Protestants are more likely to have the ESS codes just listed when they are classified as entrepreneurial. The value of p is less than .10. No relation appears when our subjects are grouped according to behavioral integration.

Finally, we must regret that the small number of cases did not permit us to examine the joint effects of the structural and behavioral integration settings on our types of Protestants. Nevertheless, we conclude that these results, taken together with those from the Allinsmith-Greening data, give our modified hypothesis enough support to justify its continued exploration.

Findings for Jews and Roman Catholics

Little can be said about the Jewish students in connection with the hypotheses of our study. Not only was their number small, but, as a result of the large number of foreign-born or self-employed parents involved, only five cases could be typed as structurally bureaucratic. Further, the range of shift scores is narrowed from that for Protestants because 33 per cent of the Jews, as against 10 per cent of the Protestants or Roman Catholics, showed signs of decreasing in interest in religion. Their lack of interest appears in more drastic form on other indices. Eighty-one per cent of the Jewish students, and only 25 per cent of the Roman Catholics and 27 per cent of the Protestants, did not select a theological topic in preference to an ethical theme on the three forced-choice items for that content. Eighty-six per cent of the Roman Catholics and 64 per cent of the Protestants said they attend religious services twice a month or more. Not one Jewish student reported such frequent attendance.

Our data are not adequate to explain this pattern among Jews. We cannot, for example, explore the possibility that it represents a rejection of a traditional religion, not as religion, but as part of a way of life from which these students now move as they try to become assimilated into a predominately non-Jewish society. Perhaps it stands for a genuine rejection of religion as such. These are problems for additional study. In any event, and whether as a result of this shortened range of responses or for some other reason, the Jewish replies are not related to our entrepreneurial-bureaucratic classification.

The Roman Catholics presented us with some similar problems for analysis. There were only 30 Catholic respondents. Most of them were rated as increasers. Thus, as with the Jews, our data provided little variation in response. No trends appear when the Catholics' answers are distributed by the structural and behavioral entrepreneurial-bureaucratic categories.

. . . . . *GENERAL CONCLUSIONS*

We find evidence for a greater frequency of self-perceived increase in interest and belief in religion among our bureaucratic Protestant respondents than among those in an entrepreneurial setting. This situation is consistent with our hypothesis and appears at a moderate level of confidence.

These trends do not appear among Roman Catholics and Jews. We have considered the possibility that this failure of prediction is due to some peculiarities in the distribution of the responses of these students as compared with the Protestants. We recognize, however, that the absence of entrepreneurial-bureaucratic differences in these two groups may be negative evidence for our theory.

In our own data and in those of another study we also have been able to find support for the hypothesis that, when degree of belief in the doctrines and practices of the denomination is taken into account, Episcopalians and Lutherans are more likely to be devoutly religious under bureaucratic rather than under entrepreneurial conditions. By contrast, other Protestants are more likely to be devout under structurally entrepreneurial conditions. We have presented a description of the nature of these two types of Protestants from which such findings can be derived.

Finally, looking toward future research on our problem, we want to suggest a possibility for which our study has no adequate data. After our data were collected we managed to give clearer formulation to an explanation suggested by the thinking in Lasswell's famous essay on the garrison state (8). He saw Americans, pressed by the threat of Soviet aggression, giving up civil liberties for national security. The integrity of the state would stand though all else failed. We have speculated that religion might prosper in this circumstance. Emphasizing traditional patterns of behavior and moral rectitude, its practice could be the sign of a citizen's integration into his society. He would be a good security-risk. At the same time, religious practices would call men's attention to their common moral community, drawing energies from the pursuit of diverse and fragmenting goals. In this view, it is not so much fear of attack as the desire for a reputation for rectitude and a visible sign of allegiance to the nation that would underlie a renewed interest in religion. What our present data do suggest is that, if this conception has merit, it may be differentially associated with the integration settings of the families concerned (9).

NOTES

[1] On this point consult: John Dewey, "The Religious in Experience," in Joseph Ratner (ed.), *Intelligence in the Modern World: John Dewey's Philosophy* (New York: The Modern Library, 1939), 1003–1037; George H. Mead, *Mind, Self and Society from the Standpoint of a Social Behaviorist* (Chicago: The University of Chicago Press, 1934), 273–298.

[2] Emile Durkheim, *The Rules of Sociological Method* (Chicago: The University of Chicago Press, 1938), 1–13.

[3] Mead, *op. cit.*

[4] Emile Durkheim, *The Elementary Forms of the Religious Life* (Joseph W. Swain, trans., New York: The Macmillan Co., 1915).

[5] The values associated with entrepreneurial as against bureaucratic organizations are derived and elaborated throughout this book. This classification of magazines was made quite subjectively from a general knowledge of the characteristic differences among them. The technique deserves special and careful research to standardize and refine such judgments. Obviously, a thorough content-analysis would provide the needed information. Without the facilities for such an analysis, however, we settled on the following groups: Entrepreneurial periodicals: *Antiques, Consumers' Research, Cosmopolitan, Good Housekeeping, Homemaking, The American Legion Magazine, The American Magazine, The Pathfinder, The Saturday Evening Post,* and *United States News and World Report.* Bureaucratic periodicals: *The American Home, The Atlantic, Better Homes and Gardens,*

Harpers, Holiday, House and Garden, The Ladies' Home Journal, Life, Look, McCall's, The National Geographic, Newsweek, The New Yorker, Parents' Magazine, Pageant, The Saturday Review, Time, Vogue, The Woman's Home Companion.

The Reader's Digest was a special and difficult case. Studies have shown its dedication to the virtues of the small town and countryside and to the small enterpriser and the rewards of persistence and ambition. It does, however, contain a considerable selection of articles that might be read simply for their informative value. We resolved the issue by deciding that the level of information obtained from its articles would be unlikely to satisfy a person with an upper middle or higher-class background, and that such persons who read the *Digest* must do so for its point of view. Therefore, we classified them as entrepreneurial in orientation. We did not include the *Digest* in our list of magazines used for classifying persons at other social class levels. An analysis of upper middle and higher-class persons who read the *Digest* (an analysis done *after* the foregoing groupings of magazines had been used to interpret our data) shows that such persons are less likely to have increased in interest in religion than are persons at the same social class level who do not read the *Digest*. Further, readers of the *Digest* are not different in religious interest from non-readers at other social class levels.

[6] The technique used for computing chi-square values for tables with more than four cells and containing small numbers of cases appears in Alexander M. Mood, *Introduction to the Theory of Statistics* (New York: McGraw-Hill Book Co., Inc., 1950), 152–164. See also J. E. Keith Smith, "Multi-variate Attribute Analysis," Engineering Research Institute, University of Michigan, August, 1953. Whenever we have successfully predicted the direction in which a finding should appear, we present the p value for one tail of the probability distribution. The method used for controlling variables in these computations is described in Milton J. Rosenberg, "The Experimental Investigation of a Value Theory of Attitude Structure," unpublished doctoral dissertation, Doctoral Program in Social Psychology, University of Michigan, 1953, 118–123.

[7] Much of the history of these developments appears in Ernst Troeltsch, *The Social Teaching of the Christian Churches* (Olive Wyon, trans., London: George Allen and Unwin, Ltd., 1931).

[8] Harold D. Lasswell, "The Garrison State," *The American Journal of Sociology,* 46 (January, 1941), 455–468. For some interesting and related developments see Edward A. Shils, "The Intellectuals, I. Great Britain," *Encounter,* 4 (April, 1955), 5–16. We cannot dismiss yet another possibility—namely that the rising interest in "religion" is really an increase in interest in moral problems generated by bureaucratization, but discussed in the theological frameworks traditional among Americans.

[9] Preliminary findings from a more recent study of Michigan undergraduates by Harry C. Dillingham indicate differences in vitality of religious belief between Protestants from structurally entrepreneurial and bureaucratic origins similar to those presented here. Dillingham's material also supports the hypothesis that higher education is associated with lower vitality of belief among entrepreneurs, that amount of education is not related to vitality of belief among bureaucrats.

I_{NDEX}

Family, bureaucratized, 197–206
  colleague, 200–206
  companionship, 197–206
  entrepreneurial, 197–206
  institutional, 197–198
Feeding, amount, 7
  bottle or breast, 6, 8, 14–15, 27, 121,
    135, 139–140, 158, 170, 217
  demand or scheduled, 6–7, 16, 27, 40,
    92–93, 97, 99, 121, 124, 131, 139,
    140, 143, 158, 165, 169, 217–218
Festinger, Leon, 263
Fiske, Donald W., 263
Frazier, E. Franklin, 176
Freedman, Ronald, 88, 145
Freud, Sigmund, 4, 94, 186–187, 210–211,
  231
Fromm, Erich, 236

Gardner, Burleigh B., 175
Gardner, Mary R., 175
Genitals, exploration of, 6, 19, 28, 41,
  85, 102–106, 117, 130–131, 133,
  139–140, 225–226
  see also Masturbation
Gesell, Arnold, 28
Gibbs, Patricia K., 145
Ginsberg, Morris, 212
Goodman, Leo A., 259, 263
Greening, Thomas, 289–290, 292
Guest, Edgar A., 101–102, 119
Gulick, Luther, 47, 59

Hartley, Eugene L., 145
Hartmann, H., 26, 29
Hastings, James, 176
Hatt, Paul K., 175
Havighurst, Robert J., 118, 121–122,
  124, 126, 128, 133–138, 145, 158,
  175–176
Hawley, Cameron, 175
Henry, William E., 55, 60
Hobhouse, Leonard T., 212
Hofstadter, Richard, 59
Holt, Luther Emmett, 15–17, 23
Holt, Luther Emmett, Jr., 15–17, 23,
  28–29
Home, ownership of, 248
Howells, William Dean, 149

Hoyt, Elizabeth E., 59
Hutt, Max L., 175

Income, and child rearing, 154–155, 180
  of family head, 247
Independence training, 6, 13, 17–18, 23,
  25, 27, 40–41, 56, 102, 104–105, 123,
  125, 144, 170, 187, 226–227
Individuated-entrepreneurial, see Entrepreneurial lower classes; and
  Entrepreneurial middle classes
Infant Care, 18–23
Inner direction, see Other-direction
Integration settings, comparison of populations in, 79–80
  described, 39, 67, 160
  homogeneity of, 75–78, 89
Internalization Indices, 92–101, 111, 114,
  124–125, 127–129, 132, 137, 149–
  150, 164, 166, 183–184, 189–193,
  239, 242
  cumulative scores, 99–101, 124–125
  reliability, 108, 191–193, 246, 256–258
  validity, 94–97, 108
  see also Self-control
Interview, plan of, 64, 66, 68, 84
  questions, 64, 84–86
  validity of responses to, 64, 86–88
Interviewers, 64–65
Isaacson, Jean, 276

Jaffe, A. J., 59
Janowitz, Morris, 175
Jefferson, Thomas, 36
Jews, 167, 276–295
Jones, Lyle V., 263

Katz, Daniel, 263
Kissing of child, 17
Knupfer, Genevieve, 89
Kris, E., 26, 29
Kruskal, William H., 259, 263

Ladies' Home Journal, 13–14, 28
Lasswell, Harold D., 60, 294–295
Lerner, Daniel, 60
Limits on child's behavior, 21–22, 185,
  201–202
Lindesmith, Alfred R., 118
Lindzey, Gardner, 89

Index **299**

Linton, Ralph, 176
Lipset, Seymour M., 175
Locke, Harvey J., 197, 212
Locke, John, 9
Loewenstein, A. L., 26, 29
Lowie, Robert H., 212
Luther, Martin, 162

Maccoby, Eleanor E., 145
Mackintosh, Hugh R., 176
Marquand, John P., 149
Marriage, age of, 126–128, 228
Martin, William E., 145
Marvick, Dwaine, 175
Masturbation, 7–8, 16–19, 41, 85, 102–103, 122, 139–140
    see also Genitals, exploration of
McClelland, David C., 118
McNemar, Quinn, 263
Mead, George H., 294
Mencken, Henry L., 187, 195
Merton, Robert K., 60, 208–209, 213
Middle classes, lower middle, 98–99, 101
    upper middle, 67–70, 91, 98–99, 101
Miller, Daniel R., 88, 118, 145, 175, 232
Misbehavior, type of, 126–127
Mobility, intergenerational, and child rearing, 149–151, 179
Modesty in children, 139
Mood, Alexander M., 119, 295
Moral relations, defined, 161
    Indices of, 166–176, 179, 189–193, 245
        reliability, 191–193, 256–258
    style of and child rearing, 159–174
Motoric skills of child, 115–116, 131, 229
Murdock, George P., 231
Myrdal, Gunnar, 175

Nail biting, 16
"Natural" child rearing, 24–25, 27, 55
Negroes, 83, 91, 155–158, 180
Neighborhood, social class composition of and child rearing, 153–154, 180
Newcomb, Theodore M., 89, 145
Niebuhr, Helmut R., 176
Norton, James, 252

Obedience, 12
Ober, Harry, 59
Occupation, expected for children, 135, 170, 229–230

Occupation, of husband, 180, 250
    of husband's father, 280
Ogburn, William F., 59
Orderliness in children, 7, 122
Ordinal position of child, 247
Other-direction, 23, 109–112, 118, 129, 131, 230

Pacifiers, 121
Parenthood, age of, 126–127, 228–229
Parents, agreement about discipline for children, 143, 225
    aid to grown children, 117, 129–131, 170
    authority of, 11–14, 54, 187
    expectations about child's occupation, 135, 170, 229–230
    information desired about child rearing, 131, 170, 224–225
    responsibility for child's behavior, 109, 113–115, 118, 129–130
    rewards gained from children, 117, 131, 133, 170, 216–217, 230
Parsons, Talcott, 101, 119, 176
Passivity in children, 41, 56, 85, 102, 104
Payne, George H., 237
Peak, Helen, 263
Permissiveness in child rearing, 9, 11–13, 26, 55, 91, 122, 139, 144
Personality, and integration setting, 206–212
    individualization of, 23
    needed for occupation, 229–230
Play, 7, 18, 20, 22
Production orientation, see Consumption orientation
Protestants and integration settings, 276–295
    child-rearing practices, 158–174, 176–177, 179
Psychoanalysis and child rearing, 4–5, 26, 85, 94–96, 185–188, 210–211
Psychosis in Chicago, 137
Punishment, by "natural" results, 13
    direct and symbolic defined, 93
    methods of, 6, 8–13, 27, 40, 56–57, 85, 94, 97, 99, 124, 131, 139–140, 143, 160, 164, 167, 171–172, 221–223, 276

Index **301**

Validity of interpretations of findings, 178–189
Variance in child rearing, amount explained, 189–193, 259–260

Warner, W. Lloyd, 89, 157, 175
Watson, John B., 17–18, 23–24, 29, 40–41, 58
Weaning, age of among primitives, 217–218
  in Boston, 139
  in Chicago, 121, 134–135, 158
  in Detroit, 92–93, 98–99, 104, 124, 131, 133–135, 165, 169–170, 217
  in the United States, 6–7, 14–15, 28, 40, 56, 95

Weaning, methods used, 7, 15, 85
Weber, Max, 176–177
Welfare-bureaucracy, see Bureaucracy; Bureaucratic lower classes; and Bureaucratic middle classes)
Wesley, John, 9
Wesley, Susannah, 9–11, 24, 40
Wheeler, G. C., 212
Whiting, John W. M., 218, 220, 231
Whyte, William H., Jr., 209, 213
Willfulness of children, 18, 20–22
  see also "Breaking the will" of children
Wirth, Louis, 36–37, 58
Wolfenstein, Martha, 18–20, 22, 24, 29
Woytinsky, Wladimir S., 58–59